The Identity
of Nations

The Identity
of Nations

MONTSERRAT GUIBERNAU

polity

First published in 2007 by Polity Press
Reprinted 2008, 2010, 2011

Polity Press
65 Bridge Street
Cambridge CB2 1UR, UK

Polity Press
350 Main Street
Malden, MA 02148, USA

ISBN-13: 978-07456-2662-8
ISBN-13: 978-07456-2663-5 (pb)

A catalogue record for this book is available from the British Library.

Typeset in 11 on 13 pt Dante
by SNP Best-set Typesetter Ltd., Hong Kong
Printed and bound in Great Britain by the MPG Books Group

The publisher has used its best endeavours to ensure that the URLs for external websites referred to in this book are correct and active at the time of going to press. However, the publisher has no responsibility for the websites and can make no guarantee that a site will remain live or that the content is or will remain appropriate.

Every effort has been made to trace all copyright holders, but if any have been inadvertently overlooked the publisher will be pleased to include any necessary credits in any subsequent reprint or edition.

For further information on Polity, visit our website: www.politybooks.com

Contents

Detailed Contents

Acknowledgements

I would like to thank those who have supported me while I have been writing and thinking about this book. Rainer Bauböck, David Held, Tony Giddens, Maria del Mar Serrano, Michel Seymour and Anthony D. Smith have read parts of earlier drafts and offered their comments and criticism.

I started this book while working at the Open University, and I would like to take this opportunity to thank my former colleagues there, in particular Grahame Thompson, Linda Jones, Eileen Potterton, Marilyn Denman and Fran Ford.

At Queen Mary University of London, I would like to thank the Department of Politics, in particular Raymond Kuhn. I am also grateful to Anne Kershen for introducing me to the fascinating history of the East End of London.

A research fellowship from the Leverhulme Trust funded the research upon which this book is based, and it permitted me to enjoy a sabbatical period as visiting fellow at the Austrian Academy of Science (Vienna). Among my colleagues there, I would like to warmly thank Rainer Bauböck, Monika Mokre and Sonja Puntscher-Riekmann. I would also like to thank Bernhard Perchinig, Kurt Richard Luther, Lothar Hoebelt, Anton Pelinka and Ernst Bruckmüller for sharing with me their knowledge of Austrian politics and society. At Polity Press, I would like to thank Emma Longstaff and Gill Motley. A special thanks goes to Caroline Richmond for a thorough copy-editing of the manuscript.

Finally, my gratitude goes to those who have unconditionally supported me while writing this book: my husband, who deserves a very special mention for his constant encouragement, my parents, Antoni and Maria Dolors, and my nephew Joan.

Cambridge, March 2007

Introduction

In 2000 I visited Montreal and Quebec City to participate in a conference on nationalism. In the opening session, and after a staunch defence of the right of Quebeckers to self-determination, a member of the audience challenged the speaker and claimed that all that rhetoric on partnership with Canada and democratic Quebec nationalism was false. He defined himself as an English Canadian feeling excluded within Quebec and fed up with Quebeckers' recurrent demands for greater autonomy, 'when in truth', he argued, 'what they really want is independence'. He added: 'How could we possibly allow this? You are a mere province of Canada. Who do you think you are?' The speaker replied: 'We are a nation'. That triggered a lively debate in which mutual recriminations and arguments were employed to support antagonistic views, not only on the current status of Quebec and its eventual political future within Canada, but also on the cultural and public policy measures adopted by Canada to reinforce its national identity.

The views of Indian nations – called First Nations – living within the territory of Quebec were also represented in the debate. They came across strongly against Quebec nationalism and the granting of further devolution to the province, their main argument being that their ancestors had signed treaties with Canada in which their status as nations was recognized. Canada had to fulfil its duties towards them and not 'dump' them with the Quebeckers, with whom they had never entered into any type of agreement. The atmosphere was tense, and the ideas and arguments being debated mattered a great deal to those defending them.

In a matter of seconds, at least four different nations with their own national identities had come to the fore. They were of different sizes and age and had different cultures, languages and traditions, and all of them were claiming their right over parts of the same territory. Thus Canada was confronted by Quebec's national demands, while simultaneously Quebec was being challenged by the existence of smaller nations, such as the Hurons and the Mohawk, claiming their rights over their own homelands currently included within Quebec's territory.

*   *   *

The complexity of the Canadian–Quebec–First Nations relationship brings to the fore territorial issues, but it also opens up questions about how to accommodate national diversity within a multinational democracy. From a cultural perspective, it raises concerns about the nature, components, strength and strategies employed in the construction of national identity; such concerns were further stressed by my own experience as a Catalan.

As an adolescent I witnessed the rise of democratic Catalan nationalism after Franco's death (1975). I observed the sanctioning of a democratic constitution in 1978 and a new statute of autonomy for Catalonia in 1979. I saw the transformation of a highly centralized, conservative and authoritarian regime into a decentralized, democratic and modern nation-state included in the European Union and NATO. At that moment, I was still unable to participate in the political process, but I remember vividly the tremendous optimism and excitement of people who, for the first time in over forty years of dictatorship, were able to vote in a free and democratic election and express their views on the constitution and the statute. People believed that the future was in their hands, that from then on they would have a voice and could make a difference. At school, our teachers were bringing newspaper articles and newly published books for us to learn about Catalonia's re-established political institutions, their background, the civil war and exile. Even more crucially, I remember a young teacher avidly learning herself and simultaneously teaching us about the ideas and practices of social democracy and political pluralism that neither she nor we had ever encountered previously.

Still today, when Catalans define themselves as a nation, they obtain a heated reaction from some Spaniards who, as the 1978 constitution declares, regard the constitution as 'based upon the indissoluble unity of the Spanish Nation, the common and indivisible patria of all Spaniards'.[1] Catalans reply that Catalonia has a distinct national identity and has constituted a nation since the Middle Ages – a time when Catalonia became a key power in the Mediterranean and enjoyed its own constitutions, independent government and laws. They regard the current lack of recognition of Catalonia as a nation as part of a legacy of years of oppression by the Castilian yoke. In the War of the Spanish Succession, Catalonia supported the cause of the Austrians against Philip V (Felipe V) of the Bourbon dynasty. The Treaty of Utrecht (1713) confirmed Philip V as king of Spain, and Catalonia was left alone to face the might of the Franco-Spanish armies. Catalonia maintained its rights and liberties until 1714, when, on 11 September, after a massive Franco-

Spanish attack that followed a siege of fourteen months, Barcelona surrendered. Philip V ordered the dissolution of the Catalan institutions and Catalonia was subject to a regime of occupation. Catalan was forbidden and Castilian (Spanish) was proclaimed as the official language.

As I was growing up in Barcelona, I became a spectator of the stark contrast between a peaceful and democratic Catalan nationalism and the recurring violence perpetrated by some sectors of the Basque nationalist movement. 'Why are the Basques prone to violence and the Catalans are not?' I have had this question thrown at me on innumerable occasions, and I must confess that I still do not have a clear-cut answer to it. The response invariably has to include some references to the different components of national identity, that is, to the historical experiences, influences, values and principles defining the nation in each case.

The symmetrical decentralization of Spain effected after 1978, and referred to as 'coffee for everyone', involved the division of Spain into seventeen autonomous communities, some of them with historical roots and a strong sense of identity – Catalonia, the Basque Country and Galicia – others artificially created where no sense of a separate identity had ever existed – La Rioja and Madrid among many others. One of the most striking consequences of Spanish devolution has been the emergence of distinct identities being constructed within the newly created autonomous communities – an indication that multilevel governance tends to favour the generation of multiple identities operating at different levels. Right now some define Andalucía as a nation and defend its right to self-determination. Of course, nations are not eternal, they are born, transformed, and some of them disappear. But when does a nation come into being? How do nations construct their identities? In what circumstances does a nation declare itself as a *demos*, that is, a community with the right to decide on its political future?

In Spain, transformations affecting national identity were not limited to a sub-state level. The victory of the PSOE (Spanish Socialist Workers Party) in the 1982 general election initiated a dramatic transformation of the traditional definition of Spanish identity inherited from Francoism and defined primarily by its centralism, conservatism, Catholicism and anti-Europeanism and the pre-eminence of Castilian culture and language. The redefinition of Spanish identity was completed after the landslide victory in 2000 of the PP (Popular Party). Since then Spain has become an established democratic, modern, progressive (no less progressive than other European countries) nation-state, which is also decentralized, prosperous, pro-European, industrialized, secular, and enjoying a welfare system in constant development. In spite of this, it could be argued that Spanish identity still includes some hindrances from the past, such as the passion for centralism and the pre-dominance of Castile; however, no one could deny that Spain has dramatically transformed its identity. How do nations transform their identities? What strategies do they employ? Is there a core that remains constant within all national identities in spite of their dynamic advancement?

★   ★   ★

It is just before 8 a.m. when I usually get off the train at Liverpool Street Station and take the 25 bus to the university. In a matter of seconds, the bus leaves the already busy streets of London's financial district ('the City'), with its combination of skyscrapers, old buildings and churches, sleepy cafes, posh restaurants and shops, and heads towards the heart of the area recently termed Londonistan.[2]

The racial, cultural and social diversity of Mile End Road is easily captured as I look through the window. The imposing silhouette of the East London Mosque on the right; a bit further, on the left-hand side, dozens of vendors are rapidly arranging their stalls in what in an hour's time will become a buzzing street market, evoking some memories of those of Lahore or Karachi. The range of produce available and the dress code of most vendors, clients and passers by reveal a profound mixture of origins and traditions. The bus gets busier at every stop: some English working-class people – only a couple today; a big Jamaican lady with her son; some Urdu-speaking young men; a quiet group of about six or seven young girls, with their blue uniforms and headscarves, heading to one of the single-faith schools in the neighbourhood; two men in their mid-twenties speaking in an Eastern European language, their hands toughened up by manual work; and myself, a white Southern European woman. I wonder how many nationalities, languages, religions and national identities fit into a single bus in one of the most heterogeneous areas of London.

My short trip to work reveals the great diversity present in most Western cities, a trend already expanding to the countryside. Immigration is not a novel phenomenon; it has been around for centuries, and London offers a very good example of it. But, suddenly, difference has acquired unprecedented relevance in some Western societies, now uneasy about the consequences of multiculturalism. Does it contribute to the reification of differences rather than to the construction of a cohesive society? To what extent does having a British passport ensure loyalty to the nation and solidarity towards fellow citizens? Is there a growing gap between citizenship and national identity? Is citizenship cherished solely as an entrance-card to a prosperous labour market and mobility within the EU while loyalty and social commitments remain elsewhere?

The Britishness of the 7 July 2005 London bombers, rising tensions between some Asian and white youth in various locations, and the emergence of areas where people from different ethnic origins never mix are raising a certain degree of anxiety among significant sectors of the population. Trevor Phillips, head of the Commission for Racial Equality, has recently proclaimed that Britain is 'sleepwalking into segregation', with some districts 'on their way to becoming fully fledged ghettos – black holes into where no one goes without fear and trepidation and from which no one ever escapes undamaged.'[3] How do citizens of migrant origin define their national identity? Has Britishness, a concept strongly connected with the British Empire, been successfully redefined to embrace a wide range of peoples of various provenance? Are indigenous populations prepared fully to accept and regard as their own fellow citizens who are physically, culturally or religiously different from the majority?

*   *   *

Reflection on the various experiences I have just mentioned triggered the project to write this book, with the aim of studying how the identity of Western nations is being transformed from below, from above and from within. The book examines the meaning and main pillars of national identity as well as the strategies employed by nation-states engaged in processes of nation-building before and after the current intensification of globalization processes. It studies bottom-up movements for recognition and self-determination organized by national minorities living within the boundaries of the nation-state. In particular, it focuses on the ways in which Western nations react to such demands and the consequences this may have on national identity and social cohesion.

At the same time, the book reflects on top-down pressure exerted by the construction of novel supranational political institutions, such as the EU, which actively seek to instil a shared sense of common identity among a diverse citizenry. A further source of transformation points at dramatic changes in attitudes, values and perceptions of ethnic and religious diversity by significant sectors of the indigenous population. This takes place at a time when some communities of migrant origin are voicing strong claims to maintain their separate distinct identity – cultural, linguistic and religious – within the nation-state of which they are citizens. Simultaneously, other ethnic communities are advocating the right to contribute to and transform the identity of the nation within which they live. Still others despise the values and principles of the society of which they are citizens and defend their right to opt out of a common project uniting the nation because they place their allegiances elsewhere.

The outcome mirrors a polyhedron reflecting various reactions on behalf of the indigenous population, which regards its own national identity, and the bonds of solidarity and social cohesion legitimizing its actions as a political community, as being under threat. Western nations are unsure about how tolerant they should be and what they should tolerate. Tragically, the West is uncertain about the content of its own values and principles and, in some cases, it seems prepared to nurture the seeds of its own decline as a civilization.

Rising doubts about multiculturalism, a greater sensitivity towards difference, fears – justified or not – of being swamped by immigrants who contribute to lowering wages, greater unemployment, crime, and the stretching of welfare services are giving arguments to the new radical right, who are playing by the rules of democracy and presenting a primarily anti-immigrant programme aimed at defending the rights of an indigenous population 'abandoned' by the political correctness, tolerance and multicultural policies implemented by mainstream parties in recent years. Renewed calls for preserving the 'purity' of national identities are on the rise.

In contrast, a cosmopolitan elite stands in favour of a hybrid cultural view of the world. They denounce the perniciousness of nationalism and often ignore and dismiss the value that national identity has for millions of people who regard the nation as some kind of extended family, as a community within which they have a stake, as a homeland within which they matter and they can expect to be assisted when in need.

Outline of the book

This book explores how the identity of nations is being transformed by the impact of devolution, migration and the construction of supranational institutions in the age of globalization. It analyses some of the reactions to the end of 'pure' identities and invites the reader to reflect on the growing influence of a primarily anti-immigrant political agenda designed by the new radical right. It also explores the nature of cosmopolitanism and its possible compatibility, or lack of compatibility, with nationalism and national identity.

The book is divided into seven chapters. Chapter 1 offers a detailed analysis of the role and relevance of national identity in contemporary societies.

It emphasizes the difference between national identity, that is, the collective sentiment of belonging to the nation – understood primarily as a cultural community – and citizenship, which basically refers to membership of the state – a political institution granting rights and imposing duties on its members. Here, I examine the strategies regularly employed by the state in the construction of a shared national identity among its usually diverse population, a national identity in the end destined to legitimize the state's own existence. In so doing, I consider the transformations prompted by globalization of traditional mechanisms destined to build national identity in modern societies.

Chapter 2 focuses on various institutional arrangements intended to accommodate within liberal democratic states the nationalism of nations without states. It argues that political decentralization, when accompanied by a substantial degree of autonomy, the constitution of regional institutions and access to significant resources, promotes the emergence of dual identities – regional and national – without necessarily diminishing the latter. Besides, this chapter shows that political decentralization does not tend to foster secession, that is, devolution does not usually challenge the integrity of the nation-state's boundaries. I justify my claims by comparing Britain, Canada and Spain as three cases which, so far, prove that decentralization – including political autonomy and federalism – tames secessionism, both by offering significant power and resources to the national minorities it seeks to accommodate and by enticing regional political elites with the power, prestige and perks of devolution.

Chapter 3 introduces the concept of ethnicity to complement the study of nations and nationalism developed in the two previous chapters. Max Weber called ethnic groups 'those human groups that entertain a subjective belief in their common descent because of similarities of physical type or of customs or of both, or because of memories of colonization or migration.'[4] This chapter focuses on migration and its impact upon Austrian national identity. It explores the role of ethnicity in the construction of national identity and analyses various integration models ranging from ghettoization to assimilation and multiculturalism. In addition, it considers the role of immigrants within the new Austria emerging after the Second World War and looks carefully at the rise of the radical right Freedom Party.

Chapter 4 investigates whether a transnational political institution such as the European Union could foster the emergence of a novel type of shared identity among its citizens. The EU provides a new environment within which individuals and groups seek recognition and organize their participation in politics. The big question concerns whether the development of a political institution such as the EU and the harmonization of Europe through the implementation of EU Directives will result in the emergence of a common identity accompanied by sentiments of loyalty and attachment to the EU or, on the contrary, whether national loyalties and interests are to prevail and prevent the emergence of a European identity.

Chapter 5 concentrates on the main challenges currently being faced by American identity. Here, I highlight the tremendous ethnic and racial diversity included in the USA. In particular, I focus on the gradual replacement of assimilation by integration within a wide range of ethnic groups endowed with their own cultures, which often include their own separate sub-economic structures. I analyse the impact of large Hispanic immigration upon America's traditional culture and monolingual status, the pervasive discrimination against African-Americans and their renewed nationalism, and the socio-political transformations brought about by the adoption of multiculturalism in the post-civil rights era. The chapter concludes by reflecting on the meaning of American identity in the early twenty-first century.

Chapter 6 examines the rise of the new radical right and its defence of what I refer to as 'pure national identities'. This chapter looks carefully at the new radical right's anti-immigration discourse and its position against multiculturalism. In so doing, I draw from the study of a range of European new radical right-wing parties – among them, the Austrian Freedom Party, the French *Front National* and the Italian *Lega Nord*. I also establish a connection between the European new radical right's defence of ethnoculturalism and white nativism in the USA.

In Chapter 7, I establish a distinction between 'global' and 'cosmopolitan' culture and focus on the ethical component absent from most theories of cosmopolitan culture and identity. The chapter compares national and cosmopolitan identity by examining five dimensions: psychological, cultural, historical, territorial and political. It concludes by assessing whether nationalism and cosmopolitanism are able to coexist and investigates the specific conditions that would render this possible. At this juncture, I argue that the political agenda for the future of nations should embrace a commitment to cosmopolitan ideals and values capable of informing political action and adding a new moral dimension to national identity. The advent of cosmopolitanism requires the pledge to eradicate social, political and economic ideologies based upon the exploitation of individuals and nations. In so far as this remains out of reach, cosmopolitanism will remain a utopian ideology.

1

What is National Identity?

This chapter explores the meaning of national identity and the relevance it has achieved in contemporary Western societies by examining its definition, components and origin. It begins by briefly analysing the processes around the nineteenth century that initially gave prominence to the concern for identity and resulted in turning it into one of the most significant features of late modernity. The chapter then moves on to study the psychological, cultural, historical, territorial and political dimensions I attribute to national identity. Some of the key issues considered include the role of elites in the construction of national identity, the relevance of antiquity, the constructed or immemorial origin of nations and national identity, matters regarding the legitimizing role of history, and the significance of territory in the construction of national identity. The chapter concludes by providing an original examination of the strategies traditionally employed by the nation-state in the construction of national identity. In so doing, it points out how some of these traditional strategies are being transformed under the influence of a growing intensification of the globalization processes.

Identity

The concern with individuality is a relatively recent phenomenon connected with the emergence of modern societies and the differentiation of the division of labour.[1] By the late Middle Ages, people increasingly learned to think in individual terms and slowly solidified concepts of the single human life as an individual totality. Before that, society operated on the basis of lineage, gender, social status and other attributes. Baumeister's analysis recalls that of Durkheim: 'The "individual", in a certain sense, did not exist in traditional cultures, and individuality was not prized.'[2]

In the nineteenth century, the prestige of the individual self reached an all-time high, but it declined in the early twentieth century when 'new social arrangements and events dramatized the relative powerlessness of the individual leading to a devaluation of the self'.[3] However, a process giving special significance to the 'uniqueness' of each individual led to a particular concern about identity reflecting the individual and collective (group) desire to be 'different'.

The key questions with regard to identity are 'Who am I?' 'Who are we?' Identity is a definition, an interpretation of the self that establishes what and where the person is in both social and psychological terms. All identities emerge within a system of social relations and representations. As Melucci observes, all identities require the reciprocal recognition of others; they involve permanence and unity of a subject or of an object through time.[4] Melucci connects identity with action. In his view, actors must have a perception of belonging, a sense of temporal continuity and a capacity for self-reflection informing a process of constant reaffirmation of one's self-identity and differentiation from others. He argues: 'We might define identity as the reflexive capacity for producing consciousness of action (that is, a symbolic representation of it) beyond any specific contents. Identity becomes formal reflexivity, pure symbolic capacity, the recognition of the production of a sense of action within the limits posed at any given moment by the environment and the biological structure.'[5]

In my view, the defining criteria of identity are continuity over time and differentiation from others – both fundamental elements of national identity. Continuity springs from the conception of the nation as a historically rooted entity that projects into the future. Individuals perceive this continuity through a set of experiences that spread out across time and are united by a common meaning, something that only 'insiders' can grasp. Differentiation stems from the consciousness of forming a distinct community with a shared culture, past, symbols and traditions, attached to a limited territory. Continuity and differentiation from others lead to the distinction between members (those who belong) and 'strangers', 'the rest', 'the different' and, sometimes, 'the enemy'.

National identity

The French love cheese and are proud of the Enlightenment and the changes brought about by their Revolution. The English enjoy cricket, tea and the countryside. They are also pleased about their old democratic legacy. US citizens are proud of the founding fathers of their nation; they love steaks and big cars. Spaniards appreciate good wine and paella and are content about Columbus's discovery of America under Castilian sponsorship.

But do all citizens of each one of these countries share such features? Surely not, and those who share them do so with different intensity and focusing on various specific features in each case. Are they 'less' French,

English, Spanish or American citizens in this case? The response depends on the value attributed to national stereotyping. If we were to look deeper into these definitions, we might discover that stereotypes have an origin, and, up to a point, they direct us to a set of characteristics which are believed to be shared by those who belong to particular nations. Stereotyping consists of selecting and often exaggerating some distinctive features of certain nationals. But is there a relationship between the attributes which are singled out to define certain nationals and the so-called national identity of these peoples?

National identity is a collective sentiment based upon the belief of belonging to the same nation and of sharing most of the attributes that make it distinct from other nations. National identity is a modern phenomenon of a fluid and dynamic nature. While consciousness of forming a nation may remain constant for long periods of time, the elements upon which such a feeling is based may vary.

Belief in a common culture, history, kinship, language, religion, territory, founding moment and destiny have been invoked, with varying intensity, by peoples claiming to share a particular national identity. At present, such a national identity is generally attributed to citizens of a nation-state. However, distinct national identities may also be shared among individuals belonging to nations without states, such as Quebec, Catalonia, the Basque Country and Scotland. Collective memories of a time when the nation was independent, endured oppression, or attained international leadership tend to strengthen a sense of common identity among those who belong to the nation, even if it lacks a state of its own.

The dimensions of national identity

National identity is constituted by a set of attributes shared by those who belong to a particular nation. The nature of these attributes stems from the specific way in which the nation is defined. Yet, in referring to the nation as a human group conscious of forming a community, sharing a common culture, attached to a clearly demarcated territory, having a common past and a common project for the future while claiming the right to self-determination,[6] I am implying that national identity has five dimensions. These are psychological, cultural, territorial, historical and political.

Psychological dimension

The psychological dimension of national identity arises from the consciousness of forming a group based on the 'felt' closeness uniting those who belong to the nation. Such closeness can remain latent for years and suddenly come to the surface whenever the nation is confronted with an external or internal enemy – real, potential or imagined – threatening its people, its prosperity, its traditions and culture, its territory, its international standing or its sovereignty.

Some scholars of nationalism insist on the subjective nature of national identity's components.[7] In my view, the most relevant quality of those components is not whether they are subjective or not, but rather whether they are felt as real by those sharing a common identity. Across the globe we find countless examples of people prepared to make sacrifices and ultimately to die for their nations, and this proves that, at least for them, national identity is real and worth fighting for. But why is this so? Sharing a national identity generates an emotional bond among fellow nationals and, as Connor puts it, this is fundamentally psychological and non-rational. It is not irrational, only 'beyond reason'.[8] This is so because, basically, a nation is a group of people who feel that they are ancestrally related. In Connor's view, the nation 'is the largest group that can command a person's loyalty because of felt kinship ties; it is, from this perspective, the fully extended family.' However, 'the sense of unique descent need not, and *in nearly all* cases *will not*, accord with factual history',[9] since nearly all nations originate from the mixing of peoples from various ethnic origins. For this reason, what matters is not chronological or factual history but sentient or felt history.

The attributes, real as well as invented, sustaining the belief in common ancestry make up national identity and foster a sense of belonging which generally engenders loyalty and social coherence among fellow nationals.

The internalization of national identity, and in particular of a distinct culture specific to the nation, results in individuals charging it emotionally. In certain circumstances, sentiments of love of the nation and hatred of those threatening it are intensely felt by fellow nationals. Political leaders and agitators are fully aware of the power of national identity, and it is not uncommon for them to mix rational arguments with the appeal to shared sentiments of belonging and love of the nation while trying to mobilize the population. Calls for action and sacrifice in the face of threats to the nation and of defeat are accompanied by appeals to the 'unique character' and 'qualities' of those who belong. Such assertions have the capacity to lift people beyond their daily lives and routines, to raise them to a higher level in which their actions acquire a novel meaning and are qualified as crucial for the survival and prosperity of the nation. The strength of emotions overrides reason, because it is through a sentimental identification with the nation that individuals transcend their finite and, at least for some, meaningless lives. Their efforts and sacrifices become decisive, even heroic, and the conviction of having contributed to a higher aim, that of preserving and enhancing the nation, increases the individuals' self-esteem as well as their own image in the minds and memory of fellow nationals.

National institutions honour some of those who defend and promote the nation within the international arena. Commemorations of heroic war actions, medals and other awards, and special receptions organized by the nation's dignitaries as a gesture of recognition to distinguished athletes or national sports teams exemplify this. Of course, some could argue that individuals endure sacrifices and seek success for their own personal sake, but most contests, in particular sports ones, are organized according to national teams, and generally only representatives of nation-states are allowed to participate.

Cultural dimension

Values, beliefs, customs, conventions, habits, languages and practices are transmitted to the new members who receive the culture of a particular nation. As mentioned above, the process of identification with the elements of a specific culture implies a strong emotional investment. Two major inferences deriving from this possess a particular significance when considering national identity. First, a shared culture favours the creation of solidarity bonds among the members of a given community by allowing them to recognize each other as fellow nationals and to imagine their community as separate and distinct from others.

Second, individuals socialized within a distinct culture tend to internalize its symbols, values, beliefs and customs as forming a part of themselves.

Deutsch defines the nation as a cultural entity and refers to the processes of communication as fundamental in creating coherent societies and cultures. In his view, 'Membership in a people consists in wide complementarity of social communication. It consists in the ability to communicate more efficiently, and over a wide range of subjects, with members of one large group than with outsiders.'[10]

Communication requires the use of a specific language known by the members of the nation. To a great extent, vernacular languages are employed, though there are some exceptions. For instance, where the vernacular language has been lost, this is often replaced by the state's language. In Scotland the practical disappearance of Gaelic, primarily due to the imposition of English, resulted in the latter becoming Scotland's national language. There are cases where more than one language is official within the nation and both are employed; this is the case in Quebec (French and English) and Catalonia (Catalan and Spanish). Yet, while French is official within Canada (together with English), and not only in Quebec, Catalan's official status is restricted to Catalonia, where it is co-official with Spanish (Castilian), the only official language in the whole territory of Spain.

The power of language springs from its ability to create unified fields of exchange and communication, which contribute to the strengthening of national identity. Two people who do not understand each other cannot be said to share a national identity.

Three recurrent questions when considering national cultures concern, first, their *antiquity*, that is whether they are ancient or modern; second, their *origin* – whether they have emerged spontaneously out of certain given attributes specific to each nation or have been constructed; and, third, whether they constitute a *mass* or an *elite* phenomenon.

Antiquity

There is a poignant confrontation between perennialists, eager to trace back the roots of contemporary national cultures to immemorial times, and modernists, who emphasize their recent origin. Perennialists do not perceive nations or ethnic groups and the cultures making them up as natural; rather, they regard them as the product of a historical and social process. As Smith mentions, for Armstrong, the collective identity defining the nation is 'a modern equivalent of pre-modern ethnic identity'.[11]

Modernists offer an altogether different picture, by arguing that a national culture is a relatively recent occurrence associated with the emergence of industrial society,[12] the advent of print capitalism and the spread of vernacular languages.[13] Others stress the recent origin and invented nature of most traditions presented as rooted in ancient times.[14] The ethnosymbolist perspective propounded by Anthony D. Smith endorses a middle-way approach to the antiquity of national culture. He acknowledges the modernity of nations and nationalism (and those elements forming them, for instance national culture), while insisting on the ethnic origins of nations. He confers great relevance on the values, myths, symbols, holy places, memories and traditions embedded in the ethnic community, as a social formation which, in pre-modern times, did not normally act as the basis of alternative polity formation.[15]

Antiquity is employed as a source of legitimacy for a nation and its culture. It binds individuals to a past stretching over their own lifespan as well as those of their ancestors. Antiquity stresses one of the key elements of identity, that is, continuity over time, and in so doing it contributes to the preservation of the collective self. Acknowledging and documenting cultural antiquity is a modern activity which also provides nations and their cultures with a distinguished pedigree, so that when individuals look back in time they are not confronted with a meaningless vacuum about their own collective origin, but reassured by the deeds of their ancestors. Antiquity feeds the subjective belief in a kinship relation right at the heart of the nation, while culture is perceived as the particular way of being in the world adopted by each nation. Its distinctive culture singles out the nation and stands as its presentation card to the international community.

Origin

Does national culture emerge naturally, or is it constructed? And, if so, by whom? Primordialists argue that 'cultural givens' such as assumed blood ties, language, custom, race and religion constitute the cultural 'essence' of nations. Edward Shils establishes a distinction between the public, civil ties of the modern state and the primordial ties embodied in kinship, religion and common ethnicity.[16] Clifford Geertz attributes such great binding power to primordial ties that, in his view, disaffection based on primordial sentiments threatens the very existence of new states. Geertz is eager to stress that 'the general strength of such primordial bonds, and the types of them that are important, differ from person to person, from society to society, and from time to time. But for virtually every person, in every society, at almost all times, some attachments seem to flow more from a sense of natural – some would say spiritual – affinity than from social interaction.'[17]

One of the main criticisms of the primordialist approach refers to its quasi-static view of 'cultural givens'. Primordialism seems to ignore that language as well as custom and religion are subject to transformation. Even race may be subject to change as a result of the variability of racial definitions and perceptions – as is the case in Brazil – and interbreeding, common not only in contemporary societies but also in pre-modern times, when colonizers, merchants, armies and migrants constantly travelled the world and mixed with the peoples they encountered.

Two further objections to primordialism concern the impossibility of determining the future development of ethnic groups or nations out of distinct primordial groups, and reasons such as personal and collective survival or interest in seeking identification with specific primordial attachments in order to be included as group members.

In contrast with the primarily essentialist view of culture defended by primordialists, instrumentalists regard cultures as infinitely malleable and susceptible to elite manipulation. Instrumentalists select and employ certain cultures, or parts of them, as an *ad hoc* supplement to their political strategies, their aim being mass mobilization in favour of their goals. Culture is to provide legitimacy to the elite's aims, and it is expected to act as the glue holding society together. Abner Cohen exemplifies this position in his study of the conscious manipulation of kinship and symbols by political entrepreneurs in urban Africa.[18]

When examining current anthropological approaches towards culture, Thomas H. Eriksen signals a shift towards the study of identities rather than cultures, which places great emphasis upon conscious agency and reflexivity.[19] He points to the abandonment of essentialism and primordialism and emphasizes that 'there seems to be good political sense in discarding the old, static view of culture'. He adds: 'The main tendency in recent years has, on the contrary, consisted of deconstructing instrumentalists' notions of authenticity and tradition, and showing not only that the internal variation within a group is much greater than one would expect but also that traditionalist ideologies are, paradoxically, direct results of modernization.'[20] Eriksen condemns reification and essentialism and insists on the existence of an infinite number of versions of each culture, none of which is more 'true' than the others.

The influence of 'post-modernist' thought and the deconstructionism associated with it denounces instrumentalists' approaches to culture and treats ethnicity and nationalism as 'political reifications or constructions of a particular authorized version of culture, freezing that which naturally flows, erecting artificial boundaries where they did not exist before, trimming and shaping the past to fit present needs, and inventing traditions where no organic traditions exist, or are not adequate, to ensure a sense of continuity with the past.'[21]

Mass or elite phenomenon

To be true to its name and contribute to the rise of a sentiment of shared identity among fellow nationals, national culture has to be a mass phenomenon. In my view, we cannot speak about national culture outside industrial societies, since only the mechanisms of mass communication allow for the expansion of vernacular languages, and I consider them as a precondition for the rise of truly national cultures.

Western countries acquired national cultures at different points in time. Stark differences among them were related to diversified literacy rates among their populations. Eugène Weber's seminal work *Peasants into Frenchmen* argues that a large proportion of people living in rural areas and small towns did not conceive of themselves as Frenchmen until 1870, while many of them still failed to do so before the First World War.[22] Walker Connor wonders whether the French experience is unique or could be generalized to other countries. In so doing, he warns that elites have sought to offer generalizations concerning the existence of national consciousness within their countries, when 'until quite recent times it is doubtful whether ostensibly nationalistic elites even considered the masses to be part of their nation'.[23] Connor signals that 'a sense of common nationhood is not compatible with a cross-cutting cleavage as deep and unremitting as that between slave and landowner', notwithstanding he also adds that democracy is not a precondition for national consciousness, as the Japanese and German cases illustrate.[24]

Connor's and Weber's theories on the rise of national consciousness prompt a reflection on the origins of national cultures, not only in terms of their timing but also with regards to the agents and processes involved in their creation. The question 'When did a national culture emerge?' could be interpreted in the following manner: At what point in time did particular cultures, cultivated solely by the elite, manage to permeate the masses so deeply that they came to regard them as their own?

A lapse, sometimes stretching into centuries, has separated the extension of some elite cultures to the masses. Involved in this approach is the belief that national culture is a top-down process by means of which elites tend to project a selected version of their own high culture upon the masses, while encouraging them to believe that, in spite of social differences, a common culture unites them. Such 'culture-based unity' between the elite and the masses stands at the heart of the conception of a shared national identity. A common culture legitimizes the existence of the nation and is employed as an argument in favour of social cohesion and unity among all sectors of an otherwise diverse national population.

The top-down theory of national culture, however, should be subjected to some scrutiny. 'Elite culture', by definition, is a high culture with an established language and a substantial body of literature and knowledge, which requires its own clerisy. Control of the learning process lies in the hands of scholars and institutions ready to preserve, develop and inculcate the culture upon a diverse population. Their mission is to achieve a linguistically and culturally homogeneous population able to communicate with each other and to work and live within that culture. Gellner emphasizes the role of the state as the 'organism [which] must ensure that this literate and unified culture is indeed being effectively produced, that the educational product is not shoddy and sub-standard'.[25] He adds, 'the state does take over quality control in this most important of industries, the manufacture of viable and usable human beings.'[26]

But how do these human beings react to such an attempt? In my view the successful initiation into a high culture – its internalization – requires an environment within which this culture is dominant, has prestige, is associated with power structures and, crucially, provides opportunities for those embracing it. As Gellner put it bluntly, 'a man's culture, the idiom within which he was trained and within which he is effectively employable, is his most precious possession, his real entrance-card to full citizenship and human dignity, to social participation. The limits of his culture are the limits of his employability, his world, and his moral citizenship.'[27]

Notwithstanding, such a theory seems to neglect the force of popular myths, symbols, traditions, rituals and languages spoken by the masses, which often did not coincide with those of the elites. I argue that elites had to make certain concessions and incorporate a sufficient number of elements from popular culture into what was to be designed as national culture, in order for the masses to identify and recognize the elite's constructed national culture as their own. I agree with Gellner when he writes: 'Admittedly, nationalism uses the pre-existing, historically inherited proliferation of cultures or cultural wealth, though it uses them very selectively, and it most often transforms them radically.'[28] Tom Nairn reinforces this point by arguing: 'The new middle-class intelligentsia of nationalism had to invite the masses into history; and the invitation-card had to be written in a language they understood.'[29]

It is my contention that the top-down dissemination of a common culture has to be compensated for by some bottom-up contributions, even if these are substantially transformed in this process. Undoubtedly elites play an irreplaceable role in the construction of national identity, since they are better equipped, generally benefit from greater access to the media, and have an incomparable influence upon political institutions.

Through traditions, symbolism and ritual, elites and masses unite as members of a single nation, which is then placed above and beyond social differences. Its prosperity and success are presented as meaningful and desirable for elites and masses alike. By sharing a common culture, history, attachment to a particular territory and project for the future, elites and masses come to regard themselves as a community of fate.

In the quest for national mobilization, no stronger argument can be invoked than the shared belief, by both elites and masses, in the need to unite against a common enemy. Feelings of national identity are strengthened by shared memories of joy as well as sorrow endured by the nation.

Suffering caused by war, invasion, natural disasters and terrorism, as well as the belief, real or imagined, in the exclusion, discrimination and oppression endured by the nation, contribute to developing a sense of community.

The intrinsic complexity attached to the process of constructing a distinct national identity is further complicated whenever some 'alternative' national elites and masses oppose the cultural and linguistic homogenization led by the state, as is the case in some nations without a state of their own.

The cultural and linguistic homogenization of Western nation-states has been a very slow process, which in most cases was successfully accomplished only by the first half of the twentieth century. Nonetheless it is interesting to observe that, approximately during the same historical period (late nineteenth and twentieth centuries), a considerable number of social movements aiming to preserve and encourage the cultural and linguistic development of national minorities took place. Initially, and under the spell of German Romanticism, such movements displayed a cultural orientation; however, later on they came to embrace political aims. Catalonia, the Basque Country, Flanders, the Veneto, Wales, Brittany, Corsica and Sardinia are cases in point.

The irony is that, precisely at the time when it becomes credible to speak about national cultures within Western nation-states, national minorities as well as ethnic communities of migrant origin are vindicating their distinct cultures and languages. They are questioning state-sponsored national cultures and, in some cases, demanding the right to protect and develop their own cultural, religious and linguistic distinctiveness, while pressing for a redefinition of the national identity of the societies of which they have become citizens. In some instances, this has resulted in some nation-states embracing multiculturalism and adopting as their own carefully selected items originating from the national and ethnic minorities included within their territories. I will come back to the issues raised by the presence and demands of ethnic and national minorities later on in the book.

Historical dimension

When ascertaining the roots of a nation, how far back in time should we go? A century? Five centuries? Fifty years? There is no written rule about this. In fact, while nations such as England and France can easily uncover their origins to medieval times, others such as Palestine and the Jewish nation go back to antiquity. In contrast, the United States of America, Australia or Canada can claim a mere two or three hundred years of history. Does it make a difference? And, if so, to whom?

Members of a nation tend to feel proud of their ancient roots and generally interpret them as a sign of resilience, strength and even superiority when compared with other nations unable to display a rich past during which the nation became prominent. Greeks are proud of their classic legacy encompassing art and philosophy, the introduction of democracy and the Olympic Games – regardless of their current status as a nation, and neglecting the sharp distinctions between Sparta and Athens to be found in antiquity. Castilians, belonging to Castile, the dominant nation within Spain, still commemorate the date Columbus first landed on American soil, and Italians, at least many of them, celebrate the Roman Empire.

Nations remember admirable and awesome experiences, but they also evoke dreadful moments of national humiliation and suffering. For instance, Catalonia's national day commemorates the occupation of Barcelona by Franco-Spanish forces led by Felipe V (11 September 1714) and the subsequent abolition of Catalan autonomous institutions, the proscription of the Catalan language and the imposition of an occupation regime. Jews observe key dates of the Holocaust and revere the sites of concentration camps such as Auschwitz where millions lost their lives. A more recent example concerns the terrorist attacks perpetrated on the World Trade Center in New York and the Pentagon in Washington on 11 September 2001. This date has already acquired meaning for millions of US citizens, who unite in grief to remember those killed or injured.

The selective use of history provides members of a nation with a collective memory filled with transcendental moments in the life of the community – events and experiences that allow people to increase their self-esteem by feeling as do members of a community which has proved capable of great things, and which might be ready to become once again a beacon to the world. All nations evoke some features that make them special and, in a certain way, 'superior' to the rest. They all excel in something, no matter what, that makes them and their members unique. History contributes to the construction of a certain image of the nation and represents the cradle where the national character was forged.

History makes us closer to our ancestors, and strengthens the subjective belief of being part of an extended family. It is through identification with our ancestors that we rejoice in their victories and feel for their suffering and humiliations throughout history. People feel aroused when reading about their common past, watching movies that reproduce heroic moments and golden ages, and listening to political activists and leaders who invoke and revive joyful as well as outrageous past shared experiences. Celebration, pride and self-esteem as well as hatred and thirst for vengeance can equally be instilled in people's minds by appealing to history. Feelings of transcendence and immortality are infused into individuals made aware of their role as pieces of a chain that, in spite of some transformations, remains constant and unique. The feeling of continuity with the past and projection into the future unites fellow nationals eager to explore their roots and sensitive to the collective dimension of their lives.

Throughout time, nations have attributed variable significance and value to history. Learning from the past is not endowed with the same prominence in all nations. In spite of this, the cultivation of disciplines such as archeology, anthropology, history of art, philology and ethnography, among others, reflects a willingness to explore the nation's past. These disciplines include a comparative component that not uncommonly has led to claims of superiority on behalf of some cultures and nations above others. Their endeavour also assumes the existence of specialized scholars who become authorities in the various fields of knowledge. Their findings tend to be utilized as a source of legitimacy by national political leaders and activists willing to mobilize those who belong.

Territorial dimension

For centuries, the life of individuals evolved around a small territory where family, work, and religious and administrative structures were concentrated. In turn, the individual's identity was defined by the roles he or she played within that limited territory.

But does the sense of national territorial boundedness vary depending on whether an individual forms part of the elite or is a member of the masses? Probably yes. I argue that elites acquired a much more accurate sense of the territorial boundaries of the nation as soon as they had access to education. The masses did not attain notable levels of literacy until the late nineteenth century, and in some areas they had to wait until the early twentieth century. A great shift was required for people to conceive the nation as their home, since large sections of the population had never travelled around their own nation's territory and could not imagine it as clearly bounded and distinct. Even today, a fair number of people lack direct knowledge of significant parts of their nation and only attain an accurate sense of its territorial limits through the media and education – two decisive elements that enable people to 'imagine' their nations as territorially bounded, distinct and sovereign.

Print and other forms of media have contributed to individuals being able to imagine their nations and regard them as homelands.[30] International media and communications have brought greater awareness of the territorial limits of nations and of the different peoples and cultures inhabit-ing them.

It is widely accepted that globalization has increased interconnectedness, and that it has brought about greater worldwide interdependence. But how do ordinary people react to events taking place outside the territorial bound-aries of their nation? Do they feel with the same intensity about loss of life, natural disasters or great sports achievements regardless of where they take place? Surely not. While it is true that events happening miles away can have an impact upon our daily lives – the Tokyo stock exchange, ecological disas-ters – we do not react in the same manner to famine, war, epidemics, ter-rorist attacks or world sports records if they occur beyond the boundaries of our nation and if they have 'foreigners' as their subjects. In addition, within the nation, we tend to feel more intensely about events happening closer to us, that is within our region, city or local village. Certainly it appears much more difficult to feel for 'strangers', yet not all 'strangers' are the same. Thus, in Britain, a US citizen may be perceived as closer than an EU citizen, and be seen as 'almost' a fellow national when compared with a Japanese or an Algerian national.

Globalization conveys visibility and awareness of the 'other', but for the large majority of peoples the territorial boundaries of the nation signal the limits of their homeland, and fellow nationals are usually regarded as if they were more 'humane' than the rest, as deserving our full support, concern and nurture. Filial sentiments towards fellow nationals with whom we iden-tify are not matched by feeling for 'foreigners', 'unknown peoples', 'strang-ers', maybe potential 'enemies'.

In spite of globalization and emerging cosmopolitanism, which so far are primarily elite phenomena, local and national attachments remain strong, and I expect them to continue to be so in the foreseeable future. This is not a process opposed to cosmopolitanism, but a process parallel to it. So-called citizens of the world are bound to be concerned primarily about their nations, and this should not prevent them from displaying greater awareness and increasing sensitivity towards 'strangers'. Unfortunately, however, human beings only rarely feel with the same intensity about their family, the com-munity they belong to and the wider world. It is my contention that this operates as an efficient mechanism to protect our emotional stability. Our capacity for joy and sorrow is limited and concentrated on ourselves and on those we regard as closer to us. It is only by identifying with others that we can feel their happiness and pain as our own.

Our homes, our villages and cities are located in the nation's territory. It is normally considered as a tragedy to have to leave one's own home; in a similar way, it is also devastating to be forced to leave one's own nation, as is the case with refugees and those displaced by means of war or natural or man-made disasters.

Further to that, territory has traditionally been the people's primary source of nourishment, and even today home products and natural resources possess great significance and constitute a crucial component of the nation's wealth. When turned into landscape, territory achieves a completely different meaning for those who belong, those able to discern particular sites where memorable battles and events took place and to identify particular landmarks and sacred places constituting the distinctive character of the nation. People come to regard the landscape as embodying the traditions, history and culture of the nation they share with their ancestors. The landscape, be it urban or rural, also represents our heritage to future generations. This is why, in nationalist thought, it becomes highly relevant to be concerned about the preservation of the national environment – a feature with the potential to establish a connection between nationalist and ecologist groups.

The landscape is also a source of beauty, admiration and exploration. It is turned into a symbol of the nation which embodies traditions, ideas, aspirations and sentiments, some of which evoke a strong sense of national belonging.

Political dimension

Most literature on national identity tends to define it as a property shared by citizens of a nation-state. I argue that this is an incorrect assumption based upon the common error of conflating nation and state.[31] National identity refers to those attributes shared by those who belong to the nation, and it is essential to bear in mind that not all nations have a state of their own.

The political dimension of national identity derives from its relation with the modern nation-state. From its foundational moment, the nation-state pursued the cultural and linguistic homogenization of an otherwise diverse population. That is, the state selected and generally imposed the culture and language of the dominant group within its territory and sought to create a single nation out of the various nations or parts of nations forming it.

Throughout time, conquests, annexations and marriages brought together peoples who were foreign to each other. The distance between elites and the masses was epitomized in the 'foreign' character of some rulers who shared very little, if anything at all, with their subjects, and it was often the case that rulers could not understand or be understood by their subjects. It was quite common to find rulers of this type because they spoke languages different from those of their subjects. For centuries nobody objected to the legitimacy of such political arrangements.

Enlightenment ideas of popular sovereignty and democracy were first postulated around the American Revolution (1776) and the French Revolution (1789). Their finest contribution to politics was to place the legitimacy of government in the support received by the members of the nation. The whole process of translating the ideas of popular sovereignty into universal adult suffrage required a long and hard struggle, during which the ideas of 1789 began a slow but compelling progress, and permeated to varying degrees first the educated classes and then the masses in the various European countries. Another relevant feature of the French Revolution is the emphasis it placed on education, creating as a result 'the first comprehensive system of national education to raise new generations of virtuous and patriotic citizens.'[32]

This framework made possible the rise of modern nationalism, a device that proved to be exceedingly useful for refocusing a people's loyalty away from the monarch. Monarchy by divine right was an elegantly simple device for evoking emotional attachment. But an aggregate of sovereign citizens could hardly perform that function. Then the nation, personified through symbols and rituals which symbolically re-create a sense of 'people', became the focus of a new kind of attachment. Thus, the French Revolution politicized the cultural concept of nationality and national identity.

It was the nation, then, to which was attributed the function of providing legitimacy to the power of the state, although this involved a long and arduous process which progressively granted more and more people the status of citizen. Citizenship, that is, membership of the state, entitles individuals to have a say in how their country is ruled. Citizens share duties and rights, and they are commanded to remain loyal to the state and to uphold its values.

The political aspect of national identity, when applied to the nation-state, focuses upon those actions of the state destined to construct a cohesive society through a set of strategies designed to generate a culturally and linguistically homogeneous citizenry. By creating a national education system and national media, and by promoting a specific 'national' culture and an 'official' language, the nation-state contributes to the dissemination of a distinct national identity among its citizens. Some of them, however, may already have a different national identity, or originate from beyond the nation-state's boundaries. Others may legally be citizens of a particular state but place their loyalty elsewhere.

In some cases, the national identity of those who belong to a nation without a state may stand in opposition to the national identity instilled by the state within which that nation is included, for instance Quebeckers in Canada and Basques in Spain. For this reason, the strength of the state-instilled national identity may vary greatly among members of particular nations without states and ethnic minorities, depending on whether or not they already hold a strong separate identity. Significant differences come to light when comparing the power and resources in the hands of both nation-states and nations without states engaged in the construction and promotion of their own separate identities.

Constructing national identity

Among the main strategies generally employed by the state in its pursuit of a single national identity capable of uniting its citizens are:

1 the construction and dissemination of a certain *image* of the 'nation', often based upon the dominant nation or ethnic group living within the state's boundaries and comprising a common history, a shared culture and a demarcated territory;
2 the creation and spread of a set of symbols and rituals charged with the mission of reinforcing a sense of community among citizens;
3 the advancement of citizenship, involving a well-defined set of civil and legal rights, political rights and duties, and socio-economic rights. By conferring rights upon its members, the state facilitates the rise of senti-ments of loyalty towards itself. It also establishes a crucial distinction between those *included* and those *excluded* from the community of citi-zens, that is, between those entitled to certain rights and those deprived of them within the boundaries of the state;
4 the creation of common enemies. The prosecution of war has proven crucial to the emergence and consolidation of a sense of community among citizens united against an external threat, be it imminent, poten-tial or invented;
5 the progressive consolidation of national education and media systems as key instruments in the dissemination of a particular 'image of the nation', with its symbols and rituals, values, principles, traditions and ways of life, and common enemies, and, even more crucially, a clear-cut definition of a 'good citizen'.

Significant changes in the context within which these strategies are carried out have been registered in the last twenty years or so. Most of these changes are closely connected to the intensification of globalization processes and the emergence of the post-traditional nation-state.[33] But what are these changes? How can we best understand them? What new challenges do they pose to traditional conceptions of national identity? This is an ambitious task which cannot be fully accomplished within the limited scope of this chapter. For this reason, in what follows I am able to sketch only some of the major transformations affecting the way in which national identity is already being constructed in the era of globalization.

Challenges to a homogeneous national identity

At present, demands for political autonomy or independence are often grounded on the principles of popular sovereignty and democracy. Such claims hold the potential to seriously subvert the idea of a homogeneous national identity which generally ignores intra-state diversity. By advancing their own distinctive identities, national minorities and ethnic groups challenge the state-created myth of a culturally homogeneous people living within its territory – a myth adopted and sought after with varying degrees of intensity and success by different nation-states. It could be argued, however, that social movements pressing for the rights of ethnic groups and national minorities existed well before the era of globalization. Nevertheless, globalization has added very distinctive features to these movements by providing, to those who can afford it, potent means to promote their own languages and cultures, denounce unfair situations, create virtual resistance networks and organize political action where co-presence is not a necessary condition. Globalization has radically transformed the ways in which information and culture can be created and disseminated.

In addition, globalization has added visibility to the ways in which nation-states conduct politics and deal with their national and ethnic minorities. Visibility contributes to the denunciation of unjust situations but, so far, has not proved very efficient in halting repression or changing them. The visibility associated with globalization has placed greater pressure upon nation-states to characterize themselves as democratic, either by genuinely democratizing their functioning and structure or by skilfully seeking to hide their non-democratic practices, something which is becoming increasingly difficult. Greater visibility of national and ethnic minorities has revealed that, in spite of continuous attempts to homogenize their populations, most nation-states remain multinational and multi-ethnic. This fact, so long hidden and/or neglected, reveals the urgent need for European states to find alternative strategies for the construction of national identity on a more integrative basis. Failure in this respect inevitably threatens social cohesion and fuels further claims for devolution and secession which, in many parts of the world, are already leading to the state's break-up.

The Spanish transition to democracy illustrates how increasing visibility of the democratic claims for recognition put forward by Catalans and Basques, together with the desire to be accepted by Western supranational institutions such as the EU and NATO, prompted a fundamental redefinition of Spain. Such redefinition stimulated changes in the Spanish state structure and, to some extent, Spanish national identity. During the Francoist regime (1939–1975) the state imposed an image of Spain defined by centralism, conservatism, Catholicism and the pre-eminence of Castilian culture. The 1978 constitution transformed the nature of Spain. Democracy forced the Spanish state to recognize the differences that existed within it and to confer the status of autonomous community upon Catalonia and the Basque Country in the first instance, thus proceeding to a radical modification of the Spanish model of the state. In the new democratic Spain, the creative role the state plays in relation to nationalism in the interconnection between Catalonia and Spain applies reflexively. The country's definition has to be examined and reformed in the light of incoming information about Spain itself; this concerns the nations or, in the terms of the 1978 constitution, the 'nationalities and regions' forming Spain.

The power structure through which the Francoist state was able to impose its own constructed Spanish national identity, persuading social actors – when necessary by force – to adjust at least their public life to it, has now been eroded. Spanish national identity is being defined in relation to its constituent nations, while these nations are at the same time struggling to recuperate and develop the key elements of their specific national identities suppressed under Franco. The very definition of Spain is at stake here: by defining themselves as nations, Catalonia, the Basque Country and Galicia challenge the model of a homogeneous Spanish national identity defended not only by Francoism but also by some conservative sectors critical of the substantial autonomy they have already acquired.

Cultural confrontation, competition and dialogue

Although nation-states are able to generate and disseminate common symbols and to reproduce rituals destined to enhance a sense of community among their citizens, they can no longer count on their exclusive capacity to exert cultural control over their territories. The new technologies associated with globalization have loosened the state's ability to impose a single culture upon its population and rendered cultural homogenization difficult. Yet, this assertion has to be qualified because, as we have already mentioned, never before did the nation-state have such potent technology at its disposal to produce and disseminate a particular culture and to control its population. The post-traditional nation-state seeks to present its national symbols and rituals in isolation from those belonging to other cultures and peoples. But, instead of cultural isolation, we are witnessing increasing interdependence, which manifests itself through cultural confrontation, competition and dialogue. Of course, this is not an even phenomenon which affects all nations equally; rather, it stands as a constantly expanding feature in the age of globalization.

National identity and citizenship

The whole process of translating the ideas of popular sovereignty into universal adult suffrage required a long and hard struggle. The achievement of citizenship rights was by no means a process which could be taken for granted, since we can find a contrast between its defence among certain intellectual circles and the strong resistance to it on the part of the more privileged sectors of society.[34]

Citizenship established a clear-cut distinction between those entitled to direct engagement in governance processes and those excluded from them. In the West, the concession of further rights to citizens grew quickly after the Second World War, and diverse welfare-state models were established in various countries. Since then, and due to the impact of globalization upon the proliferation of international and supranational institutions, the nation-state's traditional role as a rights-giver *par excellence* has been challenged by institutions such as the United Nations and the European Union. For this reason, some scholars argue that a 'post-national' type of citizenship alongside the existing 'national model' may be emerging in Europe.[35] At this stage, it is not clear how potent and widespread this new model will become.

In the last fifty years, greater emphasis has been placed on human rights as defined and, to a certain degree, guaranteed by the United Nations. As Held argues: 'The 1948 UN Declaration of Human Rights and subsequent 1966 covenants of rights raised the principle of egalitarian individualism to a universal reference point: the requirement that each person be treated with equal concern and respect, irrespective of the state in which they were born or brought up.'[36] This entails the recognition of single persons as subjects of international law and, in principle, as the ultimate source of political authority. Further to this, 'human rights entitlements can trump, in principle, the particular claims of national polities; they set down universal standards against which the strengths and limitations of individual political communities can be judged.'[37] However, in spite of the emergence of some cosmopolitan trends in legal and political developments since the Second World War, a new deep-rooted structure of cosmopolitan accountability and regulation has yet to be established. Nation-states remain strong and their rights are usually affirmed alongside more cosmopolitan leanings.

The definition of specific rights to be conferred upon EU citizens is much more recent. It represents a major step in so far as it breaks the nation-state's unique status as rights-guarantor and opens up the possibility for EU citizens, dissatisfied with some aspects of their countries' legislation, to appeal to EU institutions whenever the right in question has already been granted by the EU to its citizens. This specific situation reflects an anomaly based upon the lack of total harmonization between EU laws and regulations and those of its member states, and explains why, in some cases, the EU Court of Justice has overridden some countries' rulings.

Once fully defined, EU citizenship could make redundant a great deal of the EU member states' legislation.

So far, the nation-state's status as guarantor of its citizens' rights has contributed to strengthen its ability to infuse a still incipient sense of common national identity. However, the progressive supersession of the traditional role of the state and its replacement by supranational institutions holds the potential to weaken its citizens' loyalty. Consciousness of forming a group with a shared history, culture and territory plays a fundamental part in the construction of national identity, and it is unlikely that such a potent emotional attachment could be easily replaced by membership of larger political institutions such as the EU. But this argument should not underestimate the fact that not all citizens feel with the same intensity the emotional bond which connects them to their nation-states. In this respect, the intensity of the emotional attachment of Scots, Welsh, Irish (in Northern Ireland), Catalans, Basques, Flemings, Quebeckers, Corsicans and Bretons to their respective nation-states would require careful consideration. For instance, it might be worth analysing whether greater devolution to nations without states when combined with the consolidation of European citizenship could eventually contribute to weakening the nation-state's capacity to infuse a homogeneous national identity among its citizens. In addition, one could question to what extent the strengthening of the EU could affect the relationship between different levels of identity. A further concern refers to the force of the emotional attachment of ethnic minorities to the nation-states within which they live and work.

Finding new common enemies

An essential strategy in the generation of national identity consists in uniting people against a common enemy. Since their foundational period, nation-states have been engaged almost continually in the fighting of war. Territorial, religious, ethnic, political and economic arguments have been employed to justify fighting against a wide range of external enemies.

Wars have contributed to the dissemination of the idea of the nation as a community of fate. Besides, they have generated sentiments of solidarity towards fellow citizens and loyalty to the nation-state. Yet, while in some parts of the world conventional war continues to operate as a practical tool in dealing with enemies and contributing to the construction of a strong sense of national identity, in the West the absence of war – except for wars waged away from the national territory, for instance in Iraq and Afghanistan – poses some questions about how national identity may be built in peacetime. A possible response to this question points to the emergence of new kinds of external and internal enemies. Among the former are more abstract enemies, such as the threat of international terrorism, 'Islamic fundamentalism', organized crime or ecological disasters. The latter may include some national and ethnic minorities, migrants, refugees and asylum-seekers as groups which, for various reasons, represent the 'alien' and the 'different', and generally prompt the reinforcement of the state's national identity. Quite often, immigration ends up strengthening the nation-state. In selected cases, some of these 'alien' groups are portrayed as posing a potential threat to the stability, order, prosperity and/or well-being of the nation-state. Some political parties and associations employ these types of arguments to justify their stand against migrants, refugees and asylum-seekers, while they coincidentally display a negative attitude towards devolution. Arguments for exclusion grounded on ethnic and national differences can lead to vehement hostility whenever racist and xenophobic ideas are added to them.

Media and education

The nation-state actively seeks to retain control of the national media and finds its backing crucial in moulding public opinion. The role of the media in general, regional and local elections has proven decisive in determining the fate of contending political parties and providing legitimacy to state actions and policies.

Even more important, national education continues to play a fundamental part in defining the national community and supplying a sense of continuity and purpose to the very existence of the nation-state. National education, as Gellner demonstrated,[38] equips individuals with the language and culture which will allow them to live and work within a given society. The importance of controlling the national curricula becomes apparent when the nation-state decides on such vital issues as:

- the content of national history;
- whether to include the languages and cultures of minority nations and ethnic groups as forming a part of the national culture;
- what religions, if any, should be taught to students;
- how other countries, peoples and cultures are to be presented.

As a consequence of globalization, the nation-state is gaining greater control over the education system and fighting to increase its control over some of the media. Simultaneously, however, globalization has fostered the generation of continuous flows of information that cut across state boundaries. There is some kind of inherent contradiction concerning the effects of globalization upon the nation-state's capacity to impose a homogeneous image of the nation.

At a time when the nation-state has the most potent means successfully to accomplish the cultural homogenization of its citizens, the proliferation of global flows of information hampers its objective and breaks its monopoly upon culture and the media. There is great tension between these two consequences resulting from globalization. Matters are further complicated by acknowledging that not all nation-states possess the same power and resources to become global players, and that not all external information and cultural flows have the same ability to reach ordinary citizens in different parts of the world. Furthermore, the status and social class of citizens determine the variety and quality of the information to which they have access; a very substantial number of citizens still remain deeply influenced by the national education and media system.

A crucial question when dealing with the impact of globalization upon culture concerns whether we are moving towards a unitary global culture of a cosmopolitan nature or whether, on the contrary, globalization will contribute to the blossoming of particular cultures.

The creation of national identity, I argue, responds to a complex process by which individuals identify themselves with a set of symbols and traditions, and a culture and language, that have the power to unite and stress the sense of community. This process of identification involves a continuous flow between individuals and symbols, in the sense that individuals do not merely have to accept already established symbols, but rather have constantly to re-create them and attribute to them new meaning according to the changing circumstances through which the life of the community develops. Tradition has to be reinvented and persistently actualized. All groups need symbols and rituals in order to survive, maintain cohesion and reaffirm the collective ideas which they create.

2

National Identity, Devolution and Secession

In recent years, the proliferation of nationalist movements in nations without states, such as Catalonia, Scotland, Flanders, Wales, the Basque Country and Quebec, has raised some issues about whether devolution could be regarded as a threat to the national identity instilled by the state. This chapter focuses on the impact of devolution on national identity by addressing two key issues. First, it examines whether devolution fosters the rise of dual identities – regional and national – within a single state and, second, it considers whether devolution encourages secession or, on the contrary, stands as a successful strategy in accommodating intra-state national diversity.

The chapter compares three Western liberal democracies – Canada, Spain and Britain – which include some territorially circumscribed national minorities – among them, Quebec, Catalonia and Scotland, all of which are endowed with a strong sense of identity based upon the belief in a common ethnic origin and a sense of shared ethnohistory. It begins by offering a detailed examination of the processes since the early 1960s leading to the accommodation of Quebec within Canada; this is the particular period in which Quebec modern nationalism emerged and initiated a sustained campaign for the cultural and political recognition of the province within Canada. Quebec's demands are studied in relation to the Canadian nation-building strategies set up by former Canadian prime minister P. E. Trudeau.

The chapter then moves on to consider whether devolution fosters the emergence of multiple identities within a single state. At this point, recent data on regional and national identity in Canada are compared with data measuring similar variables in Spain and Britain. To conclude, the chapter investigates whether devolution feeds separatism by assessing support levels for current devolution arrangements in Canada, Spain and Britain.

The rise of modern Quebec nationalism

Traditional Quebec nationalism was conservative and strongly influenced by Catholic values. It was not separatist, but it possessed a strong ethnic orientation and aimed at preserving the specificity of the French-Canadian nation within the federation, the key components of Quebec identity being the French language, the Catholic religion, a common history and, more ambiguously, territory.[1] Its main ideologist was the Abbé Groulx and its most clear expression can be found in the Tremblay Report (1954). Traditional Quebec nationalism 'was an ideology opposed both to individualist liberalism and to collectivist socialism, emphasizing instead the Catholic social doctrines of personalism and subsidiarity, anti-materialist and imbued with spiritual values.'[2]

A radical shift in Quebec nationalism took place in the 1960s and gave rise to the so-called *Revolution Tranquille* (Quiet Revolution), which coincided with the election of the Liberal government led by Jean Lesage. Demands for socio-economic change resulted in a modernization programme which strengthened and redefined nationalism. Language remained a key identity-marker of Quebeckers, but substantial transformations affected civil society. Among these were the secularization of nationalism, the spread of liberal values, the rise of a francophone middle class, the expansion of organized labour and the wish of the population to take control over their own affairs, encapsulated in Lesage's slogan *'maîtres chez nous'* (masters in our own house).[3] The Quiet Revolution[4] awakened a nationalist movement which denounced the second-class treatment received by French Canadians within the federation.[5] Education, employment and language emerged as three major areas in which French Canadians were discriminated against.

Accommodating Quebec

Prime Minister Lester Pearson (1963–8) thought that the only way to tame the emerging separatism was to accommodate Quebec's demands. He created the Royal Commission on Bilingualism and Biculturalism, its objective being to 'recommend what steps should be taken to develop the Canadian Confederation on the basis of an equal partnership between the two founding races, taking into account the contributions made by the other ethnic groups to the cultural enrichment of Canada and the measures that should be taken to safeguard that contribution.'[6] Pearson's conception of Canada included a sense of asymmetry between the provinces capable of acknowledging the distinct nature of Quebec within Canada. In 1963 he declared that, 'while Quebec is a province in this national confederation, it is more than a province because it is the heartland of a people: in a very real sense it is a nation within a nation.'[7] Pearson's approach materialized in a series of initiatives to accommodate Quebec, including the elaboration of the notion of 'cooperative federalism' providing the same opportunities to all provinces, but assuming that only Quebec would be prepared to take advantage of them. For instance, he established 'contracting out', that is, the opportunity given to all provinces to take full responsibility for programmes managed jointly by the federal and the provincial governments, or even by Ottawa alone, a responsibility that only Quebec was willing to take on. Among others it was applied to the youth allowance and the student loan programmes established by Ottawa in 1964. The most prominent of all the programmes from which the provinces were allowed to 'opt-out' was the Canada Pension Plan. Quebec was the only province to 'opt-out',[8] and in so doing it was clearly engaging in a nation-building project which, in principle, should be compatible with its status as a member of the Canadian federation. For Quebeckers accommodation implied the tacit recognition of the French as one of the two founding peoples of Canada.

Canadian nation-building: Trudeau's vision

The new prime minister, Pierre Elliot Trudeau (1968–79 and 1980–4), adopted a radically different policy towards Quebec from that of his predecessor. While Pearson sought to accommodate Quebec, Trudeau despised nationalism and was determined to eradicate it by incorporating Quebec francophones into a new pan-Canadian identity. Trudeau, a francophone from Quebec, albeit of mixed British–French descent, regarded Quebec as a backward society and defined its nationalism as the enemy of democracy, individual rights and social and economic justice.[9]

Trudeau was strongly committed to a type of individualism rooted in the Catholic doctrine of personalism coupled with an abiding commitment to human rights. In his view, the individual should be supreme and all collectivities were suspect. He condemned the emotional character of nationalism and argued in favour of federalism as a superior form of organization. The strength of Trudeau's personality and his determination to transform Canada led him to defend a 'rational messianism'[10] founded on the idea that Canada had the moral responsibility to defeat Quebec nationalism. In doing so, Canada would defend reason above emotion and fulfil its historic mission. It might or might not have escaped Trudeau that such a strong sense of historic purpose could easily be turned into a solid basis for the emergence of a new Canadian nationalism, even if he was opposed to the use of such an expression and decided to define it as something else.[11]

Trudeau offered a new image of Canada at a time when the British connection had weakened as a result, among other reasons, of the dismantling of the British Empire and the spread of the United States of America's influence and power around the world. Many anglophone Canadians welcomed Trudeau's proposals for a renewed, modern and strong pan-Canadian identity ready to confront a rising Quebec nationalism.[12]

Trudeau sought to shift Quebeckers' primary allegiance to Quebec by promoting a brand new pan-Canadian identity which ultimately should strengthen Canadian unity and weaken Quebec's nationalism. A tense relationship between Canada's and Quebec's nation-building strategies was to unfold and turn into one of the key challenges to the Canadian federation for years to come. Trudeau's vision of Canada involved:

- defence of language rights for francophones throughout Canada;
- defence of individual rights as superior to collective rights;
- opposition to the notion of the Royal Commission on Bilingualism and Biculturalism (B&B Commission) of biculturalism based upon the recognition of two culturally distinct communities with a territorial basis, that is, French and English Canada;
- recognition of the equality of all provinces, which, in turn, implied the defence of symmetrical devolution;
- opposition to recognizing Quebec as the primary base of francophone language and culture within Canada;
- the renewal of Canadian federalism;
- the construction of a new pan-Canadian identity.

The pillars of Trudeau's nation-building project were official bilingualism, multiculturalism, and renewed federalism involving the patriation of the constitution and a new charter of rights.

Bilingualism

Trudeau's objective was to make Canada bilingual, an idea rooted in his goal of defeating Quebec nationalism. In Trudeau's view, being able to understand each other in French and English should ultimately contribute to uniting Canadians. He argued that competence in both official languages would break the territorially grounded claim of Quebeckers to constitute the only French linguistic and cultural enclave in North America. As McRoberts points out, 'historically, very few Canadians have been bilingual. In 1961, only 12.2 per cent of Canadians said they could carry on a conversation in both English and French . . . [and] 70 per cent of bilingual Canadians had French as their mother tongue.'[13] The 1969 Official Languages Act granted equal status to French and English in federal institutions, guaranteed federal services in both languages across the country, and established the Office of the Commissioner of Official Languages to police implementation.[14] The same year, the Royal Commission on Bilingualism and Biculturalism revealed that the cultural and linguistic privileges of the English minority in Quebec were combined with a considerably better economic situation.[15]

The federal government was strongly committed to promoting bilingualism, but the outcome of its campaign, in terms of promoting national unity and a new pan-Canadian identity, was mixed. It is true that the use of French in the federal government increased substantially.[16] The number of anglophone Canadians who made the effort and became competent in French was remarkable, and this somehow contributed to generating a hostile reaction towards Quebec's continuing demands for recognition. The decision of the Quebec government to abandon linguistic equality with Bill 22 and Bill 101 prompted a negative reaction among many anglophones. They were unsympathetic to the idea that such measures were needed to strengthen the use of French in a primarily anglophone Quebec economy and to integrate immigrant children into a francophone society.[17]

Multiculturalism

In 1971, Trudeau proclaimed, 'there are no official cultures in Canada.'[18] Canada was to be a multicultural state, a measure highly disputed in Québécois[19] circles, where it was argued that multiculturalism was an instrument to water down their nationalist claims and the primarily bilingual and bicultural nature of the Canadian federation. The adoption of multiculturalism contradicted the B&B Commission's assertion that Canada contained 'two dominant cultures . . . embodied in distinct societies'.[20] Multiculturalism was endorsed by representatives of ethnic groups, and as a policy it shifted from the preservation of cultures to the promotion of equality. Initially it received the support of largely white, second- and third-generation Canadians of non-British, non-French descent. Later, from the mid-1960s, it appealed to new non-white immigrants, who denounced inequality and stood for the need to break down social and racial barriers. Limited resources were allocated to the promotion of multiculturalism, bilingualism remaining Trudeau's key concern and priority. To sum up, multiculturalism has had a mixed impact on national unity and the generation of a new pan-Canadian identity.

- It has widened the gulf between anglophone and francophone Canadians.[21]

- 'It has robbed Canadian identity of any real core, if Canada lacks an "official culture", then it is difficult to designate any set of values that are common to all Canadians.'[22]
- It has undermined the particular status of French as an official language. 'Not only has biculturalism become multiculturalism but, in the minds of some English Canadians bilingualism has become multilingualism.'[23] Yet how can cultures be meaningfully supported without also supporting their languages?[24]
- It has obtained support from many anglophone Canadians who regard multiculturalism as a feature distinguishing Canada from the USA and the melting pot model it is presumed to represent.[25]

Constitutional reform

The election of the Parti Québécois (PQ) (1976), which endorsed sovereignty-association as a means to achieve an agreement between Canada's founding peoples while defending an ambitious socio-economic programme, demonstrated the failure of the Trudeau government's attempt fully to engage Quebeckers – in particular francophone Quebeckers – in his pan-Canadian nation-building project. Trudeau's plan involved the eradication of Quebec nationalism and the end of asymmetrical devolution,[26] and Quebeckers were not prepared to support it.

Trudeau's direct response to the PQ's victory involved the creation of the Task Force on Canadian Unity, also known as the Pepin–Robarts Task Force. Its report advocated a renewed federalism able to accommodate the distinctiveness of Quebec; it rejected Trudeau's orthodoxy and supported Bill 101. The federal government reacted by signing a bilateral agreement with Quebec on immigration – the Cullen–Couture Accord (1978) – and by softening its tone, thus showing a much more flexible approach towards Quebec's demands. It was within this newly generated environment that the Quebec referendum on sovereignty-association took place on 20 May 1980. Quebeckers failed to envisage that a resounding victory for the 'no' platform would encourage Trudeau to pursue his programme of constitutional reform and to ignore the recommendations of both the Pepin–Robarts Report and the Beige Paper, produced by the Quebec Liberal Party under the influence of Claude Ryan.

The inclusion of a constitutional amendment, the Canadian Charter of Rights and Freedoms, was enacted in 1982 when Canada patriated its constitution from the British parliament without the consent of the people of Quebec. This constituted an injustice from the Quebeckers' perspective because it violated one of the fundamental rules of federation: what affects all must be agreed to by all or by their representatives. Opposition to Trudeau's constitutional patriation package came from beyond the Québécois nationalist camp. The Liberal Party leader, Claude Ryan, stood against it, and most of the Liberal members boycotted the ceremonies.[27] The charter protected individual rights and granted special status, to be defined at a later stage, to the First Nations. It also entrenched the policies of the Official Languages (Articles 16–20, 23) and multiculturalism (Article 27).

Peter Russell[28] identifies three main unifying and nation-building aspects within the charter. First, its symbolic aspect, in so far as its audience, through a set of rights and a discourse of shared values, are 'Canadians from coast to coast'.[29] Second, by promoting national standards, the charter results in homogenizing policies which cannot be touched by the National Assembly in Quebec, for example language policy. Finally, 'the judicialization of the Canadian political system meant that issues ceased to be regionally defined and addressed by provincial representatives and instead took on a non-territorial and "national" character'; in addition, 'the Canadian judicial system is hierarchical, and the Supreme Court's jurisprudence is binding on all other courts.'[30]

The charter reduced the powers of the Quebec government. Notably, the new amending formula did not grant Quebec a veto over all forms of constitutional change – a right which the province had enjoyed in the past. As Tully emphasizes, 'although the Supreme Court ruled that the convention would be breached, nine provinces and the federal government, all of whose consent was given, proceeded without the consent of the Quebec Assembly, and with its express dissent, even though Quebec was affected the most. This was unprecedented.'[31] Since then, several attempts have been made to solve this anomalous situation. McRoberts argues: 'rather than uniting the many Quebec francophones who continued to support the Canadian federation, constitutional patriation served to divide them – with far-reaching consequences for all Canadians.'[32] He adds, 'The Constitution Act, 1982, can best be understood as the imposition by the Trudeau government of its own conception of Canada. . . . To defend its course of action, the Trudeau government invoked its right, as the national government, to act on behalf of the Canadian nation.'[33]

Failed attempts to recognize Quebec as a 'distinct society' within Canada

In 1987, under the auspices of Prime Minister Brian Mulroney (1984–93), the premiers of the ten provinces drafted the Meech Lake Accord, which increased provincial power and contained a clause in which Quebec was defined as a 'distinct society' within the Canadian federation. Much concern and unease emerged about the meaning and significance of the term 'distinct society' applied exclusively to Quebec. The accord attracted growing opposition, and it finally collapsed in June 1990.

The Charlottetown Agreement, drafted in 1992, substantially increased provincial powers and weakened the federal government while granting Quebec a 'distinct society' status. Decentralization went further than it did in the Meech Lake Accord. In the Charlottetown Agreement, the so-called Canada clause proclaimed the 'equality of the provinces' and Canada's 'linguistic duality', and proposed to entrench the inherent right of aboriginal self-government in the constitution.

The most irreparable damage to the Charlottetown Agreement resulted from the stand adopted by the Native Women's Association of Canada (NWAC). Their major concerns were the exclusion of women from the negotiating table, and the primacy given by the Agreement to native culture and traditions over gender equality rights.[34] Charlottetown gained further opposition from the First Nations' chiefs' caution about the possible erosion of treaty rights. In Quebec, the 'Canadian clause' insistence on the 'equality of provinces' reawakened an ever present resentment which would re-emerge whenever Quebec was treated as a province just like the others. In the 26 October 1992 referendum on the Charlottetown Agreement, Quebec and the rest of Canada (commonly referred to as ROC) voted 'no' for opposite reasons.

Quebec nationalism: a recurrent phenomenon

Trudeau's struggle for Canadian unity and his attempt to generate a new pan-Canadian identity have had a long-lasting impact upon the country. However, instead of eliminating Quebec nationalism, they seem to have prompted its recurrent resurgence. The federal government's implementation of some measures regarded by Quebeckers as a threat to their distinct identity and status within Canada has consistently resulted in an upsurge of separatist support.

The final years of the Trudeau administration were dotted with examples of the new pan-Canadian nationalism born out of the prime minister's wish to unite Canada and promote equality among its provinces. For instance, after the defeat of the 1980 referendum on sovereignty-association in Quebec, Ottawa announced the new prices of oil and gas without prior consultation with the provinces, in contravention of what had become a common practice throughout the 1970s. In 1983, again omitting the usual consultation practice, Ottawa made substantial changes and cuts to its fiscal transfers to the provinces.[35] Simultaneously, the Canadian government decided to run 'parallel' projects with the provinces and adopted a more proactive policy in delivering benefits and services directly to citizens in areas of clear provincial jurisdiction. McRoberts points out that, 'by reinforcing English Canadians in their resistance to any recognition of the continuing Quebec identity within the Canadian federation, it left Quebec sovereignty as the only alternative.'[36]

Later on, the failure of Meech and Charlottetown were resented by many Quebeckers and played a crucial role in the 1995 Quebec referendum, which showed a remarkable increase in the vote for sovereignty. The government led by René Lévesque coined the expression 'sovereignty-association', currently referred to as 'sovereignty and partnership'. This involved redefining the relationship between Quebec and Canada as equal, and did not aim to achieve outright independence. The 30 October 1995 referendum on Quebec's sovereignty, while maintaining a partnership with the rest of Canada,[37] was lost by only 54,288 votes, which allowed for a 1.16 per cent majority for the 'no' camp.[38] The referendum result prompted two main reactions in the rest of Canada: incomprehension as to the causes of such a significant 'yes' vote, and anger over the threat to the survival of Canada. Moreover, it cast a shadow upon the assumption that Quebec could flourish and evolve within the newly created conception of Canada as a bilingual and multicultural nation. Canadian nation-building had gone wrong in Quebec, and it had managed to split the vote.[39]

Political and intellectual elites outside Quebec[40] devised Plan A and Plan B as possible responses to the situation created after the near 'yes' victory in Quebec. Plan A sought to accommodate Quebec, but the Chrétien government's initial responsiveness towards Quebec's demands came to a halt in 1996, when a radical shift in favour of a Trudeau-style attitude was adopted. This included the creation of the Canada Information Office, with a $20 million budget, whose aim was to promote Canadian identity and unity.[41]

Plan B involved considering how Canada should respond to an eventual majority in a future referendum in favour of Quebec sovereignty. In 1996, and responding to a plethora of criticisms, the federal government referred three questions to the Supreme Court of Canada regarding the constitutional ability of the province of Quebec to secede unilaterally from Canada.[42] In 1998, the court rendered its opinion: Quebec could not proceed with a unilateral secession.

The detailed ruling of the court indicated that the secession project is legitimate if it is supported by the people through a 'clear' referendum: 'the referendum result, if it is to be taken as an expression of the democratic will, must be free of ambiguity both in terms of the question asked and in terms of the support it achieves.' It added that the democratic legitimacy of the secessionist project denoted a constitutional obligation on the rest of the country to negotiate, in so far as 'the continued existence and operation of the Canadian constitutional order cannot remain indifferent to the clear expression of a clear majority of Quebeckers that they no longer wish to remain in Canada.'[43] The obligation to negotiate is based upon four funda-mental principles: federalism,[44] democracy, constitutionalism, and the rule of law and the protection of minorities. Further to this, according to the Clarity Act (C–20), the Canadian government becomes the sole judge of what constitutes a 'clear' question and a 'clear' majority.[45]

In Quebec, debates about the specific consequences and meaning of the Supreme Court ruling have been accompanied by opposition to further nation-building policies implemented by Ottawa, perceived by many Que-beckers as undermining federalism. Among such measures are the Frame-work on Social Union (1999), innovation funds and the Millennium Chairs of Excellence programme.[46]

★   ★   ★

So far I have examined the tensions between accommodation and assimi-lation of Quebec within Canada. In what follows I assess the impact of the nation-building policies inaugurated during the Trudeau era upon the Quebecker's desire for sovereignty and partnership. In order to contrast Quebec's support for separatism with that of other Western nations without states, I introduce similar data concerning Spain and Britain. My aim here is to consider whether devolution – encompassing federalism and both symmetrical and asymmetrical devolution – fosters separatism.

Canadians: for federation in spite of dissatisfaction with the government

The main difference between federation – as a form of government or a country in which power is divided between one central and several regional governments – and political autonomy lies in the much higher degree of decentralization, which is constitutionally established and guaranteed when-ever a federal structure is set up. In objective terms, and from the point of view of the degree of self-determination a nation without a state can enjoy without becoming independent, this is the most advantageous arrangement.

However, there is not one sole interpretation of federalism, or, at least, there are remarkable differences between different federal structures. In Graham Smith's view, federalism is both a political ideology and an institutional arrangement.[47] As a political ideology, it assumes that the ideal organization of human affairs is best reflected in the celebration of diversity through unity. As an institutional arrangement, federations vary widely in their content depending upon historical, economic, social and political circumstances.

Federalism represents an ideological commitment. This is why the mere creation of federal structures does not necessarily lead to a federalism which assumes both respect for diversity and a strong commitment to accept the union of the federation. In some cases, the commitment of political leaders to federalism produces a 'federalizing influence' in the articulation of the state without arriving at federation. Spain is a case in point.

Federation embodies a particular articulation of political power within a clearly demarcated territory, which is informed by the desire to acknowledge, protect and encourage diversity within it, while at the same time maintaining the territorial integrity of the state. The constituent units of a federation, as Burgess writes, are not mere local authorities subordinate to a dominant central power: 'On the contrary, they themselves are states with states' rights.'[48] As Elazar puts it, 'the very essence of federation as a particular form of union is self-rule plus shared rule.'[49]

At the centre of the federalist idea lies the assumption of the worth and validity of diversity. For this reason federations have often proved highly useful political tools in protecting national minorities concentrated in particular territorial areas within the federal state. For instance, Quebec, as the only French enclave in North America, is one of the most active nations without a state in struggling to secure its linguistic and cultural development, in principle, within the Canadian federation.

Quite often there is a tension between the desire of some members of the federation to expand the scope of self-determination and the state's wish to increase federal control. This tension varies in each case, and its intensity depends a great deal on the reasons which prompted the creation of the federation. Ideally, federations should be the outcome of an agreement between independent states which freely decide to start a federal project that allows them to shoulder common interests jointly while dealing separately with their domestic affairs. Quite often, however, federations are born out of the pressure exerted by territorially circumscribed ethnic groups which are dissatisfied with the treatment they receive by the unitary state containing them, and have enough power to force its transformation. This would be the case in Belgium. There a strong Flemish nationalist movement has progressively pushed for the recognition of its specificity within a once unitary Belgian state, which has recently turned into a federation to accommodate the nationalist demands of Flanders. In other cases federations do not respond to pressure from below, but are created from above. The Soviet Union and India illustrate this point.

While there are no outstanding movements questioning Canada's federal structure in the rest of Canada, the *Portraits of Canada Survey*[50] shows that the citizens in seven out of the ten Canadian provinces felt that they were poorly treated by the federal government, with 84 per cent of the population feeling that they were badly treated in Labrador and Newfoundland, and 55 per cent in Quebec; 83 per cent of ROC's citizens and 80 per cent of Quebeckers consider that the federal system is 'too slow' to make needed changes.

According to CRIC,[51] 75 per cent of Quebeckers are favourable to the idea of their provincial government playing a very active role to help the Canadian federation work better, while 19 per cent are opposed. It is even more significant to see that 61 per cent of Quebeckers think that federalism can satisfy both Quebec and the rest of Canada, a percentage which has remained unchanged since 1998. Also unchanged between 1998 and 2003 was the 49 per cent of Quebeckers who agreed that 'Canadian federalism has more advantages than disadvantages for Quebec'. When questioned about their preferences, 41 per cent of Quebeckers supported a renewed federalism and 30 per cent declared themselves in favour of 'sovereignty-partnership' with Canada. Those who support the status quo represented 16 per cent of Quebec's population; only 8 per cent stood for total independence. If a sovereignty and partnership referendum had been held in September 2003, 47 per cent say that they would have voted 'yes' and 53 per cent 'no'. When asked how they would vote in a referendum that did not mention partnership but asked simply 'Do you want Quebec to become a sovereign country?', 38 per cent say 'yes' and 54 per cent 'no', while 8 per cent were undecided.

Table 2.1   Quebeckers' preferred choice of state model, 2003

Renewed federalism	41%	(down 3 points from 1999)
Sovereignty-partnership	30%	(up 4 points from 1999)
Support the status quo	16%	(up 3 points from 1999)
Total independence	8%	(down 2 points from 1999)

Source: CRIC, *Opinion Canada*, vol. 5, no. 39, 6 November 2003.

In stark contrast to the above data stand the findings of *Portraits of Canada, 2004.*[52] According to them, voting intentions in support of a sovereign Quebec in a partnership with Canada have risen to 49 per cent, its highest level since *Portraits of Canada* began tracking the issue in 1998. Support for sovereignty-partnership has risen steadily since 2004. At the time of writing, a new opinion poll of CROP-La Presse corresponding to July 2005 shows that 55 per cent of Quebeckers would vote 'yes' in a referendum on sovereignty-partnership, signalling a historical record since the 1995 referendum. When asked about whether they would be prepared to support Quebec's sovereignty without partnership, 45 per cent of Quebeckers say 'yes', while 49 per cent stand in favour of the federalist model. A further question concerns whether a new referendum should take place if the Parti Québécois was to attain power. At present, 53 per cent of Quebeckers support this idea, while 42 per cent are against a new referendum.[53]

In terms of ROC's attitudes towards Quebec, the proportion of Canadians who say that they have become more hard-line towards Quebec has been cut by half since 1998, from 52 per cent to 25 per cent. 'Yet, in a separate question, 57 per cent of respondents outside Quebec say almost nothing would satisfy Quebec (up from 48 per cent since 2003).'[54] In contrast, 37 per cent of Canadians outside Quebec believe that, with some effort on the part of the rest of Canada, Quebec can be made to feel happy within the country (down from 49 per cent in 2003). The gap between Quebec and the rest of Canada seems to have widened, and 70 per cent of Quebeckers agree that 'English Canadians often tend to think that French Canadians are inferior to them'. This is the highest level of agreement since this question was first asked in 1980. Such perception has to be balanced against the 67 per cent of Quebec francophones who say that in the past thirty or forty years, when compared with anglophones, they have made some or a lot of progress in economic terms.

The data examined here show overall support for Canada's federal structure in spite of a critical assessment of the federal government. It also shows strong support for federalism in Quebec, coupled with a record of rising support for sovereignty-partnership in 2004 and 2005. It is crucial to realize that sovereignty and partnership does not entail outright independence; rather, it stands for what I refer to as 'qualified independence', involving sovereignty with an offer of political and economic partnership with Canada.

Spain: symmetric devolution

After forty years of dictatorship, the 1978 constitution provided a new political framework within which Spaniards could organize their lives. One of the major issues faced by the new regime was the national question, particularly acute in Catalonia and the Basque Country.[55] The new constitution radically transformed the centralist non-democratic socio-political regime inherited from Francoism and made possible the creation of the Autonomous Communities System based on symmetrical devolution. The lack of violence in the transition to democracy, the almost immediate acceptance of Spain by NATO and the European Community (now the European Union), and the rapid expansion of the economy engendered a socio-political dynamism which stood in sharp contrast to the backwardness and conservatism of the Franco years.[56]

The makers of the constitution opted for a model based upon symmetrical devolution – what has been referred to as 'coffee for everyone' (*café para todos*).[57] Yet, instead of directly responding to the nationalist demands of Catalonia and the Basque Country as nations which had enjoyed their own institutions and laws until the eighteenth century, and which still maintained their own separate identities, specific cultures and languages, they decided to divide the territory of Spain into seventeen autonomous communities.[58] Some of them were historically and culturally distinct – Catalonia, the Basque Country and Galicia – but others were artificially created where no sense of a separate identity had previously existed – for instance, La Rioja and Madrid. While Catalonia, the Basque Country and Galicia could immediately initiate the process towards full autonomy, other regions had first to fulfil a five-year 'restricted autonomy' period. Once full autonomy is achieved, however, the constitution makes no distinction between the communities.

Currently, Catalans and Basques are not fully satisfied with symmetrical devolution, and they manifest their desire to be recognized as nations within Spain.[59] They demand greater autonomy and show increasing reluctance to accept blindly the 'coffee for everyone' option.[60] Pressure to change current devolution provision and funding is already piling up in various autonomous communities, including, among others, Catalonia, the Basque Country, Andalucía and the Balearic Islands.

In Catalonia dissatisfaction with current devolution arrangements has resulted in the elaboration of a new statute of autonomy sanctioned in June 2006. In turn, the Basque government has launched the so-called Plan Ibarretxe, already endorsed by the Basque parliament and rejected by the Spanish parliament. It suggests that the Basque Country should become a 'free state' associated with Spain, a project falling short of outright independence within the EU[61] and close to the Quebec sovereignty and partnership plan.

A large number of Catalans and Basques favour an alternative model of the state based upon asymmetrical devolution. This would entail the recognition of the distinct status of the historical nations[62] – Catalonia, Basque Country and Galicia. In their view, such an arrangement would reflect the multinational, multicultural and multilingual nature of Spain in a more accurate manner.

In favour of devolution

An opinion poll (2003)[63] shows that the majority of Spaniards are against a unitary state model. The autonomous community (AACC) which attains the highest score in favour of a unitary state is Murcia, with 19 per cent in favour of a single central government. The lowest scores are registered in Navarra and the Basque Country (2 per cent), La Rioja (5 per cent), Andalucía (6 per cent) and Catalonia and Galicia (7 per cent). This shows that historical nations such as the Basque Country, Catalonia and Galicia are strongly against a unitary model of state. Curiously, a newly created community such as La Rioja displays a similar attitude, and so does Andalucía, a region with a rising sense of shared identity.

The majority of Spaniards endorse the current devolution model. Again a recently created autonomous community, La Rioja, offers the highest support (66 per cent) for the status quo. Madrid, also a recently invented autonomous community, scores 60 per cent. At 28 per cent, the lowest score is registered by Catalonia, closely followed by the Basque Country (30 per cent).

However, quite a significant percentage of Spaniards are in favour of greater devolution for the autonomous communities. Catalonia shows the largest support for greater devolution (42 per cent) while Madrid shows the lowest (13 per cent). In contrast, the Basque Country (23 per cent), followed by Catalonia (17 per cent), shows the largest support for a state model prepared to recognize the right of its autonomous communities to become independent nations. The lowest scores in favour of opening up the possibility to secede are to be found in Murcia (0 per cent), La Rioja, Extremadura, Castilla-La Mancha, Asturias and Aragon (all with 1 per cent) and Andalucía and Castilla-León (2 per cent). Madrid registers 4 per cent in favour of a state prepared to recognize the right of autonomous communities to become independent.

To sum up, the majority of Spaniards support the current devolution model. In Spain, devolution has not fostered separatism, but it has generated a strong desire for greater autonomy in Catalonia and the Basque Country.

Table 2.2   Percentage of population favouring various state models in selected autonomous communities

AACC	Centralized government	Current model	Greater autonomy	State acknowledging right to independence of AACC
Catalonia	7	28	42	17
Basque Country	2	30	27	23
Galicia	7	53	27	3
Navarra	2	64	15	9
La Rioja	5	66	16	1
Madrid	14	60	13	4
Andalucía	6	51	24	2

Source: CIS (2003).

Still, it would be simplistic to assume a direct correlation between the two and to ignore the extent to which historical nations – in particular Catalonia and the Basque Country – feel somehow frustrated by the content, speed and financial arrangements derived from the devolution process set up in the late 1970s and early 1980s. In addition, the neo-conservative, neo-centralist policies and attitudes of the Aznar government, once it attained a majority in the Spanish parliament (2000–4), undoubtedly contributed to radicalizing regional nationalism in Spain and indirectly fed separatism.[64]

It was during José María Aznar's mandate that the 'Plan Ibarretxe' in favour of the Basque Country becoming a 'state associated with Spain' was devised. In Catalonia, the spectacular rise in support for the only pro-independence Catalan political party, Esquerra Republicana de Catalunya (Republican Left of Catalonia, or ERC), also occurred during Aznar's term in office. Support for independence has remained strong, and the ERC is still holding its position as a third political force in the Catalan parliament after the Catalan election on 1 November 2006. Again, it should be noted that the ERC stands for Catalan independence within the EU.[65] In both cases, the impact of the Aznar government's attitudes and policies played a major role in exacerbating nationalist feelings. However, there were also other factors, national as well as international, that contributed to it. Their study is beyond the scope of this chapter.

Britain: asymmetric devolution

Once in power (1997), the Labour government decided to implement an asymmetrical devolution model granting differing degrees of autonomy to Scotland, Wales and Northern Ireland. In doing so, they sought to respond to different demands for devolution based upon particular national identities existing within Britain.

The British model stands in sharp contrast to the symmetrical devolution programmes implemented in Germany after the Second World War, where all its *Länder* enjoy similar degrees of devolution, and with post-Francoist Spain, where its seventeen autonomous communities are due to enjoy similar powers once the devolution process is completed. So far, devolution in the UK has been confined to Wales, Scotland and Northern Ireland, omitting the 85 per cent of the population that lives in England, something which could find a remedy if elected regional assemblies are finally created there. Some argue that in this omission lies the inherent instability of British devolution, quite apart from the different settlements already in place.[66]

In support of devolution[67]

Among the English, 57 per cent support the current model of government for England, 22 per cent are in favour of English regions having their own assemblies, and 16 per cent consider that England as a whole should have its own new parliament.[68]

When questioned about their preferences regarding the British model of the state, 53 per cent of Scots,[69] 25 per cent of Welsh and 12 per cent of Northern Irish are in favour of the current devolution settlement. In addition, 37 per cent of Welsh and 31.4 per cent of Northern Irish consider that their assembly/parliament should enjoy tax-raising powers, and only 5.6 per cent of Scots think that their parliament should not have tax-raising powers, as it currently has. In addition, 18.6 per cent of Scots, 7.2 per cent of Northern Irish and 6.5 per cent of Welsh support the independence of their region within the European Union. Scotland shows greater support for the status quo, while both Wales and Northern Ireland stand for greater devolution.

When questioned about whether the long-term policy for Northern Ireland should involve its remaining part of the UK, unifying with the rest of Ireland or becoming an independent state, it is interesting to observe that 25.3 per cent of English people and 51 per cent of Northern Irish consider that it should remain in the UK. It is also quite striking to note that 55.4 per cent of the English and only 25.8 per cent of the Northern Irish consider that it should unify with the rest of Ireland. Only 0.65 per cent of English and 6.4 per cent of Northern Irish think that it should become an independent state.[70]

When compared with results obtained in Spain, the percentage of non-English British citizens in favour of a unitary state without devolution is greater (22.5 per cent in Wales, 13.3 per cent in Northern Ireland and 9 per cent in Scotland).[71] In Spain, the highest percentage against devolution is to be found in the autonomous community of Murcia (19 per cent), followed by Aragon (14 per cent) and Madrid (10 per cent).[72]

According to the above data, in Britain post-1997 devolution has not fostered separatism. However, the asymmetrical model adopted by the state may have contributed to a desire for greater autonomy in Wales and Northern Ireland in order to follow the Scottish example. A further characteristic of British devolution when compared with the models in Canada and Spain concerns the fact that, so far, not a single nationalist party in Wales or Northern Ireland has obtained a majority in regional elections. The victory of the Scottish National Party (SNP) in the Scottish elections of 3 May 2007 has created an unprecedented political scenario in which the government of one of Britain's nations is being presided over by a pro-independence party. The SNP's victory has broken a tradition according to which British-wide parties had been ruling devolved institutions in Scotland and Wales since they were re-established in the late 1990s. In contrast, nationalist governments have been or are still in power in Quebec, Catalonia and the Basque Country.

Does devolution promote single or multiple identities?

Devolution has strengthened regional identity in Spain, Britain and Canada, and, in all three cases, it has promoted the emergence or consolidation of dual identities – regional and national. I am aware that other types of identity such as local or transnational identity are often present and sometimes strong, but they are not being analysed in this chapter since they are beyond its limited scope.

In Canada, regional attachments are very strong. In Newfoundland and Labrador, 97 per cent of the citizens feel attached to their province. This figure is 88 per cent in British Columbia, 91 per cent in Alberta and a slightly lower percentage, 85 per cent, in Quebec (including anglophone as well as francophone and allophone Quebeckers). When questioned about whether they also feel attached to Canada, positive responses account for 96 per cent in British Columbia, 95 per cent in Alberta, 92 per cent in Newfoundland and Labrador, and 79 per cent in Quebec.[73] Such an attachment prevails in spite of the fact that the population in seven out of the ten Canadian provinces feels poorly treated by the federal government. The highest scores are registered in Newfoundland and Labrador, where a striking 84 per cent feel badly treated, compared to only 16 per cent of respondents who feel that their province is treated properly. The respective data for Quebec are 55 per cent and for Alberta 42 per cent.[74]

Overall, Canadians display very strong dual identities, provincial and federal, in spite of being highly critical of the federal government. National identity, that is identification with Canada, obtains much higher scores among Canadians than does identification with Spain and Britain among Spanish and British citizens.

In Spain,[75] the highest score for citizens who feel 'only Spanish', 30 per cent, is to be found among those living in the autonomous community of Madrid. In contrast, only 12 per cent of Catalans and 5 per cent of Basques display a single Spanish national identity. In addition, 8 per cent of Catalans and 3 per cent of Basques feel 'more Spanish than Catalan or Basque'.[76]

Citizens who identify 'only' with their autonomous community represent 25 per cent in the Basque Country, 16 per cent in Catalonia, 7 per cent in Galicia and 15 per cent in the Canary Islands. Those who confer priority on their identification with their autonomous community above identification with Spain ('feel more Catalan, Galician, Basque . . . than Spanish') register the highest scores in Catalonia (24 per cent), Galicia (25 per cent) and the Basque Country (19 per cent). This clearly shows that a significant percentage of the population in Catalonia (40 per cent), the Basque Country (44 per cent) and Galicia (32 per cent) identify more strongly with their region than with the Spanish state.

Devolution has contributed to the consolidation of dual identity in Spain. The highest scores concerning equal dual identification, national and regional (that is, those who feel 'as Spanish as Catalan, Basque, Andalucian, etc.'), are to be found in Extremadura (75 per cent), Aragon (73 per cent) and Andalucía (70 per cent). In contrast, the lowest are in Catalonia (37 per cent) and the Basque Country (34 per cent), while Galicia scores 58 per cent. Such data reflect the separate sense of identity manifested by Catalans and Basques when compared with that of Galicians – also citizens of a historical nationality, although one with a much weaker sense of identity – and the population in the rest of Spain.

In the Basque Country, those who feel 'only Spanish,' plus those who feel 'more Spanish than Basque' and those feeling 'as Spanish as Basque', show that under 50 per cent of the population, 42 per cent, exhibit some sense of 'Spanish identity'. The above data point to the Basque Country as the autonomous community with the weakest sense of Spanish identity, since identification as 'Spanish only', plus dual identification prioritizing identification with the state, scores only 8 per cent. In the Basque Country, however, the overall percentage for those declaring some kind of dual identity is 56 per cent. In Catalonia, it corresponds to 69 per cent of the population.

In Spain devolution has not resulted in the weakening of Spanish identity. On the contrary, the reconfiguration of post-Franco Spanish identity as democratic, pro-European, secular, modern, industrialized and in favour of decentralization has promoted a dual identity among large sections of the population. For instance, it has made it possible for many Catalans and Basques, as well as for other Spaniards, to identify with the Spanish state, for many an untenable position during the years of the dictatorship, when they regarded Spain as an oppressive, limiting and alien state.

In Britain,[77] 17.7 per cent of English, 36 per cent of Scots and 23 per cent of Welsh identify solely with their nation, that is, England, Scotland or Wales, and not with Britain. In addition, 13 per cent of English, 30.5 per cent of Scots and 22 per cent of Welsh prioritize their national identification over identification with Britain. In contrast, those who feel 'more British than English, Scots or Welsh' correspond to 9 per cent in England, 3 per cent in Scotland and 11 per cent in Wales. Very low scores are registered when citizens are questioned about whether they feel 'only British': 11 per cent of English, 4 per cent of Scots and 11 per cent of Welsh.[78]

Forty-one per cent in England, 23 per cent in Scotland and 29 per cent in Wales have equal dual identification, much lower percentages than in Spain. Those declaring some kind of dual identity (regardless of whether greater emphasis is placed upon regional or national identity) are 63 per cent in England, 56.5 per cent in Scotland (a similar percentage to that obtained in the Basque Country) and 63 per cent in Wales. Curiously, according to the above data, the overall Catalan's sense of dual identity is greater than that of the English, Scots and Welsh.

Overall, identification with the region only (regions correspond to 'nations' in Britain and to 'autonomous communities' in Spain) is much higher in Britain than in Spain, except for the Basque Country and Catalonia. In my view, this could be explained by invoking the long-standing recognition of Wales, Scotland and England as nations constituting Britain and the almost complete assimilation of the English between English and British identity reinforced during the empire. At that time Scots, and to a lesser extent Welsh, were permitted to cultivate their own separate identities and have a strong influence in separate sections of the vast British Empire. In Spain, the unsuccessful assimilation of Basques and Catalans is connected to a long history of oppression marked by repeated attempts to annihilate their specific cultures, languages and identities while dismantling their autonomous institutions. Recent memories of exclusion and repression aimed at Catalonia as the last bastion, together with Madrid, in resisting Franco's troops and, above all, Spanish hostility against the nationalist demands of both Catalans and Basques, contribute to accounting for their separate sense of identity in contrast with those in other parts of Spain.

Similar percentages identify 'only' with the state (Britain or Spain) in both countries, and again similar percentages grant priority to state above regional identification. The English show the highest sense of dual identification, as English and British, a feature connected with the long-term unspecified distinction between Englishness and Britishness.

In conclusion, I argue that devolution strengthens pre-existing regional identities and fosters the emergence of novel identities where they did not previously exist. It promotes the development of dual identities – regional and national – invoked at different times. In the cases of Spain and Britain, a further layer of identity, which I have not considered in this chapter, concerns the rise of an incipient European identity.

Among some elites it is to be expected that the strengthening of EU institutions will foster the genesis of a further layer of identity among European citizens. The current Western socio-political framework points to the consolidation of strong dual identities, often accompanied by local and European forms of identity of various strengths. This invariably seems to lead our societies to the coexistence of multiple identities of a cultural, a territorial and, often but not necessarily, a political nature. To coexist, such identities should be compatible, that is, individuals and groups should not face a situation in which they are forced to choose between them. In some instances, as the cases considered here indicate, various national identities coexist within a single state. This occurs where the identity of some national minorities coexists with the national identity promoted by the state.

Does devolution foster separatism?

Most Western nation-states have embraced federal political structures or some type of devolution. Nevertheless, the rationale for devolution varies according to each particular case, and the aims and mechanisms to implement it are also specific to each country. Geographical, economic, administrative, cultural and historical reasons are invoked by states when they decide on the boundaries of their regions.[79]

In my view, Canada, Spain and Britain share four main characteristics. First, they have opted for various devolution models encompassing federation and symmetrical and asymmetrical devolution. Second, devolution models have not remained static throughout time. Third, the three cases contain one or more strong national minorities, endowed with their own sense of common ethnicity and ethnohistory, cultures and identities, which have developed relatively powerful nationalist movements demanding self-determination, be it in the form of greater autonomy or secession. Fourth, up to the present time, none of the three cases considered has witnessed the rise of a separatist movement sufficiently robust to force the independence of the region it claims to represent. In spite of substantial support for Quebec, Catalan, Basque and Scottish nationalism, all these movements seem to have been somehow accommodated through the device of particular devolution structures which, so far, have prevented secession and weakened pro-independence claims. Yet the main nationalist political parties within these countries do not stand for outright independence, rather – and this may lead some to question their 'nationalist' character – they advocate greater devolution or some form of 'qualified independence', such as the 'sovereignty and partnership' model defended by some Quebeckers. As Keating argues, 'autonomy is no longer a question of establishing a state, or using it to pursue a strategy of economic autarky. Rather it involves the creation of a national project, mobilization around it and an ability to engage in policy making in a complex and interdependent world.'[80] An independent Quebec would be reliant on the rest of North America. It would have to negotiate its place within NAFTA, and 'in face of the United States and Canada it would be more of a rule-taker than a rule maker, having to accept rules made elsewhere.'[81]

Should we then conclude that devolution acts as an antidote against secession? And, if so, why? Secession entails national self-determination and sovereignty. That is, it empowers the people to decide upon their political destiny by drawing up their own laws and constructing their political institutions and national identity. At the same time, a newly created state, to function as such, requires the international recognition of its status as an equal partner by the international community of nation-states. There is a strong reluctance on the part of Western nation-states to contemplate the possibility of new states emerging out of the break-up of their own territories.

Western nation-states feel threatened by the ghost of secession and are strongly opposed to altering their territorial boundaries. They are also aware that a single successful secessionist movement leading to the constitution of a new nation-state, as was the case in the former USSR after 1989, could trigger a domino effect and foster the intensification of nationalist movements seeking independence elsewhere. Should we then infer that hostility towards secession has prompted nation-states to regard devolution as a remedial strategy to placate the nationalist demands of some of their national minorities? A cautious response is needed, since each case study is subject to specific nuances. For while Catalans, Basques and Scots sustain long-standing demands for self-determination, Quebeckers are in favour of greater devolution and sovereignty and partnership. In Wales devolution was rejected in the 1979 referendum and supported by a narrow majority in 1997. In spite of this, I believe that I am justified in arguing that the above data on Canada, Spain and Britain confirms that the various devolution models implemented in each case have, so far, contributed to deter secessionism.

Pro-independence nationalist movements in Catalonia and the Basque Country are in favour of maintaining some kind of partnership with Spain and membership of the EU. In Quebec the pro-independence movement supports 'sovereignty and partnership' with Canada. In Scotland and Wales political parties standing for greater autonomy obtain larger support than those advocating outright independence. A radically different scenario exists in Northern Ireland, where the two successive suspensions of the Stormont assembly since its re-establishment in 1997 reveal the profound difficulties of power-sharing within a divided society marked by many years of hatred, discrimination and violence.

The cases considered confirm that devolution does not fully satisfy self-determination claims, but it does tend to weaken them. It locks regional movements and political parties into a dynamic which involves an almost permanent tension with the central state generally grounded on ongoing demands for greater autonomy and recognition. Yet, devolution also entitles national minorities to enjoy substantial powers. In my view, the following are some of the outcomes of devolution which contribute towards explaining its deterrent power against secession.

1 The creation of devolved institutions – parliaments, assemblies, provincial governments, etc. – contributes to the dynamism of civil society for two main reasons. First, it requires the reallocation of resources to facilitate discrete policies and regional budget planning. These processes, in turn, contribute to revitalizing civil society, encouraging local and regional initiatives including cultural, economic and social projects. Second, among other endeavours, devolved institutions tend to promote regional businesses, restore and preserve the regional heritage, and create regional cultural networks such as universities, museums and libraries. As I have shown in this chapter, none of this is necessarily inconsistent with sustaining an overall national identity.

2 The constitution of devolved institutions invariably tends to foster a sense of common regional identity where it did not previously exist – as is the case in the non-historical Spanish autonomous communities. In those cases where a pre-existing sense of identity was already in place, devolved institutions tend to strengthen it by promoting the culture, language, regional art, and selected meaningful landscapes of the area in question. But while some of these elements originate in the local cultures, others are the products of recent invention. Whether indigenous or invented, old or new, cultural distinctiveness both generates and restores regional collective identities.

Often regional cultures question some national symbols if they are perceived as divisive. So I would argue that the devolution of power – and, with it, the creation of regional institutions corresponding to communities with or without previous historical or cultural identities – leads to the emergence and, thereafter, the strengthening of separate regional identities. Nowhere is this more so than within communities where there is a clear connection between past and present experiences of self-determination, law and a separate political and/or cultural identity and language that accounts for the sheer force of nationalist feelings. Catalonia, the Basque Country, Scotland and Quebec are cases in point. As Max Weber wrote, 'shared political memories are elemental in the construction of a common national or ethnic identity, which are more likely to persist for long periods after these communities have lost their political independence.'[82]

3 Devolution generally results in the emergence of dual identities, regional and national. As I have shown above, the promotion of regional identity seems to be compatible with holding an overall national identity.

4 Devolution reinforces the sentiment of forming a community at the regional level. Citizens are enabled to participate in decisions concerning their common political destiny and usually feel better represented by their own regional leaders. Furthermore, projects to promote the culture, economy and well-being of the region's citizens tend to increase the individuals' self-esteem by encouraging a sense of leadership among them. This is not to ignore the disappointment that some may sense when faced with insufficiently funded devolution settlements, self-interested politicians, occasional corruption and a growing bureaucracy.

5 Devolution allows the construction and consolidation of a regional political elite enjoying various degrees of power and prestige. Such an elite benefits from some privileges and acquires a distinguished status within regional circles.[83] Generally, only a few members of the regional elite play a significant role at the state level. Yet their relevance within the region

depends on whether they are perceived as politically, economically and culturally powerful and influential.

A substantial degree of devolution when accompanied by sufficient – or even moderately generous – resources automatically raises the profile of regional political elites. Members of the regional government, key figures among the indigenous bourgeoisie – if there is one – and some distinguished intellectuals dominate the elite. Moreover, selected political leaders representing various tendencies are almost invariably incorporated within the regional elite.

Regional political leaders are usually engaged in an ongoing power struggle with the central state, a struggle which often lacks a deadline. They are prepared to maintain, intensify and sometimes alleviate such a conflictual relationship, but only rarely are they prepared to risk turning their backs on the status quo in order to make a radical move of unpredictable consequences towards independence. In my view, devolution tames secessionist leaders by enticing them with some doses of political power and prestige. There is a certain 'comfort' arising from devolution, which tends to turn secessionist aims into never-ending demands for greater power and recognition.

6 Devolution tends to strengthen democracy in as much as it brings decision-making closer to the people. Problems are identified, analysed and resolved where they emerge. Regional politicians usually have greater awareness of the needs and aspirations of their electorates.

3

The Impact of Migration on National Identity

Migration is not a recent phenomenon; the movement of people across the globe has been a constant in world history. What is fundamentally new about migration in late modernity concerns the relative ease with which people are able to travel around the globe on account of the radical transformations experienced by the transport industry.[1] The media plays a key role by disseminating images, accurate or not, of what some potential immigrants may expect to find in what they often perceive as a land of opportunity that could improve their economic situation or could serve as a safe haven for those fleeing war and persecution.

The diversity of migrants is greater than ever before. Wherever they settle, migrants act as carriers of distinct cultures and languages which in some cases are similar to those of the host society, while in others they are completely alien to them. Not all immigrants are regarded as 'the same' by the host society; thus perceptions and attitudes towards them frequently depend on physical appearance, culture, traditions, religion, language and behaviour. The number of migrants concentrating in any single area is also a significant issue, since only a 'noticeable' presence of migrants tends to raise fears about a potential threat to the country's national identity and culture, and also about the labour-market impact of their presence.

The social class within which migrants integrate is also relevant. For instance, at times of economic prosperity migrants may be perceived as 'useful', even 'necessary', and this may result in greater toleration of their presence. In some cases, particular countries invite immigrants to work and settle in their societies. In contrast, tensions are exacerbated when the economy slows down and unemployment rises among the indigenous population. In such situations attitudes towards migrants are often harsher, in particular among low-skilled workers, who may invoke the migrants' presence as a scapegoat for their socio-economic troubles. Groups of immigrants sharing the same origin and culture tend to form ethnic communities within the host society.

What is an ethnic group?

The terms 'ethnic community', 'ethnic group' and 'ethnic minority' are employed to refer to different groups of people. For instance, they refer to communities of migrant origin who settle in urban environments: non-European migrants in European cities and Hispanics in the USA are cases in point. They apply to indigenous peoples such as First Nations in the United States and Canada, Maori in New Zealand and Sami in Finland. Furthermore, the term 'ethnic minority' refers to distinctive cultural communities within colonial and post-colonial societies, that is 'plural societies' according to both Furnivall and Smith.[2]

The expression 'ethnic minority' does not refer to the size of the group but focuses primarily on its lack of power and resources. Thus, an ethnic minority is a group which is subject to disadvantage and, often, racism. When considering a particular ethnic minority we should be aware not only of its 'self-definition' – including the common culture and the myths, symbols and ways of life of the community – but also of its 'other-definition', that is, how outsiders portray the minority.[3]

But what exactly do we mean by 'ethnic groups'? Max Weber defines them as 'human groups that entertain a subjective belief in their common descent because of similarities of physical type or of customs or both, or because of memories of colonization and migration'.[4] Weber stresses the significance of this belief for the propagation of group formation and emphasizes the irrelevance of whether an objective blood relationship exists among its members.

Ethnic membership is a presumed identity, and this is what distinguishes it from kinship. Probably the most important feature of ethnic membership is that, in itself, it does not constitute a group but 'facilitates group formation of any kind, particularly in the political sphere'.[5] Weber stresses that it is the political community 'no matter how artificially organized, that inspires the belief in common ethnicity', a belief which 'tends to persist even after the disintegration of the political community, unless drastic differences in the custom, physical type or, above all, language exist among its members'.[6]

The belief in common ethnicity has the capacity to create boundaries which separate the ethnic group from the outside world and from other groups. It makes the group unique and different while fostering feelings of solidarity among its members. The belief in a common ethnicity contributes to the construction of a political community in as much as membership of a political community nurtures the belief in a shared ethnicity.

Weber refers to the belief in a specific 'ethnic honor' accessible to all group members regardless of their status and social class. A common language, common myths, collective rituals and religion, coupled with different dress codes, food and eating habits, style of housing and gender labour division, encourage feelings of forming a distinct group. I argue that the combination of all these factors generates a specific collective identity shared by group members. Of course, perceptions of a shared identity are not homogeneous, and different people at different times will place greater emphasis on different selected elements of a single culture. It is also true, however, that a shared identity tolerates significant variations such as dialect and religious differences. In theory, all peoples belong to specific ethnic groups but, in practice, the term 'ethnic group' is almost exclusively adopted to refer to ethnic minorities.

It is vital to establish a clear-cut distinction between an ethnic group and a nation. By 'nation' I mean a human group conscious of forming a community, sharing a common culture, attached to a clearly demarcated territory, having a common past and a common project for the future, and claiming the right to rule itself. This definition attributes five dimensions to the nation: psychological (consciousness of forming a group), cultural, territorial, historical and political.[7] Thus, Scotland, Wales and England are nations within Britain, while the Pakistani and the Bangladeshi communities form distinct ethnic minorities within Britain – a nation-state.

The absence of a claim to self-determination is what distinguishes an ethnic group from a nation. Moreover, ethnic groups, in particular those formed by communities of immigrant origin, are not always attached to specific territories, while members of a nation always share a strong affection for what they regard as the nation's homeland. Throughout time, some ethnic groups may turn into nations if and when, for various and indeterminate reasons, they develop a collective desire for self-government within a specific territory defined as their homeland. In a similar manner nations may, after long periods of time, and because of a myriad of reasons, including foreign domination, natural disasters, cultural and economic decay and occupation by external settlers, dissolve into ethnic groups.

But yet another term needs to be defined and distinguished from the ones I have just mentioned – the state. By 'state', taking Weber's definition, I mean 'a human community that (successfully) claims the monopoly of the legitimate use of physical force within a given territory',[8] although not all states have successfully accomplished this, and some of them have not even aspired to accomplish it.

Ethnicity and the nation-state

The nation-state is a modern political institution originating in late eighteenth- and early nineteenth-century Europe. It is characterized by the formation of a kind of state which has the monopoly of what it claims to be the legitimate use of force within a demarcated territory, and seeks to unite the people subject to its rule by means of cultural homogenization. Most so-called nation-states include more than one nation and several ethnic groups within their territories; internal diversity is the rule.

The nation-state has traditionally based its legitimacy upon the idea that it represents the nation, in spite of the fact that, often, the state, once created, had to engage in nation-building processes aimed at the forced cultural and linguistic assimilation of its citizens. From its inception, the nation-state selected the language and culture of the dominant nation or ethnic group within its territory and proclaimed them as official. The pre-eminence of the English language and culture within the UK, the Castilian language and culture in Spain, and White Anglo-Saxon Protestant (WASP) culture and values in the United States of America illustrates this. The selected official language and culture are studied, promoted and protected by the state. The education system, the institutions of the state, the media and the army become instruments of the state's cultural and linguistic homogenization of its citizens (see Chapter 1).

The nation-state's aim was to build a homogeneous nation out of a diverse population while simultaneously constructing a distinct national identity destined to foster sentiments of belonging and solidarity among its members. In my view, this proves that the nation-state is not ethnoculturally free and that nation-building is ethnically charged. This assertion contradicts the position defended by scholars of liberalism such as Michael Walzer,[9] who argue that the liberal state is 'neutral' with regard to the ethnic make-up of its citizens. Kymlicka disagrees with Walzer and argues that, from a liberal position, it makes sense to defend minority rights precisely because the liberal state is not blind to ethnic difference. In his view, minority rights are consistent with liberal culturalism[10] if they protect the freedom of individuals within the group and promote relations of equality (non-dominance) between groups.[11]

Notwithstanding, while national identity refers to the sentiment of belonging to the nation, citizenship refers to the political bond which defines membership of the state. Yet, while members of a single nation-state share the same citizenship, they may not share the same national identity. For instance, citizens of Wales, Scotland and England are all British citizens, but they still retain Welsh, Scottish and English national identities. In a similar manner, British citizens include, among others, members of the Pakistani and the Indian communities, as well as people of Afro-Caribbean and Chinese origin, who may, in turn, feel that they belong to various nations, some of which may not even be included in the United Kingdom.

Immigration, citizenship and national identity

Citizenship acts as an entrance-card to a particular nation-state, since it designates equality of rights in terms of civil, political and social rights.[12] Initially, and whenever possible, immigrants seek the necessary permits that will allow them to reside and work in the host society. Some of them, in particular those seeking permanent settlement, are interested in obtaining citizenship, whose content may vary according to different countries. Stephen Castles and Mark J. Miller distinguish four ideal-models of citizenship.[13]

1 *Imperial*: 'definition of belonging to the nation in terms of being a subject of the same power or ruler . . . it allowed the integration of the various peoples of multi–ethnic empires (the British, the Austro–Hungarian, the Ottoman).'
2 *Ethnic*: 'definition of belonging to the nation in terms of ethnicity (common descent, language and culture)', for example, Germany.
3 *Republican*: the nation is defined as a 'political community, based on a constitution, laws and citizenship, with the possibility of admitting new-comers to the community providing they adhere to the political rules, and are willing to adopt the national culture.' It is exemplified by the French assimilationist approach.
4 *Multicultural*: the nation is defined as a 'political community, based on a constitution, laws and citizenship, with the possibility of admitting new-comers to the community providing they adhere to the political rules, while at the same time accepting cultural difference and the formation of ethnic communities.' Canada, Australia and Sweden have adopted this model, which is also influential in Britain, the USA and the Netherlands.[14]

Modern migration includes people escaping religious and political persecution, fleeing war, famine and natural disasters. It also involves economic migrants. For our purposes here, it is crucial to differentiate between various types of immigrants according to their ethnic identity.[15]

First, there are immigrants who are culturally and socio-economically similar to the majority in the host society – for instance British in New Zealand and the USA, and Germans in Austria. Second, there are immigrants who were initially discriminated against, such as the Irish in Britain or the Italians and the Poles in the USA, and who tend to form ethnic communities within which they maintain their cultural and linguistic heritage, but who have now fully integrated within the host society and attained citizenship. Finally, there are immigrants who tend to share some phenotypical traits distinguishing them from the majority of the population, who live within relatively closed ethnic communities, and who are often the subject of racial discrimination and socio-economic disadvantage. Yet while some countries, such as Britain, register high levels of naturalization for Asians, others such as the USA have comparatively low naturalization rates for Hispanics, by far the largest immigrant group in the country. In Austria, large numbers of Turks have become naturalized since the late 1990s, and in Germany many Turks have become naturalized after Germany reformed its citizenship law in 1999.

Immigrants also vary according to the length of time they plan to spend away from their homeland. Thus some are seasonal immigrants, some spend a considerable part of their lives in the host country, and others decide to settle permanently in the new country.

Several factors account for the impact of migration on national identity. Among them are the number of immigrants received by a single country; the time-scale of immigration; the immigrants' ethnic identity, skills and socio-economic position within the host society; the attitude and legislation of the host country regarding immigration and the degree of difficulty in obtaining citizenship; and the willingness (or lack thereof) of immigrants to integrate into the culture, language and values of the host society. It is also crucial to bear in mind the value different groups of immigrants attribute to the components of the host society's national identity. All these factors should be considered against the backdrop of the specific integration model adopted by each particular country. In general terms, assimilation, ghettoization and multiculturalism – endowed with specific nuances in each case – presuppose different views and depend on different attitudes prevalent both in the host country and among the immigrants themselves. Among them are

- the open or fixed nature of national identity;
- the degree of cultural and religious toleration of the host society;
- the economic, civil and political rights granted to immigrants in each particular country;

- the opportunities for immigrants to integrate and participate creatively in the political, social, cultural and economic life of the host society;
- the significance attributed by the dominant ethnic group to phenotypical difference as a marker of ethnic identity;
- the attitudes of ethnic communities towards the culture, language, values, religion and ways of life of the host society;
- the significance attributed by ethnic communities to fully integrating into the host society. By this I refer to the degree of willingness to integrate and to the extent of compatibility between dual 'loyalties' and 'identities' encompassing the country of origin and the host country, an idea reflected in the emerging literature about 'transnational identities' among immigrants.[16]

Integration models: ghettoization, assimilation and multiculturalism

Ghettoization

Ghettoization presumes the isolation of ethnic communities which live within selected neighbourhoods and so keep their contact with the host society to a minimum. They contribute to the labour market, act as consumers and benefit from some aspects of welfare, such as the national health service and education; however, they are alienated from the rest of society and form closed communities. Ghettoization is usually a consequence of socio-economic marginalization and, often, racism. Such situations tend to foster resentment among ethnic communities, who perceive the host country and its citizens – those belonging to the dominant nation or ethnic group – as alien. The economic status of the community plays a very significant role in its attitude towards the host society. Yet while some closed communities live on the margins of society and suffer from severe economic, social and political exclusion, others manage to attain a better economic situation and status which allows them to organize their lives according to their culture and traditions, thus forming some kind of parallel society to the mainstream. In spite of living in a situation of ghettoization and being critical of the status quo, some ethnic communities perceive their current situation as better than the one they had (or would have) in their country of origin.

The degree of identification with the host society and its national identity tends to be minimal or non-existent among a population able to conduct their lives within a ghetto-like structure. In turn, they often seek to maintain a national identity linked to their country of origin. In recent years, new advanced media and communications technology have radically transformed the possibilities available to those seeking to maintain an intense relationship with their homeland. In some cases, this has the potential to strengthen the ghetto micro-society within which they live by favouring the reproduction of socio-cultural patterns similar to those of their countries of origin.

Assimilation

Assimilation assumes that immigrants should give up their own cultures, languages and specific identities and replace them with those of the host country. They have to adopt the national identity of the host society and pledge loyalty to their new home country. The assimilationist model implies a 'one-sided process of adaptation', which should be facilitated by the state.

The Chicago School first formulated the concept of assimilation applied to American society in the early 1920s. Park and Burgess defined assimilation as 'a process of interpenetration and fusion in which persons and groups acquire the memories, sentiments, and attitudes of other persons and groups and, by sharing their experience and history, are incorporated with them in a common cultural life'.[17] To be more specific, Park defined 'social' assimilation as 'the name given to the process or processes by which people of diverse racial origins and different cultural heritages, occupying a common territory, achieve a cultural solidarity sufficient at least to sustain a national existence'.[18]

Various definitions of assimilation coexisted in early sociological literature, a problem solved only after the publication of Milton Gordon's seminal work *Assimilation in American Life* (1964). Crucially, he established a distinction between acculturation – the minority group's adoption of the 'cultural patterns' of the host society – and 'structural assimilation' – understood as 'entrance of the minority group into the social cliques, clubs and institutions of the core society at the primary group level'.[19] Gordon assumes that acculturation takes place in stages and that, in the American case, acculturation implied progressive compliance with ' "middle class cultural patterns of, largely, white, Protestant, Anglo-Saxon origins," which he also described with Joshua Fishman's term as the "core culture".'[20]

After a period during which great emphasis was placed on the assimilation of immigrants into American values and ways of life, the 1980s saw the emergence and spread of multiculturalism. At its core was the renewed value attributed to the cultural difference associated with it. Assimilation was heavily criticized, and 'acculturation' policies, as well as policies primarily destined to foster a sense of shared national identity, were replaced by policies aimed at the preservation of and respect for difference.

At present, increasing concerns about social cohesion are leading to a 'return of assimilation' in both public policies and academic debates. Such a move has been identified by Rogers Brubaker, who has studied significant changes in public discourse in France: the *'droit à la différence'* approach, which characterized the 1980s and 1990s, is currently being replaced by the *'droit à la resemblance'*. This approach is coupled with the resurgence of a neo-republican, neo-universalist and neo-assimilationist discourse. Some of its main ideologists include Alain Finkielkraut, Pierre-André Taguieff and Emmanuel Todd.[21] But the return of assimilation is not restricted to France; on the contrary, it seems to be spreading throughout the Western world. Brubaker has also identified notable transformations in citizenship law in Germany – a country highly reluctant to grant citizenship to immigrants of non-German culture and which in the 1990s substantially eased citizenship regulations, allowing thousands of Turks to attain German citizenship. It also allowed children born in Germany to foreign parents, one of whom had resided legally in Germany for at least eight years, to attain 'provisional' citizenship. At maturity, the child will have to choose between German or foreign citizenship, and renounce the other.[22]

For Richard Alba and Victor Nee, assimilation occupies a central place in the American experience. It is their concern that assimilation contributed crucially to the Americanization of earlier waves of immigrants, most of them of European origin. This view is shared by Samuel Huntington: 'Throughout American history, people who were not white Anglo-Saxon Protestants have become Americans by adopting America's Anglo-Protestant culture and political values. This benefited them and the country . . . Millions of immigrants and their children achieved wealth, power and status in American society precisely because they assimilated themselves into the prevailing American culture.'[23] The return of the assimilation tendency is exemplified both in Alba and Nee's recent work and in writings by Huntington, Taguieff, Finkielkraut and Todd, to mention but a few authors. Of course this does not imply that the defence of a much more qualified differentialist approach is absent from political and academic discourses. John Rex and Michel Wieviorka illustrate this strand.[24]

The recent debate about the veil in Britain illustrates a significant shift in a traditional multicultural approach, which protected, and sometimes funded and even encouraged, expressions of cultural difference. The 7 July 2005 bombings in London have triggered a change in attitudes towards diversity, in particular after the discovery that the bombers were British citizens who clearly did not share either in the solidarity that citizens are expected to feel for each other or in the loyalty to and identification with the nation.

As Castles and Miller argue, assimilation was replaced by 'integration policies' in the 1960s in Australia, Canada and Britain, 'as it became clear that immigrants were becoming concentrated into particular occupations and residential areas, and were forming ethnic communities.'[25] Integration strategies 'stress that adaptation is a gradual process in which group cohesion plays an important part',[26] the end result being full assimilation into the dominant language and culture.

The question remains as to whether 'full assimilation' is ever complete. Does assimilation involve renouncing one's origins? Do people resent having to give up their culture, language and values? Do experiences of social discrimination within the host society and the failure to attain economic prosperity generate resentment and frustration among those who have made a big sacrifice to integrate, just to realize that they have become second-class citizens?

I argue that people should be neither invited nor forced to renounce their origins. Adaptation and identification with a foreign culture is a long process rarely achieved within first-generation migrants. Renouncing one's culture and language seriously damages one's sense of self-esteem, since it requires abandoning the constitutive elements of one's identity – suddenly considered as inappropriate, backward, or even barbaric by the host society – and adopting a new identity within a society which may never come to regard some people of immigrant origin as their own. Great efforts to integrate on behalf of immigrants, if not matched by the host society's provision of effective policies destined to guarantee social mobility and equality, are doomed to fail.

Multiculturalism

Multiculturalism[27] 'implies that immigrants should be granted equal rights in all spheres of society, without being expected to give up their diversity, although usually within an expectation of conformity to certain key values.'[28] A distinction should be made between 'laissez-faire' multiculturalism as practised in the USA, where ethnic communities are accepted but the state does not take upon itself the task of ensuring social justice or supporting ethnic diversity, and multiculturalism understood as a government policy, as in Canada, Australia and Sweden.[29] The latter involves the acceptance of cultural diversity and the state's willingness to guarantee equal rights for minorities.

John Rex, in his seminal work in the field of ethnic relations, defines multiculturalism as 'a society which is unitary in the public domain but which encourages diversity in what are thought of as private or communal matters'.[30] In his view, 'the crucial point about our multiculturalism ideal is that it should not be confused with . . . a society which might allow diversity and differential rights for groups in the public domain and also encourage or insist upon diversity of cultural practice by different groups.' This is often the case 'under all forms of colonialism and was represented above all by the South African apartheid system.' Also writing on South Africa, John Stone points out that migration 'can never be viewed in a political vacuum, for it has inevitable structural consequences for the society as a whole and affects the delicately poised internal balance of power.'[31]

Multiculturalism implies tolerance of diversity, equal dignity and equal rights for individuals belonging to different groups living within a single nation-state. Charles Taylor establishes a crucial link between recognition and identity, thus implying that modern identity is political. In his view, 'our identity is partly shaped by recognition or its absence',[32] and misrecognition 'shows not only a lack of due respect, but it can inflict serious harm, saddling its victims with a crippling self-hatred.'[33] He regards recognition as a vital human need because we always define our identity 'in dialogue with, sometimes in struggle against, the things our significant others want to see in us'.[34] At present, the meaning of the politics of recognition involves attributing equal dignity to all citizens – which includes the equalization of rights and entitlements – and the politics of difference – that is, the recognition of the unique identity of each individual and group.[35]

Bhikhu Parekh stresses that, from a multiculturalist perspective, 'no political doctrine or ideology can represent the full truth of human life. Each of them . . . is necessarily narrow and partial . . . the good society cherishes the diversity of and encourages a creative dialogue between its different cultures and their moral visions.'[36] Significantly, he adds that a multicultural society 'cannot be stable and last long without developing a common sense of belonging among its citizens',[37] and that this sense of belonging should be not ethnic but political.

Critics of multiculturalism such as Arthur Schlesinger[38] and Neil Bissoondath[39] share the view that it promotes a 'cult of ethnicity', which 'intensifies resentments and antagonisms, and drives even deeper the awful wedges between races and nationalities. The end-game is self-pity and self-ghettoization.'[40]

Nathan Glazer, commenting on diverse reactions to multiculturalism in the USA, argues that 'what has agitated Asian Americans is not the absence of their native cultures and languages from schools curricula but rather the discrimination they experienced in the 1980s in admission to selective colleges and universities.'[41] In his view, multiculturalism is a universalist demand in so far as it argues that all groups should be recognized; however, he adds that some groups 'have fallen below the horizon of attention'.[42] Glazer focuses on some of the key issues raised by multiculturalism such as Who are we?, What kind of nation do we want?, How are we to live together?, and sees a great challenge in how public education should respond to ethnic, religious, racial and cultural diversity. Considering the black movement in the USA, he argues that, in the 1950s and 1960s, black and liberal civil rights leaders were against segregation and demanded the same education for all. They were for assimilation, and argued that blacks should not be treated differently from whites merely because they were black. In contrast, by the late 1960s a black power movement, black Muslims and black nationalists were challenging the assimilationist civil rights leadership, and by the late 1980s multiculturalism was the norm in public schools. In Glazer's view, this reflected the blacks' frustration in a society in which a huge gap persisted between black and white achievements.

A further issue concerns how multicultural societies should deal with ethnic groups whose culture and values oppose or challenge the legitimacy of liberal norms. I argue that compliance with liberal norms has to be mandatory for those wishing to live and work within liberal societies. Yet while respect for difference is paramount to liberalism, in my view, the promotion of values undermining the principles of liberal democracy cannot be permitted, since this would seriously threaten the existence of liberal society. This raises the issue of whether there should be some limits to tolerance in liberal societies.

For multiculturalism to work, it is vital for culture not to be regarded as sacred and as a set of values and traditions which must be imposed by the state. Bhikhu Parekh[43] and Rainer Forst[44] argue that not all ethnocultural groups share the liberal conception of autonomy and culture; in fact, some value norms of authority and deference. This highlights the hardly universal value of autonomy and raises questions about the foundations of a theory of multicultural citizenship grounded on a single cultural tradition.[45]

Kymlicka establishes a distinction between immigrant multiculturalism and minority nationalism. He stands firmly in favour of multiculturalism and argues that it has to be regarded as one of the policies – not the only or even the primary one – regulating the integration of immigrants. In his view, multiculturalism 'is just one modest component in a larger package', and 'many aspects of public policy affect [immigrant] groups, including policies relating to naturalization, education, job training and professional accreditation, human rights and anti-discrimination law, civil service employment, health and safety, even national defence. It is these other policies which are the major engines of integration. They all encourage, pressure, even legally force immigrants to take steps towards integrating into society.'[46] In contrast, national minorities have only a limited range of options when confronted with these sort of nation-building policies. Kymlicka argues that

> the historical experience of the Québécois suggests that a minority can only sustain its societal culture if it has substantial powers regarding language, education, government employment, and immigration. If the minority can be outvoted on any of these issues, their hope of sustaining their societal culture would be seriously jeopardized. But they can only exercise these powers if they have some forum of collective decision-making. That is, there must be some political body or political unit that they substantially control.[47]

The main difference between immigrant multiculturalism and minority nationalism regarding their objectives is that, while the former is not engaged in nation-building processes or, at least, there is 'no evidence from any of the major Western immigration countries that immigrants are seeking to form themselves into national minorities, or to adopt a nationalist political agenda',[48] the latter, in order to survive, must use the same nation-building tools employed by the majority nation, and this often results in the formulation of a separatist agenda.

*   *   *

In what follows, I consider the impact of migration on Austrian national identity. This specific case study illustrates some of the theoretical debates introduced in this chapter by examining how the novel Austrian identity constructed after 1945 has reacted to a substantial rise in immigration during the twentieth and early twenty-first century. To begin with, I examine the processes which led to the rise of a specific Austrian identity after the demise of the Habsburg Empire, the foundation in 1918 of the First Republic of Austria, the Austrians' desire for unification with Germany, and the eventual annexation of Austria by Nazi Germany in 1938.

The birth of Austrian national identity

A specific Austrian national identity[49] was born after the Second World War with the proclamation of the Second Republic in 1945, and full independence was gained in 1955 through the Austrian State Treaty[50] concluded with the four Allied Powers.

After the Congress of Vienna (1815), Austria and Prussia consolidated their status as the strongest states within the German confederation. At that time the aristocratic elite of the Habsburg Empire identified with the multi-national imperial identity of German Austria, while the educated middle classes became attracted to the German liberal democratic and cultural nationalism of Prussia. The 1848 revolution, which aimed at unification within a larger Germany, was defeated in Austria and Hungary. In spite of this, the subsequent authoritarian, non-constitutional and pro-Catholic policies of the Austrian emperor, Franz-Joseph, strengthened a pan-German identity among German Austrians.

Commenting on the Habsburgs' defeat against Prussia in 1866 and the subsequent constitution of Bismarck's German Empire, without Austria, Bruckmüller writes: 'Thus, while the nationalistically conscious liberal "Reich Germans" were extremely opposed to Austria's membership in Germany, that very "Germany" was much admired in Austria.'[51] The Habsburg Empire was restructured in 1867, when a first constitution guaranteed basic freedoms and established a dual monarchy with Hungary, but continued to deny similar power to the other disgruntled nationalities. The internal erosion of the empire prompted by the emergence of nationalist movements in Czech, Slovak, Polish and Romanian lands was accompanied by wars of independence in the Balkans. The Austrian emperor, Franz-Joseph, tried to suppress such democratic nationalist movements unsuccessfully, and the Habsburg Empire finally collapsed after its defeat in the First World War.

A strong Great German nationalism had grown in German Austria as a result of (1) the middle classes' perception of the German language and culture as the basis for a unified German nation; (2) the German orientation adopted by emerging political parties in response to an authoritarian and ultramontane Habsburg empire; and (3) the contrast between an image of the Habsburg regime, portrayed as backward, non-democratic and anti-national, and the image of a modern, democratic and well-defined German nation.[52] After the First World War, Great German nationalist feelings arose in Austria across the political spectrum.

The First Austrian Republic was founded on 30 October 1918 and was officially named German-Austria. The National Assembly in its first meeting (12 November 1918) voted unanimously for a state law that declared German-Austria an integral part of the German Republic. Furthermore, as Willfried Spohn argues, 'The Germans did the same in Bohemia and

Moravia. Referenda in Tyrol and Salzburg voted with 99 per cent for the unification with Germany. An attempt at unification with Switzerland was made by Austria's most western province Vorarlberg.'[53] But the Allies (Treaty of Saint Germain, 1919) forbade the name German-Austria and did not permit the voluntary *Anschluß* or any further referenda on this issue. Yet while Austria understood that insisting officially on unification with Germany was unpractical, a growing German nationalism spread and turned more radical. The German identity of German Austrians 'was emphasized in the fact that officials who wanted to be accepted by the republic of 1918–19 had to give a clear declaration of allegiance to the German nation before they were accepted.'[54] In addition, history was 'pan-German', not 'Austrian', and even the churches presented themselves as German.[55]

The German-Austrian Social Democratic Party (left wing), among whose leaders were Victor Adler, Otto Bauer and Karl Renner, defended a Great German cultural nationalism and were in favour of unification. But they were not alone in their demands, since the right wing was also in favour of unification with Germany. Only the Christian Socialist Party (in power since 1922) accepted the international conditions and became the centre of an emerging Austrian Catholic nationalism,[56] although this is disputable, since the Christian Socialists also never formally renounced German nationalism or indeed defended the idea of Austrian nationhood until the *Anschluß*. In 1934 it established 'an Austro-fascist dictatorship',[57] but proved unable to prevent the annexation of Austria by Nazi Germany. In the referendum (10 April 1938) following the annexation, 99.73 per cent of the population voted in favour of *Anschluß*.[58]

The experience of the Nazi dictatorship, with the ensuing repression of political opponents, the traumatic aftermath of warfare and the German defeat, weakened German orientations among many German Austrians. A different outcome of the war would have 'enormously strengthened the German identity of the Austrians of whom, of course, the vast majority (to the extent that they were subject to military service) served in the German army.'[59] From Germany's perspective, Bruckmüller notes, 'one must not forget that the German nation had already constituted itself as a consensual unit in 1848, 1866 and 1870/1871 without the German Austrians. And on the basis of that experience, which had excluded the Austrians, the German nation could regard them as "Germans" only partially or not at all.'[60]

A specific Austrian national identity emerged only after the Second World War and the establishment in 1945 of the Second Republic of Austria, which adopted the traditions, constitution, flag and coat of arms of the First Republic, with minor variations. By 1955 the Allied occupation of Austria had ended and the country had recovered its sovereignty and independence; national borders had already been fixed in 1945 and have never been in dispute since. The Allies strictly prohibited unification with Germany. Neutrality was adopted as a key component of Austria's new national identity, cutting across political allegiances.

Austrians regarded their country 'as a small nation which had become victimized by the forced annexation through Nazi-Germany. . . . The predominant form of coming to terms with the past consisted of the suppression of, rather than the moral confrontation with, the past.'[61] In Bauböck's words: 'the new identity was projected into the recent past in order to exculpate Austria as a nation from involvement in the crimes of the Nazi regime. According to the official formula, Austria was Hitler's first victim.'[62]

The consolidation of Austrian national identity involved public discussions between the new political mainstream, arguing for a specific Austrian national identity, and the so-called third camp, whose representatives continued to stand in favour of Austria's membership of the German nation (*deutsches Volkstum*).

After 1945, the Christian Social Party (renamed Austrian People's Party, or ÖVP) and the Communist Party (KPÖ) stood for an independent Austrian nation-state. Karl Renner had defended the *Anschluß* in 1938, but in 1945 he and the Social-Democratic Party (SPÖ) were in favour of independent Austrian nationhood. The Freedom Party (FPÖ) continued the German national tradition. As late as 1988, Jörg Haider, leader of the FPÖ, referred to an Austrian nation as a 'congenital ideological abnormality' (*ideologische Mißgeburt*),[63] unleashing an intense controversy about the FPÖ's view of Austria as a recently created construct. In the early 1990s the FPÖ was to place greater emphasis on its pan-German stance and defend Austrian patriotism.[64] The FPÖ had already distinguished between German cultural nationalism and Austrian political patriotism. According to Bruckmüller, after 1945

> Right-wingers committed to the notion of *Volkstum* have continued to reproach adherents to an Austrian national identity of having, for example, abandoned the common 'house of German history', or repressed the common *Volkstum*. For their part, the 'progressives' have pilloried those who have forgotten, or repressed Austria's part in the crimes of National Socialism. These critics believe the pernicious fiction of Austria having been a 'victim of fascism' has been predicated upon this lapse of memory. According to this frequently repeated charge, the role of victim (*Opferrolle*) was in turn the pre-requisite for the establishment of Austria's contemporary national identity.[65]

The disclosure in 1986 that Kurt Waldheim, who was elected Austria's federal president in that year, had concealed his membership in Nazi organizations and denied personal knowledge about war crimes in the Balkans, where he had served as an officer, challenged Austria's self-portrayal as a victim of the Nazi regime. From then onwards, 'Austrian national consciousness was no longer able to evoke exclusively positive connotations, but could also be tied to reproaches of conscious collective oblivion and suppression.'[66] Nevertheless, Austria's critical reassessment of its role and political allegiance to Hitler's National Socialism seems far weaker than the revision processes undertaken by Germany.

A range of ongoing surveys sought to assess whether a distinctive Austrian national identity was emerging after 1955. Yet, in 1956, only 49 per cent considered Austrians as a separate *Volk*, while 46 per cent thought Austrians were a part of the German people. Table 3.1 illustrates the gradual consolidation of Austrian national identity since 1964.

The complex and recent construction of a specific Austrian national identity coincided with the arrival of a substantial number of immigrants originating not only from neighbouring countries, but also from Asia, the Middle East and Africa. By and large, the ethnic groups formed by the newcomers have been considered as being 'outside' the core of Austrian identity. In the post-war period Austria has been primarily engaged in the construction of its own national identity. Yet, while the emergence of new ethnic communities of immigrant origin has been largely ignored, Austria has decided to

Table 3.1   The development of Austrian national identity 1964–93 (%)

	1964	1970	1977	1980	1987	1989	1990	1992	1993
Austrians are a nation	47	66	62	67	75	79	74	78	80
Austrians, are slowly beginning to feel like a nation	23	16	16	19	16	15	20	15	12
Austrians are not a nation	15	8	11	11	5	4	5	5	6
No response	14	10	12	3	3	3	1	2	2

Source: Bruckmüller (2003), p. 64.

recognize and protect six historic ethnolinguistic communities as a fundamental part of the Austrian heritage.

In recent years, new ethnic groups of immigrant origin have become quite large – in fact some of them are much larger than those constituted by Austria's national ethnic minorities. To begin with I offer an overview of migration to Austria from 1945 up to the present.

Austria's migrants: origin and numbers

In Austria, legal status and the cause of migration are key criteria for distinguishing refugees and asylum-seekers from 'guest workers' who came to seek employment during the 1960s and 1970s. Citizenship is determined by *ius sanguinis* – parents' nationality – rather than *ius soli* – the place where a child is born. This is one of the contributing reasons for Austria's relatively high share of foreign nationals when compared with other European countries – 8.9 per cent of the total population (census 2001): 'Austria ranks fourth along with Germany after Luxembourg, Liechtenstein and Switzerland.'[67] Austrian citizens are entitled to all rights and duties as established by Austrian laws, and EU citizens enjoy most rights. However, the so-called third-country nationals – i.e. including irregular migrants as well as non-EU nationals living in an EU member state, and who are granted legal residence in the territory of a member state – do not have the same panoply of rights and require different permits for residence and access to employment.

Austria has consistently attracted labour migration since the mid-1960s and continues to do so. For this reason the term 'migration' is generally equated with 'labour migration'. It should be noted, however, that until now migration has never been a focus in historical research, and that migrants were not regarded as social and political actors until the 1990s. Even the most recent studies on the impact of migration on Austria's society are concerned primarily with its contribution to economic growth and technical progress, the cost of social security benefits granted to migrants, and, in the last few years, the potential benefits of further immigration. Little research has been carried out in the field of cultural diversity and the consequences of an almost total exclusion of immigrants from the socio-cultural life of the nation. The impact of migration on national identity has been neglected and has only attracted attention since right-wing political parties – such as the Freedom Party or FPÖ – turned opposition to further immigration into a key electoral issue, which has attracted significant popular support. I will consider this issue in detail later on in this chapter.

After the Second World War, around 1.4 million foreigners lived in Austria, including former slave labourers, displaced persons, prisoners of war, and war refugees.[68] Some of them returned to their countries of origin, while hundreds of thousands – mostly so-called *Volksdeutsche* (ethnic Germans), exiles and refugees from Eastern and Southeastern Europe (465,000 in 1948) – stayed in Austria.[69] Labour migration started around the 1960s, when the country received three large inflows of refugees resulting from the political crisis in communist countries: over 180,000 from Hungary after the uprising and subsequent repression (1956); around 162,000 Czechoslovakians in the aftermath of the 'Prague Spring' (1968); and about 150,000 Poles after the crushing of the *Solidarność* movement and the imposition of martial law in Poland (1981–2).[70]

Austria was particularly sympathetic to refugees[71] escaping communism – Hungarians and Czechs after the 1956 and 1968 revolutions were usually well qualified, and it was easy for them to find employment; most of them moved on to other destinations, while a certain number settled in the country. Later on, when Austria was already trying to apply tighter immigration rules, greater scrutiny was applied to Poles, who were often perceived as economic rather than political refugees. More recently, in the early 1990s, Romanians were stereotyped as 'phoney asylum-seekers'.[72] Concerning refugees, Bauböck highlights that they all shared mixed political and economic motives and became less welcome at times when their additional contribution to the labour force was not needed, and when the Cold War was beginning to thaw. In his view, Austria's willingness to admit refugees depended strongly on the temporary nature of their stay in the country, since 'below the surface, the exclusionary effects of Austria's national identity continued even during the period of rather open admission when it built up its reputation as a country of asylum.'[73]

In the 1960s, after an agreement between the employers and trade unions, a 'guest worker' immigration system, with fixed annual quotas and based on 'rotation' – guest workers were supposed to stay for a couple of years and return home – was promoted and run by state agencies. Contract labour programmes were signed with Spain (1962), Turkey (1964) and Yugoslavia (1966). Between 1961 and 1972, a total of 256,000 immigrants entered Austria; Yugoslavians represented 78.5 per cent of the total immigrant population in 1973, followed by the Turks, at 11.8 per cent.

In 1974, the return of Austrians who had been working in Germany and Switzerland, the impact of an international recession, and evidence that 'guest workers' were settling in rather than returning home prompted a radical shift in Austria's immigration policies. The country halted the recruitment of foreign workers and implemented the Law on the Employment of Aliens (1975). According to this law, Austrian citizens had to be given priority when employees were hiring, while foreign nationals had to be laid off before Austrians. 'After eight years of continuous employment, a foreigner could obtain the so-called "Certificate of Exemption" [*Befreiungsschein*] which allowed him / her freedom on the labour market, before being bound to an employer.'[74] An immediate outcome of this new legislation was the reduction by 40 per cent in the number of foreign workers in the period 1974–84.

The fall of the Berlin Wall and the subsequent disintegration of the Soviet Union, as well as war in the former Yugoslavia, resulted in a rise in the number of foreigners living in Austria, from 387,000 in 1989 to 690,000 in 1993. The percentage of immigrants in the workforce increased from 5.9 per cent in 1988 to 9.1 per cent in 1993, and during the same period total unemployment increased from 149,200 to 195,100. Net immigration rose from 64,600 people in 1989 to an average of more than 80,000 per annum in the following three years.[75] About 60 per cent of these immigrants originated from traditional migration countries such as Turkey, while the rest came from states that had previously been part of the USSR.

In the light of such an upsurge in the number of immigrants entering Austria, in 1990 the government introduced a yearly quota for work permits (*Bundeshöchstzahl*), establishing that the maximum proportion of foreign workers in the total workforce should vary between 8 and 10 per cent. Exceptions were made to accommodate refugees from the former Yugoslavia by creating the so-called temporary protected status. The new yearly quota system for new residence permits resulted in a continual descent in immigration numbers, yet between 1993 and 2001 net immigration did not exceed 20,000 people per annum (net immigration for the whole period amounted to 159,000).

In July 2004 the number of foreigners working in Austria rose to 379,000. The *Impact of Immigration on Austria's Society* report (2004) argues that such a substantial increase could be explained partly by reference to two main factors: the consequences of Austria joining the EU in 1995, a political decision which has 'diminished the national range of anti-immigration policies', and the 'facilitation of the recruitment of seasonal workers, who are allowed to stay up to one year and to reapply after a two months break'.[76]

Bauböck argues that, 'by reducing immigration control to the task of optimizing the allocation of labour while securing social welfare standards, this policy has detracted attention from conflicts between the construction of national identity and the ongoing pluralization of society through immigrant settlement.'[77]

The number of asylum applications rose from 6,719 in 1997 to 39,354 in 2002, then dropped to 32,365 in 2003. Successful applications increased from 8.1 per cent in 1997 to 28.4 per cent in 2003, including a record 50.7 per cent in 1999, due primarily to a large inflow of refugees from Kosovo.[78]

In 2003, for the first time in Austrian history, more than 40,000 foreigners were granted Austrian citizenship (to be precise, 44,694 people were naturalized).[79] During the first six months of 2004, 21,586 foreigners were naturalized. This can be explained by bearing in mind that in 2003 the large immigration cohort of 1992–3 had reached the ten years' residence requirement for naturalization, and that Turkey had made the process easier in 1995 by introducing a pink card for former Turkish nationals that would preserve most of their rights in Turkey. The last census (2001) shows that 12.5 per cent of the Austrian population was born outside the country, a higher proportion than that of the USA.

Migrants' contribution to the economy

In Austria, the majority of immigrants tend to be at the lower end of the income scale, spending a substantial proportion of their income on their basic needs and sending their savings to their countries of origin. They comply with Alba and Nee's definition of 'labour migrants',[80] who tend to have low education levels and to concentrate in ethnic communities, and who usually develop a weak sense of Austrian national identity. Indeed, restricted socio-economic mobility plays an important part in preventing greater integration. The input of immigrants into Austrian society is limited and, so far, their contribution to national identity has involved greater diversification in terms of cuisine, crafts and arts.

Empirical research shows that there is little competition between immigrants and residents because of the different segments of the workforce that they tend to join. In any case, increasing direct competition takes place only between unskilled and semi-skilled workers on the one hand and immigrants on the other, a new feature 'which is mainly evident in the negative wage impact on blue collar workers'.[81] Unemployment rates tend to be higher among migrants than among natives. However, in the last few years the 'informal sector' – those in part-time employment, marginal occupations, fringe self-employment, and casual work – has acquired some weight, and has shifted from representing 3 per cent of GDP in the early 1970s to 15 per cent in the mid- to late 1990s.[82]

Most migrants work in the textile, leather and related goods industry, food production and processing, the construction industry, tourism, personal services, cleaning and nursing, as well as in seasonal agricultural work. Recently, and as a result of migrants facing greater difficulties finding jobs in the manufacturing industry, a rising number have set up their own businesses, but the percentage of self-employed migrants in Austria is still remarkably small, in particular when compared with countries such as France and Britain.[83]

In the labour market, 'the skill composition of the foreign population has become somewhat bipolar, with strong concentrations at the lower end of the skill segment and an above average proportion in the highest skill segment. This is in stark contrast to Austrians, who tend to cluster in the middle and upper medium skill segment.'[84] In 2003, and with the aim of favouring the settlement of highly qualified foreigners, the Austrian parliament amended the Foreign Worker Law (BGB1. I Nr.133/2003, BGB1. II Nr.469/2003) to permit 'distinguished highly skilled persons and researchers to access the labour market without a prior test of labour market needs'.[85] Immigrants with higher qualifications, referred to as 'human capital' migrants by Alba and Nee,[86] tend to enjoy socio-economic mobility and access to mainstream Austrian culture and identity. In spatial terms, they tend to mix with the indigenous middle classes and to integrate.

On Austria's internal diversity: autochthonous minorities and immigrants

Autochthonous minorities

In Austria, a different legal and social framework regulates the rights of the 'autochthonous' and the immigrant minorities. Yet while the former are considered as an integral part of the Austrian nation and national identity, the latter are regarded as outside Austrian society and identity; they remain alien. With regard to immigrant minority policies, it is important to stress some of the ambivalences we encounter in Austrian society. On the one hand, Austria has had high rates of immigration combined with some of the toughest and most discriminatory laws for third-country nationals in the EU, including access to citizenship, which makes for a large resident population that is not regarded as future citizens belonging to the nation. On the other hand, however, naturalization rates have been high in recent years (they are now likely to come down again as a result of the new 2005 amendment to citizenship law), unemployment and housing concentration are less dramatic than in many other states, and Austria has, for historic reasons, a regime of recognizing religious pluralism that has been praised by Muslims as a European best practice model.

The term 'autochthonous minorities' refers to the six officially recognized ethnic groups in Austria. These are Slovenes in the provinces of Carinthia and Styria, Croatians in the province of Burgenland, Hungarians in the provinces of Burgenland and Vienna, Czechs and Slovaks in Vienna, and the Roma in all of Austria. To be precise, the term ethnic group is applied to 'those groups of Austrian citizens traditionally residing in parts of the Austrian state territory that speak a non-German mother tongue and have their own national characteristics'.[87] In legal terms they are referred to as *Volksgruppe* (ethnic groups), and their status and cultural and linguistic rights are regulated by the 1976 Ethnic Groups Act (*Volksgruppengesetz* BGB1 396/1976). To make this possible, the federal state 'recognizes its obligation to subsidize measures that safeguard the existence of the ethnic groups and their national characteristics'.[88] None of these groups claims autonomy rights; special representation rights have only been demanded by one faction of the Carinthian Slovenes, and the use of minority languages among these bilingual populations is rapidly decreasing. This is also an issue currently hotly debated in Austria because Jörg Haider, the provincial governor of Carinthia, is refusing to implement a Constitutional Court ruling that requires bilingual street signs in all municipalities with more than a 10 per cent Slovene minority population.

Immigrants

'Discriminated in most areas of public life, immigrant minority groups are not seen as a part of Austria's cultural diversity in public discourse and politics, the framework of policy on immigrants fosters social exclusion and cultural assimilation, not diversity [*sic*].' This statement opens the study *Cultural Policy and Cultural Diversity: National Report, Austria*, sponsored by the Council of Europe.[89] The report argues that Austria has not yet developed a concise approach towards the accommodation of group rights and a political framework concerning cultural diversity.

Ethnic groups[90] formed by people of immigrant origin do not enjoy similar cultural rights to Austria's autochthonous minorities. Of course, it should not be taken for granted that all immigrants form ethnic groups. Even groups initially identified and discriminated against as ethnic minorities may eventually become fully integrated or even assimilate. By and large, such a process is currently happening among former Yugoslav immigrants in Austria (the largest contingent), while it is less obvious for migrants of Turkish origin.

Nearly all mainstream parties and right-wing populists do not consider immigrant minorities as a 'relevant part of Austrian society'. But 'the Naturalization Law and the Austrian Residence Law implicitly favour assimilation. According to the 1998 amendment to the Austrian Nationality Act (BGB1 124/1998), the "integration of the applicant" was the most important criterion for the granting of naturalization.'[91] If an applicant could prove a good knowledge of German and 'sustainable personal and professional integration' to Austrian society, after six years of residence, he or she might have obtained Austrian citizenship. However, the latest amendment to the Austrian Nationality Act, in December 2005, has abandoned even this possibility. Now ten years of residence are required, even in the case of 'sustainable integration'.

Immigrants acquire a legal claim to naturalization only after thirty years of residence, while naturalization based on administrative discretion can be obtained after ten years.[92] Further to this, until 1998, the Naturalization Law specifically requested 'assimilation to the Austrian way of life' as a precondition for acquiring Austrian citizenship.

The Naturalization Law is administered at provincial level and not at federal level. Consequently there are substantial differences in the ways in which provincial governments interpret the law and define 'integration'. For instance, the provincial government of Vienna defines 'complete integration' as 'fluent knowledge of German, a sound professional education and proven activities for the coexistence of the indigenous and immigrant population in Vienna'.[93] In 1996 and 1997 this resulted in the refusal to grant residence permits to Turkish women, with the argument that, 'according to experience, even after a prolonged stay in Austria people from this cultural area do not show a complete integration in the areas of language and communication with the resident population and do not assimilate to Central European customs and ways of life.'[94] The Constitutional Court revoked these decisions, which undoubtedly exemplify the complexity and 'rather peculiar understanding of cultural diversity in the ranks of local and provincial authorities'.[95]

Austria lacks an organized response to the cultural diversity of immigrant groups. Such groups are forced to rely on private initiatives and funding to promote cultural activities outside mainstream Austrian culture. Further to this, in some cases, pressure to assimilate to Austrian society may act as a deterrent force among those wishing to preserve their ethnic identities.

In recent years, some steps have been taken to integrate immigrants. For instance, the *Integrationskonferenz* (Vienna) is a regular meeting of immigrant associations organized by the City Councillor for Integration. It does not have a legal mandate, but it represents an attempt to encourage the participation of immigrants. In addition, elected 'foreigners' councils' (*Ausländerbeiräte*), with a limited advisory capacity, have been created in several cities to promote the participation of immigrants.[96] An initiative by the Vienna regional legislature to introduce a right to vote for third-country nationals in city district elections was, however, rejected as unconstitutional by the Constitutional Court in June 2004.

In the 1970s and 1980s, immigrants' children – originating primarily from the former Yugoslavia and from Turkey – were taught in their native languages. The idea behind this was that they should be ready to 'reintegrate' successfully into their own homelands after spending a few years in Austria. Because they were not regarded as members of Austrian society but as temporary guests, visitors or workers, no emphasis was placed on trying to integrate them into mainstream Austrian society. Immigrants did not identify with Austria or adopt its national identity, but most Austrians did not expect them to do so. In turn, no contribution to the make-up of national identity was envisaged or promoted.

At that time, bilateral agreements between Austria and Yugoslavia and Turkey had been signed. By the 1980s it became clear that second-generation migrants were to remain in Austria, and the reintegration approach was replaced by an 'intercultural educational' approach introduced in 1991. This was to be implemented at all educational levels. Specific curricula for German as a second language and for the mother tongues of the largest groups were developed. According to local circumstances, schools became free to offer German as a second language, either in parallel supplementary classes or integrated into the general timetable, with two teachers working with the whole class. It is estimated that about 25 to 30 per cent of all immigrant children were attending these classes in the mid-1990s.[97]

Three-quarters of all non-German pupils in Vienna spoke Turkish or one of the languages of the former Yugoslavia as their first language. In principle, native-language teaching can be offered in any language provided that there is sufficient demand (twelve to fifteen students depending on each province) and that trained teachers are available. In 1998/9 the languages offered at primary school level were Albanian, Arabic, Bosnian, Croatian, Serbian, Bulgarian, Hungarian, Kurdish, Polish, Romanian, Slovak, Slovenian, Spanish and Turkish. In contrast, 'secondary schools do not tend to value immigrants' mother tongue and . . . rarely offer Turkish or Croatian as a regular or optional second language.'[98] In addition, native-language teachers tend to endure poor working conditions, since most of them have degrees awarded abroad that are not fully recognized within the Austrian educational system.

In Austria, Sunni Islam was officially recognized as a religion in 1912. A 1979 law recognized Islam as a religious congregation under public law with similar privileges to those enjoyed by Christian denominations. From 1983 onwards, the right to be instructed in Sunni Islam in public schools was introduced. The Congregation of the Islamic Faith designed a specific curriculum that was also approved by the Austrian school authorities, with German serving as the language of instruction and the Koran being recited in Arabic. The official Muslim representatives in Austria, who regulate the teaching and are paid by the Austrian state, nominate the teachers. All of them must have Austrian citizenship. The first private denominational Islamic secondary school in Austria was founded in Vienna in 1999.

In Bauböck's view, 'Austria is an immigration society that does not regard itself as an immigrant nation',[99] and this misleading self-perception undoubtedly contributes to explain the Austrians' overall attitude towards immigrants. The distinction between those who belong to the nation and outsiders is crucial when considering various attitudes towards immigrants. Yet while some countries have created a national consensus on 'the value of relative openness for immigration' stemming from their own emigration and immigration traditions and history, Austria's historic experiences of migration 'have become relevant by way of negation or amnesia. A strong nativist construction of identity that can be easily appealed to in politics seems to have compensated for the lack of a firm sense of a republican – or even a specific ethnic core – of Austrian nationhood.'[100]

On Austria's special relationship with South Tyrol

After the Second World War, Austria became determined to construct a distinct national identity separate from that of Germany and that of the former Austro-Hungarian Empire. Such a tremendous effort allowed for the cultural recognition of some internal diversity within the Austrian territory, and it became exemplified in the recognition of cultural rights for Austria's autochthonous minorities considered as an integral part of the Austrian nation and national identity. No autonomy rights were considered, though. This stands in sharp contrast with Austria's very active role in securing strong political autonomy rights for the German-speaking population in Italian South Tyrol (Alto Adige),[101] of whom Austria feels itself to be a protector.

After the First World War, Italy annexed the German-speaking South Tyrol – in German, Alto Adige is still referred to as South Tyrol – and the

Italian-speaking Trentino that had belonged to Austria. During the fascist regime, Mussolini engaged in a forced Italianization of South Tyrol, a process that prompted the departure of many of its inhabitants. In the 1960s a movement for the return to Austria grew strong and resulted in some violent actions and numerous demonstrations. At present, the Südtiroler Volkspartei (SVP, or Party of South Tyrol), a Christian democratic party representing the German-speaking minority, demands a pardon for those regarded as terrorists by Italy and being praised as patriots in Bolzano–South Tyrol.

Since 1948, the autonomous provinces of Bolzano and Trentino form the Trentino–Alto Adige region, inhabited by 962,000 people, 69 per cent German-speaking. The region has a special status within Italy – together with Friuli–Venezia Giulia, Val d'Aosta, Sardinia and Sicily. The wealthy Alto Adige collects its own taxes, and some other Italian regions resent the special treatment received by it – in their view, too high a price to prevent a movement in favour of separating from Italy and possibly joining Austria.

Austria has recently (January 2006) invoked its will to continue protecting the German-speaking minority in South Tyrol – *Schutzfunction* – by continuing to monitor carefully events within its former territory, and we should probably understand that the basis for Austria's position originates in its view of South Tyrolean people as belonging to Austria, at least in a cultural sense. Such a move has not been welcomed by the Italians, in particular after Austria's official acknowledgement in 1992 of the Italian character of South Tyrol.

This exemplifies Austria's attachment and concern for a community of people regarded as part of their own – seen as culturally, linguistically and historically sharing Austria's national identity – but which happens to be included within the boundaries of another state.

Renewed claims about South Tyrol also reveal the influence of the FPÖ, a coalition partner of the ÖVP during the first half of 2006. The FPÖ in its programme refers to Austria as the protecting power of the German and Ladin South Tyroleans and defends the idea that 'There must remain the possibility for South Tyrol to join the Republic of Austria in a free exercise of its right to self-determination.'[102]

Austria's attitude towards South Tyrol is in contrast to its stance towards its own autochthonous minorities and the cultural recognition received by them, as well as to the way in which those immigrants forming ethnic minorities are regarded by the Austrian state.

Migration: 'cultural enrichment' or 'cultural threat'?

Since Austria does not regard itself as an 'immigration society', immigrants have been considered primarily as temporary workers doing menial jobs and occupations that Austrians were not keen on taking. The 'temporary' nature of immigration simultaneously justified and prevented Austrians from considering migrants as social and political actors within Austrian society.

After the Second World War, Austria portrayed itself as the first victim of Nazism, a factor which prevented many Austrians from undertaking a full critical reassessment of the country's Nazi past. For some, this permitted 'a stronger cultural and political continuity of traditional anti-foreign stereotypes.'[103] The impressive economic development of Austria after 1945 acted as a magnet for immigration originating in Turkey, ex-Yugoslavia and other countries in Eastern Europe, Asia and Africa. The visibility of immigrants increased, and it awakened reactions of rejection and xenophobia. Thus, in a 1996 survey, Max Haller established that 50 per cent of the Austrian population displayed negative attitudes towards immigrants.[104] The 1998 survey 'Migration and Xenophobia', commissioned by the Austrian Ministry of Science and Transport, found out that, while 31 per cent of the population saw foreigners as an 'enrichment of Austrian culture', 40 per cent felt like 'foreigners in their own country.'[105] According to another survey, the negative attitude of Austrians towards foreigners and their 'alien cultures' decreased remarkably between 1992 and 2001 (1992: 32 per cent, 1998: 25 per cent, and 2001: 11 per cent).[106]

The public presence of migrants in Austrian public life is limited, most of their own cultural initiatives are privately sponsored and, so far, very few measures have been destined to promote their participation.[107] The book *Theatre: Encounter: Integration?* (2003), edited by the Society for Theatre Ethnology, offers the first inventory of theatre groups and cultural projects organized by Austria's ethnic and religious minorities. Its authors argue that Austrian cultural policy in general 'lacks the fundamental willingness to create a sustainable infrastructure for the development and establishment of a "migrant culture". Multicultural events often degenerate into happenings with a carnival character, where culturally active migrants are presented like exotics in former times.'[108]

In the interviews I carried out in Vienna in 2004 and 2006, Austrians from different political allegiances responded 'yes' to the question: 'Do you regard Austria as a multicultural society?' – meaning a society in which various cultures coexisted, a feature regarded by them as a *fait accompli.*[109] A very different matter concerns the relationship and interaction between these cultures. The consciousness of being a small country, a pale reflection of the mighty Habsburg Empire – weakened after the First World War and the constitution of the First Austrian Republic, and further debilitated after the Second World War, including *Anschluß*, catastrophic warfare and the Allies' occupation until 1955, when Austria recovered full national independence and sovereignty – is firmly embedded in the Austrian collective consciousness.

Austria is a country with a young, specifically Austrian, national identity born with the foundation of its Second Republic. The blending of all these factors seems to have contributed to a particular sensitivity towards 'outsiders', in particular those regarded as 'too different', which has generated some feelings of mistrust and fear of 'the other', often perceived as a threat to economic prosperity, social stability, national identity, and even public order. Significant sectors of society tend to regard immigrants as different on the basis of their origin, appearance, and socio-economic, cultural and personal background.

The substantial influx of immigrants – particularly from Turkey, ex-Yugoslavia and other Eastern European and non-EU countries – received by Austria in recent years (8.9 per cent of the total population were foreigners in 2001) has provided arguments to those who have chosen to exploit politically such perceptions. According to the 2003 *Eurobarometer*, which included the fifteen EU members plus four accession countries, 64.37 per cent of Austrians showed 'resistance to immigrants.'[110] In so doing they stood in third place, behind Greece and Hungary. In contrast, 25.15 per cent of Austrians showed 'resistance to asylum-seekers', ranking twelfth on the list.[111] In addition, 29 per cent of Austrians were in favour of repatriation policies for legal migrants. Austria ranked seventh on a list of thirty countries, which included the EU-fifteen, plus accession countries and some countries with whom formal accession negotiations had not yet started, such as Turkey.[112]

Immigrants as permanent 'outsiders': the FPÖ

In the 1999 Austrian election campaign, the Freedom Party (FPÖ) adopted an open anti-immigration stance (as it had done in all its electoral campaigns since 1986). It stood against corruption and defined itself as 'anti-establishment'. The FPÖ's message undoubtedly struck a chord with the electorate, proof being the nearly 27 per cent of the vote it obtained. After the election it entered into a coalition government with the conservative

People's Party (ÖVP). In particular, the FPÖ received considerable support from blue-collar workers.[113]

The populist radical right-wing stance taken by the FPÖ is exemplified by Jörg Haider, an articulate leader who advocates direct democratic practices such as petition campaigns and referenda, while appealing to 'the latent public feeling of dissatisfaction, resentment or fear.'[114] As Ter Wal argues: 'Haider aims to articulate the views of the ordinary Austrian, while acting as the guardian of the national identity and interests.'[115] In so doing he portrays himself as the voice of the 'silent majority'. Furthermore, by placing himself outside the establishment he seeks greater legitimacy for his claim of anti-elitism.

The FPÖ argues that 'Austria is not a country of immigration' and stands in favour of a 'freeze on immigration until an adequate solution for the illegal immigrants has been found, until there is no more problem with housing, and until the unemployment rate is under 5 per cent' (points 1 and 2 of the 'Austria First' referendum organized by the FPÖ in January–February 1993).[116] The FPÖ's main argument to justify the exclusion of immigrants is the need to grant priority to Austrian citizens who are being discriminated against and disadvantaged. Ter Wal identifies the use of a series of negative stereotypes concerning illegal immigrants by the FPÖ. In her view, 'The FPÖ defines its policy of protecting its "own people first" as "humane", thus reversing the conventional meaning of the fundamental ideological concepts of humanitarianism. . . . The FPÖ thus redefines the meaning of politically charged concepts to its own advantage.'[117] In a speech at Klagenfurt on 11 September 1999, during the launch of the election campaign, Jörg Haider said:

> It is not the issue, so to say, to forbid the foreigners a [welfare benefits] payment, but the issue is finally to think about the Austrians. First we have to take our own people seriously; first we have to pay due respect to our people. And therefore one can only say to the future government, whatever it may look like: worry more about your own people, otherwise the voter will not worry about you anymore, otherwise democracy will slowly become a farce.[118]

The FPÖ prioritizes the protection of Austrian families and children as a means of safeguarding the specific components of Austrian identity, including its language, culture, traditions and sense of shared destiny. The idea that further immigration will seriously erode Austrian mores and traditions is employed as the main argument to justify the FPÖ's stance. The party presents itself as the 'guardian' and 'saviour' of a specific Austrian national identity which replaces the pan-Germanism it traditionally endorsed until the late 1980s. The 1993 referendum slogan 'Austria First' and Haider's definition of the FPÖ as a 'classical Austrian patriot's party' signalled a fundamental shift in its ideology.[119] Since then the FPÖ has invoked what it defines as humanitarian and environmental concerns to strengthen its argument against further immigration.

A further anti-immigration argument employed by the FPÖ reasons that, instead of leaving their own countries, immigrants should stay and rebuild them, as Austrians did with their own after massive destruction caused by the Second World War. In the FPÖ's view, immigrants have no positive contributions to make to Austrian society; rather, they are considered as a serious threat to a defenceless Austrian society and its national identity. The interviews I carried out among some FPÖ members and supporters show that, basically, only 'invisible' migrants – that is, those who keep to themselves, work hard and do not cause any disturbance – should be allowed in; Chinese immigrants in Vienna were often mentioned as an example. Ethnic Germans are welcomed, since they integrate rapidly into Austrian society. Blacks are often defined as 'troublemakers' and 'noisy', with no chance of being integrated into Austrian society.

Furthermore, an opinion shared among people with different political allegiances pointed at feelings of distrust and fear of immigrants – in particular towards non-EU and non-Western immigrants – who were often portrayed as alien because of their different beliefs, traditions and ways of life. Such feelings seemed more acute concerning non-white and non-Christian immigrants. The need to control immigration and the perception of being 'swamped' by immigrants seemed to resonate among significant sections of the population.

4

On European Identity

In several respects the EU represents both a novel system of quasi-supranational governance and a novel form of political community or polity. But it is also a fragile construction, for it remains a community still in the making, with an ambiguous sense of identity and within which powerful forces are at work.

The main aims of this chapter are:

1 to stress the shifting nature of Europe's geographical frontiers and assess whether cultural frontiers have remained more stable throughout time. In particular, it examines the origins of the cultural frontiers of Europe and the main criteria which have traditionally been employed when deciding who should be included and who excluded from Europe. A different question concerns the requirements for EU membership and the monopoly of the adjective 'European' by the EU, which has somehow become exclusively identified with Europe.

2 to explore contemporary sources of European cultural diversity by examining, at a time when EU politicians have decided to further European integration and to enlarge the Union, what the main features are which unite or divide Europeans in terms of culture and identity.

3 to consider emerging forms of collective identity in the EU. This entails assessing whether conflict or consensus defines the relationship between new and traditional identities. It also involves assessing the impact of the Enlightenment and the Industrial Revolution as potent forces which radically challenged European traditional societies and fostered profound social, political and economic transformation. Further change was triggered by the experience of two world wars, in particular the Second World War, and the political, economic and social consequences associated with it.

The cultural frontiers of Europe

Europe is a cultural reality that spreads well beyond the boundaries of the European Union. In recent times, it has become common practice to identify

Europe solely with the EU. Yet when people refer to 'European integration', 'European citizenship and laws', 'European institutions' or the generation of a 'European identity', they usually employ the term 'European' to refer to the processes of consolidation and greater integration led by the European Union.

On geographical boundaries

Europe is generally understood to consist of the western portion of the Eurasian landmass, together with a number of islands not far from the mainland (Iceland, Corsica, Malta, Sardinia, Sicily, Crete and Ireland, as well as Great Britain); however, this does not provide a clear-cut idea of where Asia stops and Europe begins. Precisely where the division between Europe and Asia lies is a matter of some debate. To understand Europe as a geographical area involves an awareness of Europe's shifting boundaries. The Greeks conceived a water-bound Europe whose borders lay on the Black Sea and its northern extension, the Sea of Azov, as far as the banks of the River Don. From the eighteenth century, though, Europe has often been understood to end (or begin) with the Ural Mountains and the river that takes its name from them and flows into the Caspian Sea. But this carries some ambiguities. Following the dissolution of the Soviet Union in 1991, it leaves the Transcaucasus and the newly independent states of Armenia, Azerbaijan and Georgia in an uncertain relation with regard to Europe, while Turkey also lies to the west of the Urals.

The geographical boundaries of Europe have suffered dramatic changes throughout time, and even the most recent past offers different examples that illustrate the shifting character of European borders. The post-1989 unification of Germany, the separation of Czechoslovakia, the break-up of Yugoslavia, the independence achieved by the Baltic republics and the dismembering of the Soviet Union exemplify dramatic border changes within European countries taking place in the last fifteen years.

Further to this, we should consider the claims of countries, such as Turkey, which are currently asserting their European character and demanding the right to be included within the European Union. The 2004 enlargement of the EU to include ten new member states, and the 2007 enlargement, adding a further two, strengthens the idea that the boundaries of Europe are not fixed and that the boundaries of the EU which is often identified with 'Europe' are not fixed either. It follows from this that the definition of Europe, and indeed who is included and who is excluded, tends to change over time. The description of Europe, or any other territory, as a 'geographical' entity invariably implies the absence of more elevated claims associated with the embodiment of some general values and a sense of shared identity, as loose as it may be, among its citizens.

But how useful are geographical boundaries in defining Europe? Is Europe merely a geographical space? In the light of the evidence provided above, the answer to these questions seems to be a negative one.

But what about history? Is it possible to identify any clear elements of historical continuity pointing at a pre-existent idea of Europe? In my view, this is extremely difficult and controversial, since Europe's history is fraught with confrontation and war. This seems to indicate that geography and history are insufficient criteria to decide who should and who should not be included in Europe. What other criteria may then be applied to shed some light onto the commonalities shared by those who call themselves 'Europeans'? Many scholars and politicians have turned to defending the idea that what unites Europeans is the sharing of a certain culture and values which differentiate them from other peoples, more crucially from Eastern peoples. This argument is based upon the assumption that 'there has always been a different way of life between East and West, between the full and half European . . . between real Europeans, and those caught in a nether world between the European and Asian.'[1]

Some scholars consider Europe as a system of values and mention the impact of Christianity and the rise of a set of ideas, including those of freedom, humanism and material progress, as key elements in the construction of an incipient European identity.

The 'idea of Europe' did not begin by reference to geographical or historical divisions. Instead, it emerged as a term connected to a specific cultural and political heritage embodied in Athenian democracy. It was not until the nineteenth century that George Grote, a radical banker and historian, located the origin of European civilization in Greek democracy rather than in the establishment of Christianity towards the end of the Roman Empire. But if the idea of Europe has a cultural basis connected to Athenian democracy and some common traditions and consciousness, is it then possible to refer to the cultural frontiers of Europe? What are the main criteria to decide on where to draw the line? Furthermore, if we were to agree on the existence of a certain European culture, no matter how incipient this might be, would this be sufficient to account for the existence of some embryonic European identity?

On culture

Culture is formed by values, beliefs, customs, conventions, habits and practices which give rise to a particular identity uniting those who have been socialized within a particular society.[2] From a symbolic perspective, 'culture is the pattern of meanings embodied in symbolic forms, including actions, utterances and meaningful objects of various kinds, by virtue of which individuals communicate with one another and share their experiences, conceptions and beliefs.'[3] The process of identification with the elements of a specific culture implies a strong emotional investment. Individuals are born within cultures that determine the way in which they view and organize themselves in relation to others and to nature.

Two major implications deriving from this possess a particular significance for the analysis of whether we can refer to a distinctive European identity based upon a shared culture. First, a common culture favours the creation of solidarity bonds among the members of a given community and allows them to imagine the community they belong to as separate and distinct from others. Solidarity is then based upon the consciousness of forming a group, outsiders being considered as strangers and potential 'enemies'. Second, a common historical past which includes memories of war, deprivation, victory, repression, success, and a future common project reinforce the sense of a shared identity among members of a given community. There is a strong connection between history and culture, since crucial elements in the culture of any given community, such as symbols, language, sacred places, heroes, anthems, legends and traditions, are inextricably bound up with the community's history.[4] For our purposes here, the key question concerns whether Europeans share some cultural elements capable of uniting them and making them different from 'others'. That is, is there a sense of solidarity among Europeans which goes back to medieval times? Where are the symbols, holy places, heroes and traditions which unite Europeans to be found? What are Europe's shared values? In a nutshell, what are the criteria for establishing the cultural frontiers of Europe?

At present there is a substantial body of literature which examines the historical origins of contemporary Europe and argues that some common 'traditions' and a somewhat unspecified sense of common 'consciousness' have united the peoples of Europe since the Middle Ages. Such accounts highlight European unity above the diversity which has traditionally defined European peoples. The search for a common past and traditions responds to the need to identify or invent some elements capable of acting as pillars in the construction of a shared sense of European identity, which, ideally, should go hand in hand with greater EU integration. In spite of considerable efforts to define such elements it is proving quite difficult to agree on them, particularly since the history of European peoples is fraught with memories of war. In addition, the status of Europe as a cultural unit and a system of values at the beginning of the twenty-first century remains problematic. There is a clear contrast between Europe's strengthening institutional structures and more intensive processes of governance, on the one hand (at least so far as the EU is concerned), and the relative weakness and uncertainty of the values that underpin it, on the other.

Religion as an inclusion-exclusion mechanism

Samuel Huntington, in his most celebrated book *The Clash of Civilizations*,[5] argues that religion provides the best common means of distinguishing historically between Europeans and the rest, which in particular refers to the Judeo-Christian tradition confronting Islam. This argument, however, seems to ignore that, in the Middle Ages, most intra-European wars had a religious character. In turn, it could be argued that such wars did not imply the existence of different civilizations within Europe; rather, they consisted of wars between countries defending different and revised 'versions' of a religion which had a unique origin. It is precisely from this perspective that it seems plausible to point to religion as a key feature in constructing what we now term an embryonic European identity. Following this line of argument, Anthony Smith stresses that 'there is a clear sense, going back at least to the Crusades and probably even to Charles Martel, in which Europeans see themselves as not Muslims or as not Jews.'[6] Should we then conclude that European culture is based upon Christianity and that the cultural boundaries of Europe are determined by religion? This raises two main issues.

First, is the appeal to a shared religion a recent invention? Were Charlemagne and the crusaders convinced that the religious divide between those who believed in God and those who did not reflected a further division between Europeans and the rest? Would they have defined themselves as Europeans? Probably not. Furthermore, early Europe as Christendom already contained significant religious minorities (Jews and Muslims) – and barely included the rural masses, whose peasant status was closely linked with a 'pagan' (and thus non-Christian) outlook and presented a constant challenge to the consolidation of any regional Christian realm.

Second, if we were to assume that religion, and Christianity in particular, is the key criterion for inclusion in Europe, what do we make of the religious wars in which European countries fought each other after the Middle Ages? Reflecting on these issues, Adam Burgess writes: 'it is only with the Ottoman challenge, coupled with the social and religious crises of the fourteenth and fifteenth centuries, that Europe became the Christian continent, and therefore distinct limits were drawn . . . Significantly, however, this unity was more apparent than real. Christian Europe was moving into the schisms of those centuries, and the heresies of the sixteenth.'[7]

A further point concerns whether religion operates as an inclusion/ exclusion mechanism in contemporary Europe. This raises some questions – for instance, if religion were to be considered as the key criterion in determining a particular country's European character. Could it then be argued that some of the EU member states' opposition to Turkey's accession to the EU derives from its Muslim allegiance rather than from the economic and geopolitical concerns often openly invoked by those countries? This is a highly sensitive and controversial issue. The decision in 2004 to initiate the process of Turkey's accession – subject to a set of conditions – seems to indicate that contemporary Europe is not based upon a religious divide arising from a pre-modern religious outlook on the world. Yet, this is not to deny that religions play a major part in the cultural make-up of their followers and that most elements of Europe's secular culture to be explored in the following section have, at some point, developed in opposition, debate, confrontation and/or dialogue with prevailing religions in different European countries.

On Europe's secular culture: the impact of the Enlightenment and the Industrial Revolution

But, if religion is not an appropriate criterion to define Europe, are there any alternative secular traditions which might be relevant when deciding where to draw the cultural boundaries of Europe? While Machiavelli's work offers an incipient notion of Europe based upon secular principles, the idea of Europe did not acquire real meaning until the age of the Enlightenment.[8] During that period, a primarily elitist, consciously felt European identity came to the fore. This stronger 'European' consciousness retained a Christian outlook but was now associated with other values, particularly those of a novel and swiftly developing European civilization embodied in a rapidly changing Europe that had turned into a champion of freedom, humanism and the growing ideas of material progress. According to Den Boer, it was not until the nineteenth century, and specifically after the break with tradition prompted by the revolutionary years, that the concept of Europe was historicized and politicized. He writes:

> At the beginning of the nineteenth century the idea of Europe was projected back much further in history. A search was instigated for the roots of European civilization. Europe, which in the Middle Ages had in fact

hardly existed as a geographical expression, became an accepted historical category. The historical writings of the nineteenth century romantics made it appear that in the Middle Ages there had been a conscious idea of Europe: 'The notion gained ground that out of the ruins of the Roman empire (the Latin element), the Barbarian peoples (the Germanic element), led by the Christian church, had been amalgamated to form the true European civilization'.[9]

The ideas embodied in the Enlightenment took a specific political form in the democratic explosion of the French Revolution. Napoleon's dissemination of revolutionary ideas throughout the European mainland contributed further to the radical transformation of European societies by prompting a series of dramatic changes that would progressively affect the peoples of Europe. These transformations challenged the so-called *Ancien Régime* and fostered the emergence of an early convergence among European national elites – a factor which emphasized the wide gap separating the mass of the population from Europe's cultural, political and economic elites. These transformations involved:

1 the decline of the aristocracy and the advent of the bourgeoisie which was to become the leading component of elites throughout Europe.
2 the separation between state and church which, in turn, was to initiate a process characterized by the progressive weakening of mass allegiance to traditional religions. This would evolve in partnership with the rise of secular values grounded upon humanist principles.
3 the rise and consolidation of the nation-state as the main political institution whose power should be rooted in popular consent and whose aim was to accomplish the cultural homogenization of its citizens. This framework facilitated the rise of modern nationalism, a device which proved to be exceedingly useful for refocusing a people's loyalty away from the monarch. The nation, personified through symbols and rituals which symbolically re-create a sense of 'people', became the focus of a new kind of attachment.
4 the emergence of the concept of citizenship as a mechanism to translate ideas of popular sovereignty into universal adult suffrage. Citizenship had to be struggled for, and although it was ideally conceived as embracing all inhabitants of any given nation-state, in most European countries enfranchisement was limited to male citizens owning a certain amount of property – France in 1830 had a population of some 30 million while boasting an electorate of a mere 90,000. Religion could also disenfranchise a man, particularly if he were a Catholic in a Protestant state, or a

Jew. In Britain, Catholics had to wait until 1829 and Jews until to 1858 for the right to vote. Full enfranchisement, however, often did not take place until well into the twentieth century. For instance, in most European nation-states, universal suffrage was achieved after the First World War. Women usually acquired democratic rights some time after men – in Switzerland spectacularly so (1971).

5 a great emphasis on the importance of universal education, reflected in the decision of most nation-states to create national education systems capable of attaining the cultural and linguistic homogenization of an otherwise diverse population. Further to this, education should teach the population how to become good citizens loyal to the nation-state.

Recent literature suggests that the Enlightenment opened a fracture between the 'civilized' West and the 'uncivilized' or 'barbarian' East. It would be misleading, however, to ignore that the Enlightenment also affected the empires of Central and Eastern Europe, a feature which once more stresses the difficulty of drawing a clear-cut cultural boundary of Europe.

Enlightenment ideas triggered dramatic socio-political transformations in European societies, but they also prompted the adoption of rationality as a method and progress as an objective. It is in this sense that a connection between the Enlightenment and the Industrial Revolution could be established. Rationality involved the end of alchemy and magical arguments and fostered a scientific revolution which culminated in the Industrial Revolution. Both the Enlightenment and the Industrial Revolution challenged traditional social, political and economic patterns and prompted profound transformations in European societies.

The Industrial Revolution originated in England and Scotland in the mid-eighteenth century and expanded to the continent. In England, as early as 1850 more people were working in industry than in agriculture, a situation that would be reached in Southern Europe, including France, only a century later.[10] The social and economic development prompted by the Industrial Revolution transformed the West and established a radical division between industrializing countries and those which were based primarily upon rural economies, as was the case in most of Central and Eastern Europe, but also in Greece, Portugal, most of Spain (excluding Catalonia and the Basque Country) and Italy. Burgess argues that,

> With European development, especially through the nineteenth century, the Ottoman Empire, a part of which later came to constitute the border

of 'the East' of today, became not only 'the sick man of Europe' in Western eyes, but the embodiment of torpor and decay. The change here was not so much in the Ottoman Empire. Certainly it had stagnated, but it was hardly unrecognizable. Rather, the change was relative to the newfound dynamism of the West.

It was the vantage point of the great powers that had really been transformed. They now looked down on those who had failed to reproduce their own astonishing rate of progress and innovation.[11]

Industrialism presumes the use of inanimate sources of material power either in production or in processes affecting the circulation of commodities. It involves the mechanization of production and other economic procedures, and assumes the prevalence of manufacturing understood as the manner of production, rather than simply the creation of such goods.

The advent of industrialism transformed national landscapes. It created large factories, prompting rural migration to urban centres, reshaping and enlarging cities, greatly improving transport and communications, developing the media – in particular, favouring the proliferation of newspapers and magazines – and giving rise to a wide range of mass-produced goods.

Industrialism signalled a turning point in European societies by causing massive social change. It was based upon the division of labour and the separation between home and the workplace. In many instances, industrialism is associated with the spread of capitalism. A fundamental difference between the two should be established. Thus industrialism is based upon the mechanization of mass-produced goods while remaining 'neutral' in respect of wider institutional alignments, and capitalism is a type of production system dominant in a given society which presupposes an alignment of the 'economic' and the 'political' focused through private property and the commodification of wage-labour.[12] Only when the conjunction between capitalism and industrialism is well advanced does it become plausible to speak of the existence of 'capitalist societies', and it is precisely the constitution of such capitalist societies that could be taken as a point of reference when distinguishing between European societies and those which remained outside the industrialized world.

To sum up, after the Enlightenment, competing versions of Europe emerged: liberal and conservative, for or against revolution, constitutional or absolutist forms of government. This process of European incipient convergence initiated by the Enlightenment was greatly enhanced by the almost simultaneous emergence and spread of the Industrial Revolution. It was from that moment onwards that European societies began to share certain features which would accentuate the difference between them and those societies 'towards the East' that remained untouched by industrialism.

In spite of this, it is not until the twentieth century, and after suffering the devastating effects of two world wars, that we can locate the surfacing of a coherently defined idea of Europe which served to inspire the European Union. In this process, the division of Europe into two halves during the Cold War contributed dramatically to the redefining of its cultural boundaries. In most cases, contemporary criteria for inclusion and exclusion are connected to the role played by countries during the Second World War and even more crucially to the position held by them either within or without the area of Soviet influence.

After the Second World War, Western Europe (although strongly underwritten by the United States) was clearly regarded as more 'European' than the Soviet-dominated East, a view that supported the special role played by the EU and its predecessors in the region as a whole. The EU's economic success, sustained democracy and overall stability strengthened this conception, which still prevails following the disintegration of the Soviet Union.

At a time when the EU is moving towards further political and economic integration, we are confronted with the question of whether Europe is becoming more united in cultural and social terms or whether, on the contrary, greater divisions are emerging among member states. Currently, different voices are arguing that any new Europe has to be imagined afresh and constructed as a conscious plan of action rather than deduced from existing values. There are, undoubtedly, differing 'projects for Europe'. Again, Europe is often conflated with the EU, and although some non-EU countries claim their European credentials, the EU seems to monopolize the idea of Europe as a project, which still remains largely undefined.

In what follows I explore contemporary sources of European cultural and social diversity by examining what the main features are that divide Europeans at the beginning of a new millennium. In so doing, first I study variations in religion, wealth and social class, welfare provision, culture, gender and family life, and national and ethnic diversity. Second, I focus on those elements that signal the rise of a common European culture which could eventually lead to the emergence of a shared European identity. The elements considered here include memories of war and the Cold War legacy, the emergence of a common European political culture, the rise of new social movements, and the progressive cultural homogenization of Europe under US influence.

On what divides Europeans

Religion

European societies have traditionally enjoyed a restricted range of religious and (frequently associated) ethnic diversity which has often resulted in one or two dominant, established Christian churches. At present, traditional religions seem to be in decline, although at different speed, throughout Western Europe, with perhaps the exception of Belgium and Ireland – a feature which contrasts with church membership and participation in the USA and other parts of the world where religion plays a key role in the day-to-day life of citizens and has a strong influence in politics. Europe's secularization became one of the main features defining the continent throughout the twentieth century. Even traditionally Catholic Ireland provides some evidence of religious decline, exemplified in recent constitutional changes allowing divorce and birth control. It is my concern that, in spite of the current declining authority of religion over people's lives, its influence should not be underestimated – in particular, since traditionally religion has been a major source of conflict between European countries. The separation between Eastern Orthodox Christianity and Western European Christianity has for a long time been critical in establishing a division between Western and Eastern Europe, a division which was partially reinforced by the Cold War.

Further divisions within Western Christianity between Catholicism and Protestantism determine to a certain extent the separation between North and South; however, France and Germany stand as very significant exceptions to this. Yet France, which was traditionally Catholic, but where the Catholic Church was excluded from public life for much of the past two centuries, has witnessed the rise of Protestantism as a private religion. In contrast, Germany, which was predominantly Protestant in its origins, drifted towards Catholicism during the first four decades of the Western republic after the Second World War.[13] The Catholic character of Ireland and Belgium and the divided religious structures of the Netherlands and Switzerland further challenge the North/South divide.

A further aspect of religion is its influence in shaping European political parties, such as the Christian democrat parties, which, once created, sought to appeal to large sectors of the population beyond those who could identify with their religious core.

Socio-economic diversity

The traditional division of Europe into a wealthy and industrialized North (including Britain, Germany, Belgium, the Netherlands and France) and a poor and underdeveloped South (including Portugal, Spain, Greece and Italy) has been partially challenged in recent years. Italy has become one of the richest countries in the world, a member of the G8, while Spain and Portugal have registered a faster income growth since joining the EU.

These countries share an agricultural basis and are heavily subsidized by the Common Agricultural Policy. In spite of that, the percentage of their farming population is rapidly declining and seeking employment in urban areas, where a dramatic and necessary modernization of the industrial landscape has generated high rates of unemployment. Ireland, a poor country whose economy has traditionally been based on agriculture, has also benefited enormously from EU membership. In recent years it has managed to transform its economic basis and has turned into one of the most economically dynamic European countries.

Mediterranean countries sustain paternalistic and poor welfare-state models rooted in the dictatorships which Spain, Greece and Portugal endured until the 1970s, when they initiated their respective transitions to democracy. A common feature shared by these countries concerns a steady rising level of investment in their respective welfare systems since the early 1980s, when they prepared for accession into the EU.

In contrast, Scandinavian countries generally have small populations and are defined by strong economies dependent on world markets and universal welfare-state systems, which, to some extent, share some features with the British welfare-state model. The Scandinavian model guarantees minimum security and status maintenance. The German welfare model is also based on status maintenance and assumes employment-related coverage and extensive benefits, which include old-age pensions, disability pensions, sick pay, unemployment benefits and health services.

To address great socio-economic inequalities and, above all, poverty after the Second World War, Western European countries set in place different welfare models. Crouch[14] establishes a contrast between European countries showing a preference for welfare at the cost of high unemployment (resulting from high indirect labour costs needed to pay for welfare and labour-market regulation, as well as possibly reduced work incentives) and the US preference for high employment levels at the expense of very limited welfare provision.[15] This is a pattern which has been reversed in recent years. Thus, at present, most European countries seem to have altered their egalitarian preferences under the influence of the US model; for instance, Scandinavia has witnessed significant changes in what used to be one of the most generous welfare systems in Europe.[16] Hence, a common trend currently uniting Western European countries is growing intra-state inequality and poverty, resulting in sharper class divisions.

Differences in wealth are generally connected with varying degrees of industrialization, which in turn produce different patterns of employment. Thus only some Southern European countries (Greece, Spain) and Ireland have more than 5 per cent of their population working in agriculture and mining (sector I), while Belgium and Britain employ fewer than 2 per cent of their population in this sector.

Culture and class

A feature which has historically defined most Western European countries concerns the division of culture along social class lines. In this sense, class boundaries tended to coincide with cultural boundaries and form the basis for the distinction between 'elite' or 'high' culture and 'popular' or 'low' culture. The sharp class divisions typical of the industrial period crystallized into well-organized trade unions and political parties representing the working class.

The advent of post-industrialism, or what some authors define as advanced societies, and the emergence of the middle classes broke traditional class boundaries and tended to replace a clearly defined 'working-class' culture by a standardized 'popular culture', predominantly of US origin and transmitted through the means of mass communication.

The major trends which unite Europeans beyond these class and wealth divisions are as follows: (1) the range of goods available to the working class now compared with the range in other historical periods, above all compared with the situation in early twentieth-century Europe; (2) the weakening of the working class and the predominance of a highly diversified middle class in all European countries; and (3) the concentration of the European population in cities. A network of cities, which have become financial, political, cultural and artistic centres, characterizes much of Europe.

Gender and family life

Major changes concerning traditional gender and family structures have transformed the day-to-day life of Europeans since the Second World War. The most important of these changes is the political and social emancipation of women, involving enfranchisement, access to the labour market and the possibility, thanks to birth control techniques, of separating sexual activity from reproduction.

The percentage of women in paid work varies across Europe. Northern countries have a higher percentage of women in the labour market than southern countries, where strong family ties and weak welfare systems have traditionally resulted in women staying at home and looking after children, the old and the sick. But, at present, the rise in the numbers of women who have access to higher education and expect to go into work is challenging these patterns.

When considering birth rates, it is quite striking to compare the noticeably high birth rates registered in Northern Europe – predominantly Lutheran, having weak family links and enjoying strong welfare systems – with the very low birth rates of countries such as Spain and Italy, Catholic countries with weak welfare systems and strong family ties.

Differences in divorce rates also seem to follow a North/South divide. Northern Protestant countries, Britain and the Nordic countries, in particular, record higher divorce rates than Southern Catholic countries such as Italy and Spain. France, Germany and the Netherlands are somewhere in between. The number of births outside marriage is also higher in Northern Europe than in the South. In the North there is a significant difference between the Nordic countries and Britain. In the former, such children tend to be born to mothers over thirty years old in settled partnerships; in Britain, they are more likely to be born to single mothers under twenty years old.

National and ethnic diversity

National and ethnic minorities are key components of the European socio-cultural landscape. Most nation-states are not constituted by a single nation that is coextensive with the state; internal diversity is the rule. The nations or parts of nations included within a single state do not share similar levels of national awareness. What is more, while some define themselves as nations, have strong memories of a time when they were independent political units, and share a common identity – as is the case in Scotland, Catalonia, Flanders or the Basque Country – others have a rather weak sense of identity and are content to be referred to as regions – among them Brittany, Occitany and Cornwall.

The term 'region', as employed by the EU, does not establish a distinction between a geographical region, an economic region, a region with feeble or absent distinct cultures and a region endowed with a strong sense of identity and cultural distinctiveness.

Most national minorities have organized themselves and created social movements and political parties to defend their cultural specificity and their right to self-determination. Self-determination is sometimes understood to mean political autonomy, although in other cases it stops short of independence and involves the right to secede. There are also crucial differences between national minorities, such as the Catalans and the Scots, who have opted for peaceful means in their claim for socio-political recognition, and other minorities who have turned to violence, as is the case in the Basque Country, Corsica and Northern Ireland. I should emphasize that most nations without states are not homogeneous and contain various ethnic minorities, who may or may not identify with the nationalist claims advanced by the nation's social movements and political parties. In some cases these ethnic minorities are marginalized, but in others they are encouraged to participate actively in the political life of the wider community.

Ethnic minorities are formed primarily by people of migrant origin who, in some cases, have been living in the host country for several generations. Ethnic minorities also include migrants who have recently moved to the host country, as well as refugees and asylum-seekers. Scots, Welsh and Irish form Britain's national minorities, while Britain's largest ethnic minorities include people of Asian and Caribbean origin, most of whom hold British passports and were born in the UK. British ethnic minorities also consist of migrants from other Commonwealth countries, the EU, Eastern Europe and beyond.

Between 1950 and 1975, economic prosperity brought large numbers of migrants from Southern European countries such as Spain, Italy and Portugal to Northern European countries such as Germany, the Netherlands and France. To supplement the labour force, large numbers of migrants from outside Europe were also attracted to work in the most dynamic European economies. Caribbean and Indian people flowed into Britain, Algerians into France, Turks and Italians into Germany, and Surinamese and Moluccans into the Netherlands. The recession that followed the economic boom of the 1950s and 1960s was replaced by a deep depression, which started in the mid-1970s and considerably worsened the situation of these immigrants.

From the late 1990s into the early 2000s, the largest migrant communities in the EU are to be found in Germany, France and the UK, although rising numbers of migrants from Africa are flowing into Italy, Portugal and Spain. Since 1989 the disintegration of the Soviet Union and political and economic instability in Asia, Africa and the Middle East have resulted in large numbers of migrants coming into the EU. Immigrants increase cultural diversity within the EU and have often been subject to social exclusion in the labour market, education, access to housing and the fundamental rights of citizenship.

The nation-state's cultural diversity, which is grounded on the coexistence of various national and ethnic minorities with distinct identities and cultures, is further challenged by the presence of illegal immigrants, refugees and asylum-seekers. Rising cultural diversity within the EU has resulted in a number of opposing reactions. For instance, some extreme right-wing movements defend the 'purity' of the nation and stand against immigrants, while other movements defend multiculturalism as a mechanism that could facilitate the coexistence of culturally different communities within a shared territory. I shall come back to these issues later on in the book.

On what unites Europeans

So far, I have considered some of the main features that account for diversity among European peoples. Now I shall focus on the characteristics that unite Europeans in terms of culture and explore what might become the foundations of a future European identity, an identity that is closely connected to the idea of furthering European integration and strengthening the EU. I argue that five main characteristics have united Europeans and distinguished them from other peoples: memories of two devastating world wars and the experience of the Cold War, which fixed European borders for over forty years; the end of the colonial empires after the Second World War; the rise of a distinct European political culture; the emergence of new social movements, which reflect new concerns; and the progressive cultural homogenization of Europe under the influence of the USA.

Memories of war and the Cold War legacy

European countries were deeply affected by the devastating effects of two world wars. In particular, the Second World War and its legacy, the division of Europe into two different areas of influence, capitalist and communist, generated a sense of unity among those Europeans living in countries to the west of the Berlin Wall. Even countries that were not directly involved in the Second World War, such as Spain, could participate to a certain extent in this division of Europe between West and East. The division was primarily defined by Western connections to the United States of America and the capitalist model, and the Eastern association with the Soviet Union and the communist model.

During the Second World War, the political systems of Western Europe were for the most part destroyed. Over 40 million people were killed in battle or in acts of atrocity against civilians, and the economies of the countries involved suffered tremendous losses.[17] The war acted as a catalyst for a new surge of interest in European unity, which led to negative assessments of the pre-war political situation and economic practices.

The USA emerged from the war as the strongest military and economic power. Its involvement in Western Europe became crucial in the political, economic and military recovery of an area that had been devastated by two world wars. The so-called Truman Doctrine, outlined by President Harry Truman in March 1947, and the American announcement of the Marshall Plan later in the same year were critical in the shaping of Western European economies and political systems. The Truman Doctrine stressed the American determination to defend democracy, resist the advance of communism, and guarantee the security of the USA. It represented the pledge of a firm political relationship between the USA and Western Europe and provided strong support for the evolution of Western democracies. The Marshall Plan offered economic aid to all European states, although the Soviet Union rejected the offer. The Marshall Plan was economically as well as politically motivated, and was a necessary part of President Truman's expressed intention to organize Western Europe into an ideological alliance against the Soviet Union and communism.[18]

The American relationship with Western Europe was enhanced by the creation of the Atlantic Pact in April 1949. The USA and Canada entered into a military arrangement for the collective defence of Western Europe, along with Belgium, Britain, Denmark, France, Italy, Iceland, Luxembourg, the Netherlands, Norway and Portugal. During the early 1950s the founding members were joined by Greece, Turkey and the new state of West Germany to give rise to the North Atlantic Treaty Organization (NATO).

The Cold War period consolidated a firm relationship between the USA and Western Europe, which exerted a strong influence upon the political, social, economic and military restructuring of the latter. It impinged upon the shaping of government systems, party structures, and political and social elites, and contributed to the Americanization of Western European industry.

In my view, the Cold War years generated an unspecified sense of unity among Western peoples. In contrast, Central and Eastern European peoples, once included within the communist bloc, were subject to quite different influences from those experienced by their Western neighbours. After the recent enlargement of the EU to include some former communist countries, among them Bulgaria, Romania, Poland, Hungary, the Baltic states and the Czech Republic, and faced with the accession of some additional countries in the near future, we could question whether or not communism was instrumental in awakening a pre-existing sense of European identity, as feeble as it might have been at the time, among its satellite countries. In addition, a question about what arguments, if any, may account for unity between Western and Eastern Europe should be posed. Not in vain do many Central and Eastern European citizens argue that they were integrated by force into the Eastern bloc, dominated by the USSR, and that the end of communism provided the opportunity for them to return to where they belonged, 'Europe'. And, by 'Europe', they mean the Europe that, since the end of the Second World War, has successfully created a common and prosperous economic space and generated a supranational political institution, the European Union.

The main reasons for joining the EU invoked by former communist countries include the wish to become a part of Europe, once again, after the long impasse marked by the Cold War; the prosperity, economic progress and modernization they expect from becoming EU members; and the security and stability which the EU would provide. In addition, some countries feel quite strongly about the EU's role as guarantor of their national independence. Such feelings are particularly strong in the Baltic states, Slovakia and Slovenia.[19]

The attachment to liberal democratic practices as a means for enabling cooperation stands as a major feature uniting Europeans and has become one of the most distinctive features of the EU. Eastern and Western Europe are united by shared experiences of suffering and division caused by war and, above all, by the desire for the prosperity and progress embodied in the EU. The conflict of interests, life-styles, ruling political ideas and economic models between Eastern and Western Europe, which dominated their relationship during the Cold War, has now a real possibility of being superseded by consensus.

The end of the Cold War, marked by the collapse of the Soviet Union (1989–91), has prompted significant changes in both Western and Eastern Europe. In the West, it has fostered the transformation of socialist and communist parties and opened up the search for new political ideologies able to thrive in a world branded by global capitalism and the absence of communism. It has also conferred renewed strength on the idea of greater EU political integration and given Germany the possibility of becoming a leading power within the Union. Moreover, the fall of the Berlin Wall triggered EU enlargement to include countries in Eastern and Central Europe.

In the East, the end of the Cold War has resulted in the regained independence of some former Soviet republics. It has permitted the expansion of capitalism to the former Soviet bloc, which is currently experiencing the advantages as well as the dislocations associated with this new economic system, its values and social impact. Furthermore, the demise of the Cold War has prompted the expansion of liberal democracy and a radical institutional transformation. In addition, it has ignited ethnic conflict and confrontation in the former Yugoslavia, Albania, Georgia, and Chechnya, among other areas. At the same time, it has endorsed the reunification of Germany and the search for new political ideologies, party systems and government structures to replace communism.

The end of the European empires

From the fifteenth century onwards, Europeans began to explore previously uncharted seas and unexplored landmasses. They conquered and subdued native populations and sought to exploit their territories, establishing colonies in numerous areas previously occupied by traditional societies. Europeans used their superior military strength where necessary. Many European states acquired territories and power by building up empires outside the Western European cockpit itself. Belgium, France, the Netherlands, Portugal, Spain and Britain followed that path.

For most of the period of European expansion, colonists displayed ethnocentric attitudes and saw themselves as the agents of civilization. They exported Western political ideas, culture, manners, languages and religions while establishing a power relation between the metropolis and the colonies. This relationship was fraught with inequality and discrimination. The early period of colonialism coincided with the rise of racism, and almost invariably since then racism has permeated many of the relations between those considered by the colonizers, and their descendants, as 'non-white'.

To pose an example, in the British Empire, one of the most potent and recent ones in time, the slave trade was abolished in 1807, but only in 1834–8 was slavery abolished, with a five-year 'apprenticeship' system for the former slaves. As late as 1925, the Special Restrictions (Coloured Alien Seamen) Order prohibited black British sailors from working on British ships, and forced some black sailors in Britain out of the country.[20]

The process of dismantling the 'European empires' culminated after the Second World War. Most former colonies had turned into independent nation-states by the 1960s; one of the most notorious exceptions was Portugal's African colonies, which were to be granted independence in the

1970s. During the First World War, some European states promised concessions to their colonies in return for aid against their enemies.[21] As the war
drew to a close, two events cast an influence on the development of national
liberation movements in the colonies. First, Lenin, who had just led the
Bolshevik Revolution in Russia (November 1917), launched an anti-imperial-
ist propaganda campaign. Second, after the war, and as a response to the
human and material effort which was demanded from the colonies – many
of them already calling for the right to self-determination – Woodrow
Wilson, then US president, issued in 1918 the Fourteen Points, one of which
defended the sovereign right of colonial peoples.[22]

After the Second World War, colonial powers had to relinquish their
dominance, primarily because of a lack of resources and the growing strength
of national liberation movements led by colonial elites. European powers
reacted in different ways to the decolonization process. Britain granted independence to most of its former colonies after strong national liberation
movements pressed for it, although it sought to maintain some special relationship with them by creating the Commonwealth. In contrast, French
colonies had to fight for independence. Only military defeat, as was the case
in Indochina, and guerrilla warfare, as in Algeria, forced France to abandon
its colonial possessions.

The end of the 'European empires' signalled a turning point in European
politics and economy. It had a tremendous effect upon the nation-states,
which, after having benefited from power, prestige and economic privilege
derived from their status as colonial masters, found themselves struggling
to feed their own populations. Former imperial powers were unable to carry
out the rebuilding of their own social, political and economic structures
without US aid.

The end of the colonial empires involved profound internal transformations in some European nation-states, which had to restructure their internal
systems to adjust to a radically new situation. It was in that context that the
European powers, devastated by the experience of two world wars and
increasingly dependent on US support, progressively turned away from their
disintegrating empires. Instead of looking towards their former Asian and
African possessions, they decided to concentrate on building some institutional agreements destined to prevent another war and to contribute to
Europe's economic recovery. The seeds of the European Union are to be
found in the thoughts and deeds of those political leaders and intellectuals
committed to the reconstruction of Europe.[23] That particular generation was
the first to dream about a united Europe, which at that time, of course,
excluded the Central and Eastern European countries then subsumed within
the Soviet bloc.

European political culture

The roots of European political culture may be found in the secular ideas disseminated by the Enlightenment. These ideas contributed to the foundation and development of the nation-state as a political institution. They involved the acceptance of parliamentary democracy as a form of government, the separation between state and church, the desire for progress, and the creation of the concept of citizenship, with its associated rights and duties.

Attachment to these principles is reflected in the Maastricht Treaty (1992), which marked a new stage in the process of European integration leading to the establishment of the European Union. The Treaty recalls 'the historic importance of the ending of the division of the European continent and the need to create firm bases for the construction of the future Europe'. Consequently, it signals the end of conflict and the desire to replace it by consensus as a mechanism enabling cooperation between European peoples. From this perspective, it would be plausible to assert that what unites Europeans in terms of political culture is embodied in the text of the Maastricht Treaty, which proclaims the EU member states' attachment to 'the principles of liberty, democracy and respect for human rights and fundamental freedoms and of the rule of law' and their 'desire to deepen solidarity between the peoples of Europe while respecting their history, their culture and their traditions'. The treaty also emphasizes the member states' desire to enhance further the democratic and efficient functioning of EU institutions and their determination to promote economic and social progress for Europeans. A key contribution of this treaty was the resolution to establish a common European citizenship.[24]

In my view, the EU member states' determination to pursue social and economic progress through the strengthening of EU democratic institutions within a single institutional framework based on the principle of subsidiarity is the most important feature that unites Europeans. It responds to a top-down process initiated by national elites[25] determined to turn a somewhat unspecified idea of Europe into a well-defined political institution which will, in time, acquire a common culture and identity.

New social movements

Social movements struggle for recognition – be it the recognition of equality between men and women, of the rights of gays and lesbians, of animal rights, or of environmental rights. The main objective of social movements is to bring attention to a particular issue, to make it relevant, to denounce the unfairness and ill-treatment suffered by somebody or something, whether a group of people, animals or the environment, and to put forward a set of measures to reverse their situation.[26] The distinctive nature of the European socio-cultural and economic space brought about by the Enlightenment and the advent of industrialization set up the framework for the emergence of different social movements within European countries.

The rise of trade unionism, the suffragette movement and the anti-slavery movement embodies a novel range of social concerns which would expand and have a wide influence across national boundaries. In the twentieth century, and specifically after the Second World War, European countries generated powerful new social movements typified by revolutionary Paris in May 1968, which stood against conservatism, capitalist values and morals. A different movement, contemporary with that of Paris, and to a certain extent connected to it, is to be found in the so-called Prague Spring, which opposed communist domination in Czechoslovakia. Successive social movements have since emerged in European countries and expanded to the USA, or have been imported from the USA and have flourished in Europe, including the green, the feminist and the gay and lesbian movements. An exclusively European social movement which has taken off with renewed strength in the last twenty years or so concerns the rise of democratic regional nationalism, a movement seeking the recognition of particular communities as culturally distinct and having the right to rule themselves.

The cultural homogenization of Europe: high versus low culture

The distinction between high and low culture reflects the division between elites and masses within the EU. However, I argue that at both levels it is possible to identify some convergence. Unity at an elite level emerged earlier than unity among European masses. The strong French cultural influence exerted during the Enlightenment period was contested and resented by German elites. Germany was to displace France and turn into the leading cultural centre of Europe during the nineteenth century. German Romanticism expanded throughout Europe and replaced the cultural predominance exerted by the Enlightenment in the eighteenth century. British influence became strong in the second part of the nineteenth century and was attached to the rise of the Industrial Revolution.

Through most of the post-war era, in political terms, capitalism confronted communism and, in cultural terms, high art contrasted with national and regional popular cultures, which were progressively being eroded by the mass media and the expansion of US influence. High culture regards art's role as ennobling, its realm the nation, its organizational form the institution, its repertoire the established canon and works aspiring to join it, its base audience the cultural elite. In contrast, popular culture views entertainment as its main objective, its realm the marketplace, its form the business, its audience the masses.

These two realms of elite and popular culture are not completely detached from one another, and the connections between them could be illustrated by two examples. First, in the commodification of works of art which belong to high culture, consider for instance the popular dimension achieved by certain works by Van Gogh, Picasso, Renoir or Monet, present on millions of postcards, posters and even T-shirts. Consider also the popular use of classical music, originally composed for kings, emperors and popes, which is currently played as background music, for example, in tube stations and trains, in TV and radio adverts, and even as ringtones for mobile phones.

Second, consider the strategy pursued by most European governments aimed at widening the audience for the traditional high arts. In Britain, this strategy informed the BBC and defined the ethos of the Arts Council from its foundation by John Maynard Keynes to its high point in the mid-1960s.

In the 1960s and 1970s the new left, inspired by the new social movements which emerged during this period, sought to challenge high culture. The 1968 influence brought hostility to high culture and a rejection of the 'patrician' principles of extending the reach of high art; instead, grassroots activity for festively subversive purposes was encouraged. However, this movement failed to reach the masses, but turned into the privilege of selected elites. The 1980s and after witnessed a reversal of this trend and registered a deepening of the already wide gap between elite and popular culture.

In the post-war period, the main source of external cultural influence was the United States of America – partly from choice, as a breath of fresh air and democracy, partly from necessity, given the low state of European cultural industries. The rise of television increased the reliance on imports from the USA. As Europe prospered, concern about this dependence, affecting not only Europe but also the world, was widely expressed, especially in smaller European countries.

In the 1980s a new phase, prompted by the accelerating pace of the 'European project', was initiated. For the first time, certain cultural goals of a supranational kind were being openly considered, and the concept of a 'European cultural identity' was being discussed in European elite circles. Commitment to the development of a European project has prompted a mixed reaction among European elites keen to protect national specificity while at the same time taking steps in the construction of a European identity. The creation of a European flag and anthem, the encouragement of European sports events, song contests and the like, the EU-sponsored programmes of exchange among European students, and the encouragement of and financial support to European scientific networks are cases in point.

Towards a European identity?

The European Union is a novel political institution created by nation-states after the Second World War. Its main objectives were avoiding war, strengthening state power and overcoming the poverty and destruction caused by two world wars.

The EU is a dynamic political institution, which since its inception has experienced a dramatic expansion and growth in terms of territory and citizen numbers, coupled with increasing wealth, productivity and international presence. Right now, the EU seeks economic and political integration, and in so doing it stands up as the most ambitious project promoted by any supranational political institution worldwide. The creation of a single market, the free movement of people and goods across its frontiers, the introduction of the Euro in 2001, and its latest enlargements to include ten new member states in 2004 and two more in 2007, have turned the EU into a major global political actor. However, it is one which is still struggling to offer a united voice in some areas, for instance, international relations, foreign policy and security. The EU embraces a considerable number of nation-states prepared to relinquish some aspects of their own jealously guarded sovereignty in order to benefit from membership of an economically prosperous and dynamic internal market, which has turned the EU into a successful economic global player.

But how do its own citizens perceive the EU? Do they identify with it? What enables identification to take place? Previous experience shows that identification with the nation-state emerged only after a considerable period, involving the linguistic and cultural homogenization of citizens, the fighting of wars, taxation, the establishment of citizenship rights and duties, the construction of a certain image of the nation endowed with its own symbols and rituals (instilled by the state), the existence of common enemies, and the progressive consolidation of national education and media systems.[27]

At sub-state level, the construction of autonomous political institutions also tends to generate a sense of belonging. For instance, when considering regional identity, the study of devolution in Britain, Canada and Spain proves that the establishment of autonomous political institutions with sufficient power and resources to rule a territory, and make a difference to people's lives, tends not only to strengthen pre-existing identities but also to breed a sense of belonging and shared identity where it did not previously exist – for instance, among the citizens of newly created autonomous communities in post-1979 Spain. Furthermore, data analysed in chapter 2 prove that devolution does not tend to weaken national identity and that compatibility between national and regional identity often leads to the coexistence of dual identities invoked at different times.

If compatibility between national and regional identity goes hand in hand with multilayered government, should we then conclude that a further layer of identity, on this occasion of a suprastate nature, would automatically emerge among European citizens once they feel the political weight of the EU upon their own lives? The response depends on how we are to define such a new form of collective identity, that is, on what type of attachment we imagine. In my view, European identity cannot be expected to follow the pattern of national identity, simply because the EU is not a nation-state but a new genre of political institution born out of a new socio-political and economic environment shaped by globalization.

The EU is a novel political institution created out of the free will of sovereign nation-states, which continue to establish a sharp distinction between 'communitarian' and 'domestic' affairs in terms of policy and decision-making. For instance, devolution models and recognition of national and ethnic minorities are considered as 'internal affairs' and remain in the hands of each particular nation-state.

Ultimately, nation-states set up the aims and structure of the EU while deciding on and funding its budget. In some cases, nation-states employ the EU as an excuse for action or inaction within the domestic arena, and sometimes they even use the EU as a scapegoat, thus fuelling nationalism and reinforcing national identity. Bearing this in mind, I believe that nation-states are only partially interested in promoting a European identity focused on EU membership, since 'too much Europe' could potentially weaken national identity and eventually result in refocusing a people's loyalty away from the nation-state.

European identity, as well as national identity when instilled by the state, is a top-down institutionally generated identity designed to foster solidarity bonds among a diverse population. It is also aimed at nurturing feelings of loyalty towards the EU, yet, in my view, this is more of a project for the future than a reality.

On how Europeans regard the EU

Currently, Europeans are split concerning support for EU membership. In 2004 the percentage of those who considered membership of the EU as a 'good thing' were 85 per cent in Luxembourg, 77 per cent in Ireland, 72 per cent in Spain and a mere 38 per cent in the UK. In contrast, those who considered the EU a 'bad thing' amounted to 33 per cent in the UK, 43 per cent in Latvia, 42 per cent in the Czech Republic, and 37 per cent in both Slovakia and Poland.[28]

Sizeable changes were recorded in 2005, when the view that EU membership is a 'good thing' decreased from 54 to 50 per cent.[29] At 16 per cent, opposition to membership remained low. Negative opinions only exceeded 20 per cent of the survey population in traditionally Euro-sceptic countries, namely Sweden (32 per cent), the United Kingdom (28 per cent), Austria (25 per cent) and Finland (22 per cent).[30] In the new member states, public opinion remained rather volatile and the level of 'neutral' replies was particularly high. It recorded 47 per cent in Latvia, 46 per cent in Slovenia, 44 per cent in the Czech Republic, and 42 per cent in Estonia, Hungary and Slovakia.[31]

The perceived advantages of EU membership have also suffered a decrease of 3 points. In 2005, 52 per cent of Europeans considered that their country had benefited from EU membership, compared to 36 per cent (+3) who took the opposite view. Among those holding more positive views were Ireland (86 per cent), Luxembourg (75 per cent), Denmark and Spain (both 69 per cent), Greece (67 per cent), Belgium and Portugal (both 65 per cent) and the Netherlands (61 per cent).[32]

It is also significant to observe that a high percentage of people felt that their country had not benefited from EU membership: 56 per cent in Sweden, 48 per cent in Austria, and 47 per cent in both the United Kingdom and Finland. In the new member states, the perceived benefits of EU membership remained positive, recording an average of 58 per cent (1 point down compared with spring 2005).[33]

Still a further decline was identified. Those feeling that the image of the EU was positive decreased from 50 per cent (autumn 2004) to 44 per cent (autumn 2005). Although the EU still conjures a primarily positive image among its citizens, it is remarkable to detect that the gap between those holding a positive image and those holding a negative one is closing. Feelings of a negative image of the EU have risen from 15 per cent (autumn 2004) to 20 per cent (autumn 2005).[34]

Undoubtedly, a decline in the perception of a positive EU image combined with a decrease in support for EU membership does not contribute to strengthening an incipient European identity. On the contrary, if such trends were to continue, they would signal the inability of the EU to focus on what unites Europeans rather than allowing for a deepening of existing differences. A sustained decline in the perceived advantages of EU membership holds the potential to weaken the emergence of a cohesive European identity.

Currently, the expectations of some new member states are not being fulfilled at the speed that they had initially envisaged. If this continues to be the case it will generate resentment and the construction of deep divisions within the EU. Simultaneously, enlargement is having a considerable impact upon the socio-cultural structures and public opinion of the fifteen old member states. Enlargement is extremely recent, this is true, but the consequence of opening up markets by expanding the territorial boundaries of Europe is likely to be a powerful socio-economic impact on European societies. Some signs of this are already visible. Enlargement further problematizes existing visions for greater political and social cohesion within the EU. The strengthening of a still incipient European identity is further complicated by the accession of the largest contingent ever to join the EU at once since its foundation.

Support for the EU is mixed and, critically, different percentages are obtained when analysing overall attitudes and feelings across the twenty-seven member states, and when studying country-by-country surveys that reveal deep differences among citizens of various member states.

The EU: a 'non-emotional' identity

But what constitutes European identity? What are or could be its main components? European identity cannot be founded upon the cultural and linguistic homogenization of its citizens, a mistake too often made by nation-states seeking to annihilate internal diversity in order to create a homogeneous citizenry. National and ethnic minorities claiming the right to cultural and linguistic survival and, in some cases, the right to self-determination are now contesting such homogenization attempts. In a similar manner, European identity cannot claim to rely upon a common past, and it cannot even boast about clear-cut geographical or cultural boundaries.

In contrast, a still embryonic European identity relies on the shared consciousness of belonging to an economic and political space defined by capitalism, social welfare, liberal democracy, respect for human rights, freedom and the rule of law, prosperity and progress. In my view, these are the pillars of a European identity defined primarily by the sharing of a specific political culture and the desire to benefit from the economic advantages derived from EU membership. But are these sufficient to generate loyalty to the EU? Would support for the EU dwindle if an economic crisis were to hit it hard?

As I see it, a major economic crisis would undoubtedly question the purpose of the EU at a time when the economic prosperity associated with the Union has become of paramount importance. It acted as a magnet for those nation-states which joined in 2004 and in 2007 as well as for those currently applying for membership.

The EU is still a fragile institution and, to make it work, nation-states need to believe that they would not get a finer deal by abandoning the Union. Economic prosperity is driving EU integration, and a major failure in this area would undermine the Union's capacity to bring about political integration.

At the moment, the economic incentives of EU membership are enormous. However, the determination to protect national interests is so robust that, if a major economic crisis were to affect the EU, this could prompt some member states to believe that they could do better on their own or by establishing alternative partnerships. Under those circumstances, a still feeble and incipient European identity would suffer a major blow.

In my view, at least while in its early stages, European identity is best defined as an emergent 'non-emotional' identity, in contrast with the powerful and emotionally charged national identities of our time.

In its present form, I do not expect European identity to arouse feelings comparable to those inspired by national identity. In a similar manner, I do not anticipate the emergence of a European nationalism powerful enough to mobilize the masses in the name of Europe; it would be problematical to find common causes and interests uniting Europeans and prompting them to sacrifice their own lives in the name of the EU. So far, the nation-state retains the emotional attachment of its citizens, and when it becomes alien to them, or too wide and distant, individuals turn to regional, ethnic, local and other forms of identity tying them to more sizeable communities than the EU.

Challenges to an EU identity

In addition to economic success, several other key challenges to the consolidation of a European identity should be mentioned, among them a widening gap between the elites and the masses regarding perceptions and attitudes towards the EU. However, not even the European elites share a coherent vision: rather, there exist substantial differences concerning their ideas about the institutional shape the EU should progress towards, as well as the degree of political and economic integration it should aim at. Max Haller highlights the lack of a single project for an EU identity by signalling the existence of 'significant differences in their ideas, both among political leaders and elites in different European nation states, and between different political parties, as well as between economic, political and cultural elites'.[35]

Up to a point, the gap between elites and the masses has materialized in opposition to the draft constitution that received a 'no' vote in France and the Netherlands in 2005. Dissatisfaction with the EU's democratic deficit, concern about the future of social welfare, disagreement on the institutional model propounded for the Union, lack of representation (voice and vote) for constitutional regions such as Catalonia, Scotland and Flanders, opposition to what is perceived by many as a growing hyper-bureaucratic entity distant from ordinary citizens, inability to speak with a single voice at crucial moments (intervention in the wars of the former Yugoslavia and Iraq) and discontent about their own national governments have prompted a large number of citizens to vote 'no'. Saying 'no' to the constitution, among other issues, implies that, for some, the brand of European identity emerging from the EU's magna carta does not fulfil their aspirations. It is of crucial importance, now that the EU has been enlarged to twenty-seven countries, to pause and reflect on the message being sent by the citizens of two founding EU member states.

In my view, the emergence of a European identity requires the political will among EU members to build a common project for the future, a vision encompassing socio-economic progress, commitment to liberal democracy and the pledge to replace conflict by consensus. When constructing such a project we should be wary of grand ventures, which in the past have resulted in conflict and destruction. Mazower cautions us: 'It was thus not preordained that democracy should win over fascism and communism, just as it remains still to be seen what kind of democracy Europe is able and willing to build.'[36] 'Yet we should certainly not assume that democracy is suited to Europe.'[37]

A further challenge to the EU derives from the rise of populist right-wing nationalism, in the shape of political parties fully integrated within the democratic system which tend to exploit fears of economic and cultural takeover by immigrants (legal and illegal), refugees and asylum-seekers attracted by the EU's wealth. Fear of diversity, feelings of being worse off than newcomers regarded as benefiting from social welfare, cultural clashes, prejudice, and difference in life-styles generate anxiety and are encouraging some sectors of the population, many of whom are to be found among the working class, to support right-wing, often populist, parties prepared to be 'tough' and place the interests of their own citizens first.

Current debates on whether assimilation, integration or multiculturalism should prevail are causing heated confrontations in European societies. Evidence of ghettoization, the existence of parallel societies which do not interact with each other, discrimination, racism, clashes between some members of ethnic groups, and confrontation between migrants from different origins have ignited resentment and violence. The outburst of violence registered in France during November 2005 exemplifies this. In addition, the 7 July 2005 London terrorist attacks perpetrated by British citizens of migrant origin have shaken British society to the bone.

Mazower's idea that 'The real victor in 1989 was not democracy but capitalism, and Europe as a whole now faces the task which Western Europe has confronted since the 1930s, of establishing a workable relationship between the two'[38] expresses one of the EU's greatest challenges, since it is capitalism, and the need to stand up as a global economic player, that has prompted European integration in the first place.

Furthermore, the EU's will to assert its identity as a global political actor through the implementation of a common foreign and security policy, including the eventual framing of a common defence policy as envisaged in the Maastricht Treaty (Article B), is proving a challenging objective. Lack of accord among EU leaders has resulted in the absence of a unified response to profound crises such as the occupation of Kuwait by Iraq and the subsequent Gulf War (1991), civil war resulting in the disintegration of Yugoslavia in the early 1990s, the recognition of new independent states such as Slovenia and Croatia, and the US-led invasion of Iraq.

To assume that an emotional attachment to the EU should follow underestimates the complexity and strength of national identity, which still continues to act as the immediate frame of reference for the majority of citizens. Even accepting that the nation-state is changing and recasting its nature, I do not think we can announce that it is fading away. In my view, European identity will remain an abstract concept in the medium term, and its future will crucially depend on the socio-economic and political consequences of adopting a single currency, successfully managing enlargement and dealing with mass immigration, as well as the cultural, social and political questions associated with it.

Rethinking American Identity

Does multiculturalism pose a threat to social cohesion in the USA? Why do some African-Americans feel bitter about the social and economic consequences of new waves of immigration into the USA? In what ways could massive and sustained Hispanic[1] immigration impact upon American culture, language and identity?

The United States of America originated as a nation of settlers who initially asserted their will to create a distinct polity by opposing British rule and declaring their independence in 1776. Since then, several features have defined the forging of what is commonly referred to as 'America': a new type of nation whose national identity was not ethnically based but constructed around political values of equality, freedom and individualism; the use of the English language; and a set of moral values entrenched in Protestantism, which deeply influenced Catholicism and other religions of European origin present on American soil.

Gunnar Myrdal initially popularized the term 'American Creed' in 1944.[2] It sought to define American identity and was adopted by settlers of European origin. In Hector St Crèvecoeur's words, in America 'Individuals of all nations are melted into a new race of men.'[3] Americans regarded themselves as a 'chosen people' with a mission to expand towards a 'promised land' – no matter that, in their constant pushing of their frontier towards the west, they displaced and annihilated most of America's original inhabitants – the First Nations (also referred to as Native Americans or Indians), who ended up confined on reservations and cast out of the American dream.

Creating a nation out of a diverse population constantly growing and expanding was a mammoth task. From the beginning, compliance with the American Creed was deemed the only way of becoming American. This opened up endless opportunities for people, primarily of European origin, attracted to the image of America as a land of opportunity, equality and tolerance and by the possibility of starting a new life free from many of the prejudices and constraints – political, religious, economic and cultural – facing them in their home countries.

Currently, the significance of religious values continues to permeate American identity. Thus, according to a 2003 opinion poll, 92 per cent of US citizens said that they believe in God.[4] Samuel Huntington argues that, in the USA, the separation of church and state had as a purpose 'not to establish freedom from religion but to establish freedom for religion'.[5]

Religion and patriotism are strongly united in America: 'Civil religion enables Americans to bring together their secular politics and their religious society . . . so as to give religious sanctity to their patriotism and nationalist legitimacy to their religious beliefs, and thus to merge what could be conflicting loyalties into loyalty to a religiously endowed country.'[6] For some, the American political system of government rests on a religious base, and many Americans still regard themselves as a 'chosen people' with a quasi-divine mission. This is not to neglect the fact that an important section of America's population highlights their attachment to secular liberal values and human rights. However, as Fukuyama points out, America may have something to teach Europeans, as

> They attempt to construct post-ethnic forms of national citizenship and belonging. American life is full of quasi-religious ceremonies and rituals meant to celebrate the country's democratic political institutions: flag raising ceremonies, the naturalization oath, Thanksgiving and the 4th of July. Europeans, by contrast, have largely deritualized their political lives. Europeans tend to be cynical or dismissive of American displays of patriotism. But such ceremonies are important in the assimilation of new immigrants.[7]

In spite of the non-ethnic character of American identity, for a long time, being 'white' was considered as a prerequisite for being truly American. Many would argue that even nowadays attachment to the values and culture of the White Anglo-Saxon Protestant (WASP) tradition defines 'pure Americans', since it certainly describes the majority of those included within American elites. Non-whites, in particular blacks and Native Americans, had to wait almost two centuries to be granted civil rights. Yet the USA still remains deeply divided about whether equality for all, as established by the Civil Rights Act of 1964, should prevail over positive discrimination.

The melting pot metaphor

Since the Civil War, America has sought to define itself as 'one people', open to all those prepared to subscribe to its values, culture and political system.

However, ideology and experience have often clashed, as some racial and ethnic groups have found it consistently difficult to become American. Even after obtaining US citizenship, many of them have never been regarded as real 'Americans'. Throughout time, the definition of the American people has expanded to include groups initially excluded, for instance Native Americans and African-Americans, as well as groups of immigrant origin who were initially portrayed as belonging 'to lower "races" '[8] and were [seen as] innately inassimilable', such as the Jews, Italians and Poles. Recognition and inclusion had to be struggled for.

The predominance of group mobilization to attain specific rights within the USA not only questions the individualist idea behind the melting pot metaphor, it also underestimates the endurance of collective demands. Even today, group interests continue to mark American politics and serve to emphasize the tension between individual and group rights. Assimilationists consider such a tension as a product of the shift towards multiculturalism, which in the 1960s coincided with what Putnam identified as a decline in social capital.[9]

The first half of the twentieth century witnessed a systematic programme of nation-building in the USA, which included the design of a specific education programme devised as a tool to assimilate different groups – although this tended to ignore the fact that, to a considerable extent, differences in access to education and expectations depended on group membership and contributed to the reification of group hierarchies. At a time when emphasis on individual assimilation informed education programmes, the Ford Motor Company in Michigan sought to teach its immigrant workers how to speak English and become American.[10]

Rules were finally relaxed in 1965, after almost four decades of rigorous US immigration restrictions, and 25 million new immigrants entered the country in a thirty-five-year period. More recently, 'Legal and illegal immigration to the US accounted for a record 2.4 million between March 2000 and March 2001 [compared] to 1.2 million from March 2001 to March 2002',[11] a reduction linked to the restrictions imposed after the 9/11 terrorist attacks on the World Trade Center and the Pentagon.

The Civil Rights Act of 1964 and the Voting Rights Act of 1965 signalled a turning point in American society. In principle, they ended the second-class status of blacks as an ethnic minority systematically excluded from mainstream American life. More than that, they prohibited discrimination based on race, colour, religion and national origin while upholding that all individuals should be treated equally regardless of their group membership.

Two main attitudes emerged concerning affirmative action. First, those who, like Nathan Glazer,[12] argued that the government should outlaw racial discrimination and insist on equality of opportunity while defending a strong anti-affirmative action stance. In their view, granting special treatment and benefits to blacks and other ethnic minorities was a mistake that would only contribute to reinforcing their marginal status. Second, those who, like Ronald Takaki and Stephen Steinberg, defined the Civil Rights Act as a first step towards the realization of equality, but who firmly defended the need for affirmative action because, in their view, individualism and meritocracy reinforce racial inequality.[13] According to them, American society should acknowledge the consequences of slavery, white nativism and the near extermination of Native Americans and set up reparation measures towards these ethnic groups.

After a few years, demands for the inclusion of black studies in university curricula, the rejection of European culture, and a critical attitude towards the values and cultural tenets of traditional American identity led to what Allan Bloom referred to as a 'cultural war in education'.[14] At the same time, E. D. Hirsch described the danger of America becoming a Tower of Babel, and pointed to expanding ethnic diversity as a threat to the nation's social fabric.[15]

But the new immigrants were substantially different from those that entered the country during the nineteenth and the early twentieth centuries; they had a lower education, they were much more diverse than their largely European predecessors, and they tended to retain their own ethnic affiliations. Assimilating into the mainstream American culture and value system was not their main objective; rather, many of them integrated within ethnic communities, some of them territorially circumscribed – for example Cubans in Miami and Mexicans in the Southwest. In contrast to earlier waves of immigration, new immigrants were reluctant to follow patterns of territorial dispersion. In time, many of them have become Americans without ever assimilating into mainstream American culture.

Up until 1965, Americanization and assimilation were synonymous – although some immigrant groups, such as Italians and Jews, kept much of their own cultures. Since then, a fresh emphasis on multiculturalism has encouraged most immigrants to uphold their original ethnic identities. Pressure to assimilate has weakened considerably and double citizenship has become a valid option. As Huntington argues, 'dual citizenship legitimizes dual identities and dual loyalties . . . the lack of the need to make a choice means the lack of a comparable need for loyalty and commitment. . . . exclusivity has been lost . . . with dual citizenship, American identity is no longer distinctive and exceptional.'[16] A drop in naturalization rates in America, from 63.6 per cent in 1970 to 37.4 per cent in 2000, confirms this new trend.[17]

Nowadays, American society is enmeshed in poignant debates about whether being an economic magnet for immigrants from all over the world, and in particular for Hispanics, holds the possibility of fundamentally altering its identity. Is there a limit to how much diversity could be incorporated within a single nation? Is the melting pot yielding to the Tower of Babel?[18]

Arthur Schlesinger criticizes the excessive cult of ethnicity spreading within American society and argues that denying the essentially European origins of American culture implies falsifying its own history. He writes: 'this republic has had an Anglo-Saxon base; but from the start that base has been modified, enriched, and reconstituted by transfusions from other continents and civilizations. The movement from exclusion to inclusion causes a constant revision in the texture of our culture. The ethnic transfusions affect all aspects of American life.'[19] Still, Schlesinger is concerned about whether further transformations affecting America's cultural mosaic resulting from non-whites outnumbering whites, as current analysts forecast for the twenty-first century, should pose a threat to national cohesion.[20]

In his book *Alien Nation: Sense about America's Immigration Disaster*, Peter Brimelow[21] demanded the rolling back of multiculturalism, bilingualism and affirmative action and the abolition of the 1965 Immigration Act. He referred to America as an ethnocultural community and showed great concern about the consequences of mass immigration. He wrote:

> Race is destiny in American politics. Its importance has only been intensified by the supposedly colour-blind rights legislation of the 1960s – which paradoxically has turned out to mean elaborate race-conscious affirmative action programmes . . . It is simply common sense that Americans have a legitimate interest in their country's racial balance. It is common sense that they have a right to insist that their government stop shifting it. Indeed, it seems to me that they have a right to insist that it be shifted back.[22]

Brimelow characterized American national identity as the culture of white Americans, that is, an identity based primarily upon racial and ethnic terms – a definition which, as Fukuyama points out, ignores the great diversity and variety of origins of white Americans.[23] Brimelow was particularly critical of the consequences of what he refers to as the 'browning of America' – where the number of whites is shrinking fast, squeezed by Hispanics and Asians –

and expressed alarm at the possible 'Third Worldization' of the country. Following George Borjas,[24] he argues that, while First World immigrants 'are disproportionately skilled and successful . . . Third World immigrants tend to be "negatively selected".'[25] Brimelow concludes that current immigration is tending both to 'lower the average quality of the US workforce; and [to] stratify it, with the post-1970 immigrants tending to the bottom'.[26]

In his book, he expressed fears that Hispanics would not assimilate and therefore would become the new blacks. However, he totally neglected the fact that support for multiculturalism tends to originate among white middle-class educated people – precisely those whom he is trying to 'protect'. He emphasized the 'pernicious' impact of Hispanic immigration, which, in his view, has depressed wages, drained development funds and contributed to the upsurge in multiculturalism. He also associated this type of immigration with rising crime, pollution and disease.[27]

Brimelow's provocative assertions did not manage to obtain the support of liberals or centrists, let alone mainstream conservatives, libertarians or neo-conservatives. Instead, he found agreement mainly on the ultra-nationalist fringe.[28] His stance against immigration contained the potential to alienate millions of voters, among them thousands of Asians who had proven loyal to the Republican Party in the 1992 election.

Undoubtedly, the publication of *Alien Nation* (1995) ignited an ongoing debate on American national identity. Among those expressing more nuanced views while still displaying a critical stance against immigration are Roy Beck and Vernon Briggs, Jr.[29] In contrast, Sanford J. Ungar defends the idea that 'the United States is still a nation of immigrants, and by its very nature, it will always be one',[30] and Peter Salins offers 'an impassioned defence of immigration and assimilation as the foundation of the American greatness and the American Dream'.[31] In turn, John Isbister in his book *The Immigration Debate*[32] offers a much more balanced approach, one that defends multiculturalism and regards immigration as beneficial overall in spite of having some negative effects.

Among the most recent and influential contributions to debates on American identity are Samuel Huntington's *Who Are We?*,[33] Alan Wolfe's *Return to Greatness*[34] and Walter Benn Michaels's *The Trouble with Diversity*.[35] Samuel Huntington's main objective is to analyse the main factors contributing to what he perceives as a weakening of American identity. As ideas contributing to a widening gap between elites and the masses in the USA he mentions a much more relaxed approach towards assimilation into the country's mainstream culture, the impact of Hispanic immigration and the linguistic and cultural challenges it poses to American identity, and the consequences of multiculturalism and cosmopolitanism. His position is brought to the fore and discussed at different points within this chapter.

Alan Wolfe is critical of both conservatives and liberals for replacing a legacy of American greatness – championed by Alexander Hamilton, John Marshall, Abraham Lincoln, Theodore Roosevelt and Lyndon Johnson – with America's current emphasis on 'small-mindedness'. Wolfe argues that the Republican Party, in the past, has been able to provide strong leadership, exemplified by Nelson Rockefeller, John Lindsay, Kingman Brewster and Elliot Richardson. More recently, Republicans have made some attempts to return to the idea of national greatness; however, in Wolfe's view, these have been halted by George W. Bush's administration.[36]

Wolfe believes that, if the Democrats were to lead a national greatness movement, they should first acquire a sense of national purpose.[37] For instance, he defends the idea that America has to stand for liberty and equality, at home and abroad, and be prepared to use force to defend its ideals. The return to greatness would also require rebuilding American institutions, such as political parties, interest groups, labour unions and business firms, and infusing them with renewed energy. Even more crucially, America needs national leaders able to encourage citizens to unite around a common project. At this point, he criticizes liberals for relying too much on interest groups advancing their own private aims. He also disapproves of conservatives for waging a culture war that would not otherwise exist.

Walter Benn Michaels is concerned primarily with class. He argues that focusing on race and ethnicity seeks to avoid confronting the most poignant form of difference existing within the USA, that is, economic inequality. In his view, 'white is not better than black, but rich is definitely better than poor'.[38] He contends that a world in which class differences imply that some people do not have sufficient resources to live presents a difficult problem to solve, whereas a world of racial and ethnic differences immediately offers the appreciation of difference as a solution. In his own words:

> By giving priority to issues like affirmative action and committing itself to the celebration of difference, the intellectual left has responded to the increase in economic inequality by insisting on the importance of cultural identity. So for 30 years, while the gap between the rich and the poor has grown larger, we've been urged to respect people's identities – as if the problem of poverty would be solved if we just appreciated the poor . . . Celebrating the diversity of American life has become the American left's way of accepting their poverty, of accepting inequality.[39]

To reinforce his point Michaels maintains that, in the USA, 'there are more black people than poor people in elite universities (even though there are still precious few black people).'[40] He refers to the televised images of the effects of Hurricane Katrina (2006) to highlight that there are poor people in America and that, often, they are left to fend for themselves. It is his concern that diversity has become virtually a sacred concept in American life, so that Americans would rather get rid of racism than get rid of poverty.[41] Michaels's approach does not offer a detailed analysis of the relationship between race and ethnicity, on the one hand, and social class, on the other, and, while making a strong argument against capitalism, he appears less able to offer a well-defined alternative.

★   ★   ★

In what follows I offer a brief account of the growing diversity characteristic of American society by focusing on the consequences of the Civil Rights Act of 1964 and its aftermath. I start by considering the cultural and linguistic challenges posed by the large influx of Hispanics into the USA, then move on to analyse the current status and main concerns of African-Americans, for a long time regarded as second-class citizens within their own country. Native Americans (Indians), the only peoples with a territorial claim upon parts of the USA, represent a small minority and struggle to maintain a separate identity. Finally, I examine the proliferation of hyphenated identities and their use by white working-class US citizens of European descent. To conclude, I reflect on what it means to be American and consider the main factors currently impacting upon America's national identity.

The Hispanic challenge to American society

Never before has the USA experienced such a large and constant flow of primarily economic immigrants from a single place of origin – Mexico – carrying a distinct language, culture and identity with them. In 2000, Hispanics (of which two-thirds were of Mexican origin) constituted 12 per cent of the total US population, and their number increased by almost 10 per cent in just two years (2000–2),[42] overtaking blacks as the second largest ethnic group. At present whites remain the largest ethnic group, but they are likely to lose their status to non-whites by 2050.[43]

Illegal entry to the USA is primarily a Mexican phenomenon, prompted by their wish to escape poverty and gain access to a prosperous American society offering novel opportunities – even if most jobs are badly paid and employment conditions are harsh. Furthermore, the sharing of a 2,000-mile border with the USA unquestionably contributes to fuel Mexican illegal immigration. US border patrol apprehensions of illegal Mexican immigrants rose 'from 1.6 million in the 1960s to 11.9 million in the 1980s, and 12.9 million in the 1990s . . . estimates of the total number of illegal immigrants in the US rose from four million in 1995 to six million in 1998 and eight to ten million by 2003.'[44]

The illegal status of a large number of Hispanic immigrants – from Mexico and other Latin American countries – living in the USA seriously limits their access to education and hampers their social mobility as well as their possibilities of integrating into American society. Yet, in contrast with a high proportion of well-educated and professional immigrants originating from India, China, Africa, Western Europe and Canada, most Hispanics – legal and illegal – tend to have little education and occupy low-skilled jobs.

But what are the consequences of Hispanic immigration for American culture and identity? Are Hispanics assimilating or are they contributing to the emergence of a Hispanic-American bilingual bicultural society within some major American cities, as well as in areas such as California and Texas[45] – lost by Mexico to the USA in the War of Independence (1835–6) and the Mexican–American War of 1846–8? The latter seems to be the case, in particular, when Hispanics tend to create territorial enclaves within which they foster and maintain their own ethnic ties, culture, language and traditions. This is a practice that allows them to re-create the emotional attachments at the centre of their Hispanic identity and, in the case of Mexicans, to a *madre patria* (motherland) not so distant as to be forgotten and replaced by mighty America.

According to Robert J. Samuelson, after immigrating to the USA, most Mexicans maintain strong affective links with their motherland. In his view, this is as understandable as the wish of Americans to retain their own heritage and identity while trying to avoid turning into 'a simple collection of peoples, from various places, who happen to work here and whose main allegiances lie elsewhere'.[46] He argues that 'the US cannot act as a sponge for Mexico's poor' and warns of a possible 'Balkanization' of areas such as California and Texas. He also issues a warning against a possible backlash against immigration involving renewed discrimination against Hispanic-Americans who have been members of American society for generations, and who may now be confused with immigrants.[47]

The strength of Spanish (Castilian) means that some areas of the USA have become de facto bilingual and act as a magnet for further immigration by Hispanics, attracted by the prospect of being included within a familiar environment. In the meantime, political and intellectual American elites debate the limits of multiculturalism and wonder whether the federal republic should go on protecting Spanish and encouraging bilingual education, as many Hispanic organizations and some liberal and civil rights organizations advocate. According to the 2000 census, 'over 26 million people spoke Spanish at home and almost 13.7 million of these spoke English less than "very well", an increase of 65.5 per cent over 1990.'[48]

Although the impact of Spanish has a relatively limited – if growing – influence upon American politics, since only a small portion of Hispanics have the right to vote and participate in America's political life, its economic impact is far greater. Currently over 38 million Spanish-speaking consumers are exerting a growing pressure upon the American market. They demand specific products adapted to their own taste, and businesses do not hesitate to employ Spanish in their publicity to increase the appeal of their goods. At present, it is still unclear whether Hispanics reaching middle-class status will seek further to promote their own indigenous culture rather than assimilate into mainstream American culture, and whether second- and third-generation Hispanics will become primarily English speakers or will continue to use Spanish as their main language. The recent nature of the Hispanic phenomenon prevents us from offering a sound response at this stage.

A study by Alba and Nee in 1997 of new immigration to the USA argues that it will be hard for contemporary immigrants to move up the social ladder, since the majority of jobs available to them tend to be unskilled and badly paid. As a result, most immigrants have fewer possibilities of acquiring a good education, as was the case with previous waves of immigrants, in order to contribute to their social mobility. They even raise the issue of whether second-generation immigrants may experience 'no, or even downward, mobility unless the American economy becomes more dynamic'[49] – an issue that points to the role of economic opportunities as a major incentive for cultural and linguistic assimilation. They also highlight the ability of well-established ethnic sub-economies, such as those of Cubans in Miami or Chinese and Japanese urban enclaves, to draw on ethnic solidarity and resources.

According to Benjamin Márquez, who focuses specifically on the study of organizations run by Mexicans in the USA, Mexican-American identity politics (understood as a specific type of Hispanic identity) is driven by judgements made in three interlocking cultural and socio-political areas: race, class and culture. In his view, Mexican-Americans – a newly coined hyphenated identity – suffer racial discrimination within a mainly Anglo-dominated society and pose demands for equal treatment before the law. Mexican-Americans are confined to the lower classes, suffer economic disadvantage and are affected by poverty, low wages and unemployment. In cultural terms, Márquez argues that Mexican-American organizations have politicized the use of the Spanish language and culture – including clothing, art, traditions, extended families and friendship networks – as a means to break Anglo cultural hegemony.[50] He also denounces the fact that hundreds of Mexican-American organizations across the USA do not enjoy similar recognition to that obtained by their African-American counterparts.

African-Americans: an unresolved question

The African-American movement stood for civil rights while embracing the US flag; the main objective was to achieve equal rights for all regardless of their race and ethnicity. The participation of blacks in the First World War and, above all, in the Second World War revealed a deep inconsistency in the American Creed; up until then African-Americans were dying abroad for the preservation of a democracy they did not enjoy at home.[51] Opposing reactions emerged from the black leadership, some in favour of participation in the war effort, others, such as Richard Wright, standing strongly against enlistment.[52] At that point, some blacks initiated 'the Double V campaign: victory against the foreign enemy, Japan, and the enemy at home, racial prejudice'.[53] Renewed consciousness of such a contradiction stimulated black mobilization, provided a new impetus for expressing their grievances and finally resulted in a vigorous civil rights movement.

In the period leading to the 1964 Civil Rights Act, most African-American activists, apart from leaders of the black nationalist movement such as Malcolm X,[54] emphasized their own American identity and embraced the melting pot model. The black integrationist movement shared common interests with wider American society, and with European-Americans in particular. It advocated the constitution of interracial organizations, non-economic liberalism and cultural assimilation. Black integrationists played a leading role within the black church and enjoyed greater access to external resources; their own integrationist position was, and remains, functional in accessing external support.

But the integrationist stance has not always been welcome among white Americans; rather, until 1964 it was under attack from white supremacist organizations such as the Ku Klux Klan[55] and discriminatory practices regarding housing, schools and employment. More recently, African-Americans have denounced the pervasiveness of some hostile institutional barriers in both the private and the public sector, plus some remaining institutional and individual forms of racism.[56]

The ambivalence between a mainly integrationist and a black nationalist position has been a constant in the black leadership. The black nationalist movement has defended the formation of racially exclusive political organizations and the construction of a self-sufficient black economy and, instead of focusing on their American identity, has emphasized a black and mainly pan-African identity.

Harold Cruse, in his book *The Crisis of the Negro Intellectual*,[57] echoed the blacks' ambivalence between integrationism and nationalism. He referred to it as the 'pendulum thesis' and argued that it is not sufficient to empower individuals, regardless of the ethnic or racial group they belong to. In his view, cultural group is important, and failure to appreciate this 'is debilitating to the black community because even as individual blacks ascend America's social ladder, blacks as a group remain outcast and denigrated, consistently ranking below whites across any meaningful standard of quality of life and equality of opportunity.'[58] He argued that the melting pot is a myth hiding white supremacy.

African-Americans, except for the black urban underclass, improved their status after the civil rights movement. Many made material gains, benefited from greater access to education and enjoyed economic mobility; for the first time on American soil, some of them constituted a black middle class.

Stephen Steinberg argues that immigration flows after 1965 were possible on account of the dramatic transformations in US law prompted by the civil rights movement – for instance, abolishing national origin quotas and defending equality for all. He does not call into question the rights of immigrants and he is not 'blaming immigrants for the nation's failure to address the enduring legacy of slavery',[59] but, in his view:

> Immigrants cannot hide behind the refrain that 'our ancestors didn't own slaves', or claim that, as recent arrivals, they are exonerated from America's racial crimes. Indeed, immigrants are implicated in America's race problem through the very act of immigration. Besides, when immigrants proudly embrace American citizenship and nationality, they not only take possession of American dreams and ideals, but they also acquire some heavy baggage: moral and political responsibility for the vestiges of slavery.[60]

According to Steinberg, blacks were improving their status during the post-civil rights era, and massive immigration – 25 million since 1965, plus an indeterminate number of illegal immigrants – clearly halted black progress. The numbers of Hispanics and Asians, in particular, started overtaking those of blacks, and today they have managed to establish large and well-organized ethnic communities within the USA. But, if America is racist – an argument that has traditionally been invoked to account for the pervasive discrimination suffered by blacks – then why have Hispanics, West Indians, and Asians – all people of colour – 'made it'?, and why can't African-Americans?[61]

Some have sought to explain the status of African-Americans by appealing to negative qualities associated with being black, for instance moral degeneracy, lower intelligence and laziness. For instance, Richard J. Herrnstein and Charles Murray's *The Bell Curve: Intelligence and Class Structure in American Life*[62] argued that scientific evidence shows that human intelligence is measurable, largely hereditary and varies between races. Neo-social Darwinist views also came to the fore to deny that racism and white supremacy ever led to any pernicious consequences in American history. Spreading support for such theories was employed to legitimize a critical stance against affirmative action and to shift the focus away from societal racism.

In time, 'affirmative action' was replaced by an emphasis on the protection of 'diversity' – a move regarded by Steinberg as detrimental to blacks and positive for immigrants. In his view, 'the extension of race beyond the binary of black and white, the admission of permutation in the middle, has deflected attention away from the unique and unresolved problems of race *qua* African Americans . . . the nation congratulates itself on its "diversity" and celebrates its "multiculturalism", while the problems of African Americans continue to fester from neglect.'[63] He concludes with a controversial assertion: 'Immigrants have a political debt to pay to African Americans whose protest movement led to the immigration reform that allowed them to come here in the first place.'[64]

Native nationalism in the USA

The term 'nation' was initially used by European settlers to refer to the different communities inhabiting North America. To recognize Indian nations as distinct, independent political communities implied that their right to self-government was inherent and not the outcome of a delegation of powers from the US government. To legitimize control over Indians (also referred to as Native Americans), their status had to be changed and their sovereignty extinguished or, at least, limited. In 1924, Congress granted citizenship to all Indians. This was a crucial move with decisive implications. Pressure to assimilate Indians into mainstream US culture increased and was manifested in the termination policy implemented by Congress in the 1950s. Termination involved the extinction of treaty rights and tribal political existence. The supporters of termination argued that there was an implicit contradiction in the idea that a government could make treaties with some of its own citizens, as some Indians opposing termination demanded.[65]

In the 1960s the controversy continued, and many civil rights supporters regarded the Indian position as anti-American. Indians showed great scepticism and often hostility towards a policy which would give them civil rights while abolishing their treaty rights.[66] Increasing concern about the preservation of Indian identity and land became a key issue which attracted widespread support among Indians belonging to different tribes. A new Indian social movement immediately began to take shape. The Indian discourse defended their right to choose and live according to a set of values and traditions endangered by the progressive incorporation of Indians into American life and by a set of laws which were threatening their own separate status within the USA.[67]

Some young urban Indian activists initially led the Indian movement. Most tribal councils were unsympathetic to their demands to revise old treaties, but support came from some full-blood Indians living on reservations. Full-blood Indians had opposed tribal councils set up under the Indian Reorganization Act of 1934 on the basis of treaty rights and usually acted as leaders in tribal religious ceremonies. With their support, the movement gained strength and attracted new followers. The 1969 Indian occupation of Alcatraz, the 1972 Twenty Points March, the 1973 confrontation at Wounded Knee and the 1978 Longest Walk to Washington are landmarks in the Indian movement.

The Indians insisted on the restoration of treaties, demanded the recognition of tribal sovereignty, and wanted to take an active part in the economic development of their areas. They were strongly against termination, since they considered that this would break the treaties signed between their ancestors and the USA, which had agreed to look after them. In return, Indians had ceded their lands. The Indians' argument was that, if their ancestors had known that the USA would unilaterally abolish the treaties, they would have never signed them. In 1970 Richard Nixon, shortly after being appointed US president, abandoned the termination policy and referred to it as 'wrong'.[68] He also valued cultural pluralism as one of the strengths of the USA and mentioned the need to develop Indian self-determination by encouraging Indians to take an active part in the decisions and projects which concern them.[69]

Rebecca L. Robbins defends the right of Native Americans to self-determination and acknowledges the diverse meanings that self-determination may adopt when applied to different communities.[70] Indians have limited resources to exploit and are dependent on US funding. Water, oil and uranium are the most important natural resources present on some Indian land, which permit some Indians to have a substantial source of income through direct exploitation or by leasing contracts. Probably the most visible manifestation of Indian sovereignty, at least to the general public, has been Indian gaming. However, it seems that the cultural and political survival of Indians depends to a considerable extent on US support.[71] Thus, pressure for self-determination is mixed up with increasing demands for more elaborate links between tribal communities and the surrounding society.

A key problem faced by Indians is how to make their communities viable without destroying their indigenous identity, since the prospect of economic development often causes internal divisions. Communal sense is threatened when communities are to be reorganized on the basis of market needs. There are at least two sets of crucial issues concerning Native Americans: (1) the tension between the demand for self-determination and the demand for support from the USA; and (2) the possibilities for survival of Indian identity and culture and their role within American society. Although Indian symbols have become more visible as a consequence of the success of the Indian movement, there are serious questions about whether this cultural re-emergence will be realized in actual patterns of life and action or will remain at a superficial level. Indians are progressively being acculturated to the US life-style and values.

Parallel to a growing demand for enhanced self-government, we encounter a rising Native American nationalism based upon the rejection of Western institutions and values with which Indian communities have been forced to compromise. Native nationalism is based upon re-examining the roots of the political and cultural institutions and traditions which lie at the heart of Indian communities. It condemns the colonizing strategies imposed upon them by the newcomers and blames Western institutions and principles for the sometimes irreparable erosion of Indian culture.

European-Americans: the new ethnicity

There are at least two main ways in which ethnicity has re-emerged among white Americans since 1965. First, as a mechanism for accessing socio-political advantages conferred on ethnic groups and, second, as a boundary securing a certain status and prestige in the light of new immigration.

Michael Novak[72] coined the term 'new ethnicity' to highlight the re-emergence of ethnic identity among some whites of European origin who still felt some kind of attachment to their original homelands, primarily Polish, Irish and Slavic working-class people who arrived after 1800 and were experiencing disadvantage when compared with African-Americans and Hispanics. They felt discriminated against, since most welfare programmes were destined to improve the situation of ethnic groups rather than focusing on class.

The 'new ethnics' rejected the idea that they had melded into American culture, arguing that they lived in a world far removed from that of American elites exemplified by WASPs, whose value systems and social and cultural experiences were completely different from theirs.[73]

The reaction of the 'new ethnics' amounted to a white backlash against America's attempts to redress racial inequalities at the expense of neglecting its own white indigenous working class. By politicizing their ethnicity, the 'new ethnics' sought to form interest groups able to improve their own situation. As Daniel Bell[74] once put it, politics was progressively replacing market forces as the chief instrument of distribution.

At the present time, in particular when faced with new immigration, social boundaries based on ancestry – including race and ethnicity – are highly relevant. It is true that, in America, the contours of ethnic identity can be reshaped in relatively short historical periods; however, ethnic identity continues to play a major part.

Richard Alba regards the emergence of what he calls 'European-Americans' as a strategy to emphasize the role played by one's ancestral group in the construction of the American nation. Thus membership in a hyphenated European-American group is associated with a sense of social honour deriving from the sacrifices endured by previous generations who actively contributed to building the country.[75] Nowadays, old-stock families tend to define themselves as 'American' only, while those arriving after 1800 usually employ the term European-American.

European-Americans display what Herbert Gans refers to as 'symbolic ethnicity', that is, an ethnicity 'of last resort' in the light of their progressive Americanization and the loss of specific ethnic structures. According to Alba, 'ethnic identities fit well with the individualism of American life, and accordingly they will become increasingly personal in nature, largely creatures of individual inclinations and tastes rather than social attachments.'[76] Retaining a specific ethnic identity has become a means of locating oneself and one's family against the panorama of American history, against the backdrop of what it means to be American.[77]

What does it mean to be American?

Basically, to be American indicates that an individual is a member of the most powerful nation on earth in political, military and economic terms. The status of being 'American' is further enhanced by the country's commitment to equality and freedom, so that its power and influence are often associated with a high moral standard entrenched in the American Creed and acting as a source of legitimacy for US actions. Being American is frequently regarded as something to be proud of.

While abroad, most Americans would tend to endorse this particular view of national identity, but do they perceive being American in a different manner when they are at home? Then, to be American means being a US citizen entitled to participate in a polity defined by equality, freedom and individualism. It assumes that you are an English speaker living within a multicultural society, and it also grants you access to the welfare system. Racial, ethnic and social differences matter more when you are at home, and they are closely connected with life-chances and life-styles.

At the beginning of the twenty-first century, America's identity is being problematized. In what follows I examine some of the main challenges currently facing it.

1 *Multiculturalism* implies tolerance of diversity, equal dignity and equal rights for individuals belonging to different groups living within a single nation-state. According to its critics, however, multiculturalism is eroding the pre-eminence of the original Anglo culture and has already helped to weaken the traditional emphasis on assimilation to the extent that, today, it is possible to become 'American' without ever assimilating into most of the original tenets of the American Creed. Citizenship classes and ceremonies are trying to counteract such trends, but at present this seems quite difficult. Critics of multiculturalism argue that emphasizing what divides Americans rather than fostering those features uniting them may cause a breakdown in social cohesion, resulting in the consolidation of some elites and the reification of social barriers.

In contrast, intermarriage rates show that Americans are mixing. According to the 2000 census, Americans' racial attitudes have witnessed an apparent sea change. For instance, a Gallup poll conducted at the end of 2003 established that 86 per cent of black, 79 per cent of Hispanic, and 66 per cent of white respondents would accept a child or grandchild marrying someone of a different race.[78] Interracial marriage has increased across most racial groups, escalating 'from less than 1 per cent of all married couples in 1970 to more than 5 per cent of couples in 2000'.[79] In addition, the number of children growing up in either interracial or inter-Hispanic families has grown from 900,000 in 1970 to 3 million in 2000.

2 *Heavy Hispanic immigration* has already resulted in the emergence and progressive expansion of largely bilingual and bicultural areas. Spanish is expanding rapidly, and the relentless pace of Hispanic immigration tends to reinforce this trend. Hispanics not only arrive with a different language and culture, but also exemplify some qualities that, at least for the time being, oppose American individualism. The strength of ethnic ties, a conception of extended families, and wide networks of friends stand in opposition to American individualism. In my view, ethnic ties are reinforced by the need to overcome the socio-cultural barriers that Hispanics encounter when moving to the USA. Furthermore, Hispanic immigration is territorially circumscribed, and this increases the sense of being at home among recent arrivals, a factor that simultaneously contributes to weaken the urge to assimilate.

The most distinctive trend of recent immigration refers to the origin of immigrants: 'more than one-half (52 per cent) of current immigrants are from Latin America, and another 26 percent are from Asia . . . Net immigration to the US since 1970 has been responsible for 30 percent to nearly 40 percent of US population growth.'[80]

3 *Pervasive discrimination against African-Americans* Although there have been some successes in terms of social and economic mobility and access to higher education, African-Americans, except for a limited middle class, continue to feel discriminated against and to suffer the consequences of slavery. They are disappointed at the halt of affirmative action programmes. They are also critical of a fundamental shift in American policy which has replaced a major emphasis on reversing the legacy of slavery with the promotion of diversity. In this new context, African-Americans have become one ethnic group among many, and they are currently reacting to this novel situation by revitalizing black nationalism.

4 *The proliferation of hyphenated identities* Some authors regard this trend as a strategy allowing people to identify with the two sides of the hyphen and helping them to overcome the isolation of modern life.[81] An alternative way to look at it is to consider whether being 'American' is enough to define identity. Implicit in this is the idea that there is more than one way of being 'American', and it follows that assimilation into mainstream culture may not be essential. By stressing their ancestral origins and connecting themselves to lands they may have never visited, and to peoples and cultures that remain largely alien to them, some US citizens are expressing a longing for roots. They are seeking to achieve a higher status and, above all, they wish to

acquire an identity making them unique and fundamentally different from 'other' Americans, whom they may happen to distrust or even dislike.

5 *A growing gap between the elites and the masses* The melting pot was envisaged as giving life to a new American people with a fresh culture and novel values and traditions, an aim which has been only partly achieved. Beyond that, in economic terms the USA is an unequal society – one of the most unequal societies in the Western world, if we focus on the wide gap between the richest and the poorest. However, this gap also extends to patriotic attitudes, given that an important section of America's elites displays a cosmopolitan attitude which stands in sharp contrast with the patriotic feelings of the masses. The cosmopolitanism of elites places them beyond nation and religion, and it accentuates even further their distance from the majority of the population. According to Desmond King, 'the expectation that a process equivalent to a melting pot will drive all Americans into a cosmopolitan post-ethnic identity in which the lingering commitments of race, ethnicity, or national background have vanished is fanciful.'[82]

6 *The end of the Cold War and the rise of the 'War on Terror'* The USA, as is the case with many other nations, has constructed its own identity in opposition to a set of external and internal enemies.[83] The shift from a bipolar to a unipolar world following the demise of the USSR has robbed the USA of an enemy against whom to unite and construct its own distinct identity, an enemy that was able to mobilize the population regardless of ethnic and other differences. The 9/11 attacks in New York and Washington signal the rise of a new enemy, that is, global terrorism sponsored by Islamic fundamentalism, which has managed to reawaken a sense of unity and common fate among Americans. After the attacks, the declaration of a 'War on Terror', involving the invasion of Iraq and other military operations in the Middle East, prompted almost massive support among Americans. But it is unclear whether unity will prevail in the face of growing difficulties surrounding the US military campaign. The threat of global terrorism conveys the existence of a potent enemy, and not only the USA but also Spain (Madrid) and the UK (London) have experienced its brutality. It is still uncertain whether its menace will have a long-lasting effect as a unifying factor within American society.

6

Reactions to the End of 'Pure' National Identities

What do we mean by 'pure' national identities? Have they ever existed? It could be argued that 'purity' is a myth, since many different components from diverse origins have contributed to the construction of particular national identities throughout time; however, it is also true that each national identity seems to have a core formed by a set of key elements which account for the specific symbols, values, culture, traditions, language and memories shared by fellow nationals. Of course, nations are not homogeneous communities and their members may not share all these elements; even if they do, they may not experience them in exact terms or with the same intensity.

At the moment, strong concerns have been raised about whether citizens of the same state but belonging to communities of migrant origin share a single national identity. For instance, in Britain, the realization that the perpetrators of the London bombings (7 July 2005) were British citizens whose parents or grandparents had come to the country as immigrants horrified not only the political class but also most of their fellow citizens. Questions about the degree of cohesion within British society were raised and are still currently being discussed in intellectual and political circles. Did the bombers identify as 'British'? Did other identities – national, ethnic or religious – prevail to the extreme of allowing them to regard their fellow citizens as 'enemies'?

Concerns about social cohesion and national identity are not restricted to Britain. At present they are also emerging among some sectors of the population in other European countries. For some, rising numbers of immigrants, refugees and asylum-seekers are posing a threat to national identity while contributing to transform the cultural, linguistic and religious make-up of receiving societies. For others, greater immigration results in lower wages and loss of jobs for the indigenous population. In this context, radical right populist parties assert that uncontrolled immigration contributes directly to increase crime and to the creation of ghetto areas within cities – entire neighbourhoods being turned into centres of crime, prostitution and drugs.[1]

Furthermore, within a climate of welfare reform, some resent the social benefits allocated to 'foreigners' and stand in favour of granting preference to nationals. In Western Europe such a situation has prompted calls for the preservation of national identity and, with it, a reaction against cultural diversity and multiculturalism.

This chapter analyses the reasons prompting renewed concerns about the need to protect the 'purity' of national identity at a time of intense social, political and economic change driven by globalization. In so doing it focuses on the study of the new radical right, which, by presenting itself as primarily anti-immigrant and by defending the national preference principle, is appealing to an electorate dissatisfied with mainstream political parties and genuinely concerned about the effects – cultural as well as economic – of greater migration into their prosperous societies. In recent years the new radical right's political discourse has struck a chord with the voters and experienced a substantial increase in electoral support, allowing it to enter into coalition governments in Austria, the Netherlands, Italy, Switzerland and New Zealand.

The chapter offers an outline of the main transformations affecting Western societies as a consequence of an intensification of globalization processes. It then moves on to analyse the political discourse of the new radical right, in particular its highly critical stance against the functioning of Western-style liberal democratic systems and its unsympathetic assessment of rising immigration. The chapter also examines the origins of the new radical right and the arguments it employs to justify the need to preserve national identity, along with its position towards immigration and multiculturalism.

Globalization as a transformation agent

The pace of socio-economic change is being accelerated by globalization, and this is making a major impact upon the lives of individuals. Consumption, production, leisure, media, education, travel and politics are all affected by increasing interdependence and speed in communications. But not all individuals have access to the means of globalization, that is, the sophisticated technological tools which have made it possible. In a similar manner, not all are equally affected by its consequences; social class and education tend to fuel a growing divide between those competent to move around and benefit from living in the global age and those on the margins.

The transition from industrial to post-industrial society requires rapidly adapting individuals, capable of surviving within a dislocated society where moral norms, values, ideologies, traditions and knowledge are constantly challenged and revised. In this context, only a few achieve an elite position, while a substantial underclass, having few chances of escaping its situation, multiplies at the bottom. Inequality is rampant not only between different areas of the world but also within particular societies, and this generates resentment and fragmentation.

Globalization is contributing to the expansion of certain values, ideologies and products, resulting in a pervasive, if uneven, cultural and linguistic homogenization characterized by US influence. A significant number of nations and ethnic groups share a genuine concern about the eventual disappearance of certain languages and anxiety about the worldwide expansion of English. For instance, the French are extremely preoccupied with the predominance of English and, in particular, with the progressive displacement of the use of French within EU institutions, as well as the introduction of English expressions into the French language.

Furthermore, cultural, ethnic and religious communities of immigrant origin have settled in the West and are experiencing a dramatic expansion. The substantial influx of refugees and asylum-seekers recorded in the last fifteen years or so is contributing to an enhanced perception of diversity in Western Europe and North America, where, in many instances, indigenous cultures are being challenged, rejected, and confronted by those of the newcomers. Moreover, some sectors of the indigenous population display a growing mistrust and even hostility towards some of the newcomers' cultures and values. Such attitudes are generating heated debates about various models of integration, their success and desirability; they also open up the debate about what should be the basis of a cohesive society and whether this requires the sharing of some cultural, linguistic, religious and civic values among all citizens. Ultimately, it poses some questions about the conditions for the coexistence of different identities within a single nation, thus directly addressing a reflection on the limits of toleration within liberal democracies.

The impact of globalization is not restricted to culture and values; it also affects the economic and the political spheres. For instance, world trade and the labour market are currently being guided by capitalist principles, resulting, among other things, in the displacement of manufacturing industry away from traditional industrialized Western societies, where production is more expensive, to Eastern Europe, Third World countries and other countries where labour regulations are less strict, wages lower and workers' rights weaker and sometimes non-existent.

The collapse of communism has irremediably weakened socialism and trade unions, together with the traditional values underpinning them. Solidarity and equality have been replaced by competition, individualism and the survival of the fittest. Market capitalism has been radicalized and, while a successful elite benefits from operating in a global flexible market, a growing number of low- and medium-skilled workers are filling the ranks of the unemployed. Among them there is an escalating sense of vulnerability and defeat, often accompanied by an increasing lack of self-esteem. The idea that immigrants come into their countries to 'steal' their work – disregarding the generally precarious conditions in which immigrants tend to find themselves and the often unwillingness of nationals to take up certain jobs done by immigrants – added to the view, objective or not, that asylum-seekers and refugees receive greater social benefits than nationals, is contributing to breed resentment towards the state and towards society as a whole. In addition, the visibility of difference associated with alien cultures, traditions and ways of life fosters fear, lack of trust and open hostility and, in some cases, results in xenophobia and racism against those regarded as different.

In the political arena, the ascendance of the neo-conservatism formulated in the USA has added to a political radicalization, often accompanied by strong anti-system movements beyond the control of traditional conservative parties – a factor which in some instances has crystallized in the constitution and development of radical right-wing populist parties.[2] Additionally, the progressive erosion of democracy – owing to lack of transparency, corruption and other problems associated with it – has resulted in the alienation of significant sectors of the population, who feel disenchanted and who often opt to remain on the margins of institutional politics.

The new radical right and identity in Western Europe

The rise of the new radical right partly reflects the insecurity and instability brought about by the end of a bipolar division of the world led by the USA and the former USSR – substantial changes concerning the restructuring of the world economy and a technological revolution which has far-reaching social, cultural and political consequences. Betz considers that 'the rise of radical right-wing populist parties has coincided with a marked increase in public disaffection and disenchantment with the established political parties, the political class and the political system in general.'[3] In his view, public political distrust and resentment have created a climate favouring the emergence of new radical right-wing populist parties.[4]

According to some theories, there is a link between the revival of the radical right and the *anomie* experienced by some citizens in the West. They argue that 'traditional social structures, especially those based on class and religion, are breaking down. As a result, individuals lose a sense of belonging and are attracted to ethnic nationalism, which according to psychological research increases a sense of self-esteem and efficacy. For similar reasons, they may be attracted to family and other traditional values.[5]

The new radical right has managed to capture feelings of insecurity and uncertainty encouraged by a world defined by rapid change, and it has addressed them through a political discourse based on underlining the distinction between those who belong and the 'others'. This position has marked the emergence of some kind of ethnic nationalism, cutting across social-class cleavages and emphasizing the need to preserve national identity against foreign influences.

Western societies are profoundly individualistic. However, there is a dimension of the individual which can only be satisfied by his or her sense of belonging to a group. This social aspect is generally fulfilled in situations within which individuality is transcended through experiences of feeling in unison with others, that is, by sharing some common interests or objectives which enable individuals to transcend their profound isolation and the angst accompanying awareness of the brevity of life, as well as feelings of ontological insecurity. National identity has proven capable of playing this role, and the new radical right has become not only fully aware of the relevance of a shared identity but also strongly committed to jealously protecting it against what it perceives as foreign contamination and downgrading.

According to Pippa Norris, 'the comparison of the social class profile of radical right voters, including indicators of social inequality, suggests that they are disproportionately over-represented both among the petite bourgeoisie – self-employed professionals, own-account technicians and small merchants – and among the skilled and unskilled working class'[6] – with the exception of Hungary, Italy and Israel, where the petite bourgeoisie prevails and is overrepresented. In her view, however, we should adopt a sceptical attitude towards theories which establish a causal relationship between growing levels of unemployment, or increasing dissatisfaction among low-skilled and low-qualified workers, and rising support for the radical right, highlighting that 'the socio-economic profile is more complex than popular stereotypes suggest'.[7]

Pippa Norris attributes the radical right's growing support to 'the way in which formal institutional rules set the context of, and thereby interact with, both party supply and public demand in any election'.[8] She claims to show that 'no significant relationship exists at national (aggregate) level between the national share of the vote cast for radical right parties and a wide range of indicators of ethnic diversity',[9] while simultaneously arguing that, 'at individual level, however, support for cultural protectionism does indeed predict who will vote for the radical right, as expected, with anti-immigrant and anti-refugee attitudes remaining significant variables even after applying a battery of prior social and attitudinal controls.'[10] In my view, her analysis fails to spell out clearly that, in spite of dramatic social, economic and political transformations, it is not their intensity and scope that prompts specific reactions. Instead, it is the manner in which they are 'perceived' and 'interpreted' by individuals as well as particular societies that determines public opinion and voting behaviour.

Although a large percentage of those supporting new radical right-wing parties are to be found among the ranks of the working classes, it is quite striking to note that support also comes from some well-educated middle-class people who regard the impact of migration as a deadly threat to national identity. Basically, they are concerned about the levelling down of their own cultures as a result of hybridization.

The new radical right seeks to rob elites of moral and political legitimacy and is vociferous against the corruption affecting Western-style democratic systems.[11] A sharp anti-elite rhetoric that claims to replace dominant values with the 'common sense of the people' occupies a key place within the new radical right's discourse, which often adopts a populist style.

In spite of its extremely critical view of the functioning of liberal democratic systems, the new radical right does not advocate their replacement by some kind of fascist-style political system; on the contrary, at least theoretically, it stands in favour of a radical regeneration of democracy. In this respect it is sometimes referred to as a promoter of 'hyper-democracy'. Programmatically, the new radical right's doctrine 'involves a claim for genuinely popular participation and representation by means of radical reform of the established political institutions and the whole political process'.[12] In line with this, it defends the use of referendums and open lists in elections. As Margaret Canovan stresses, it seeks to undermine and discredit issues and projects associated with the political establishment, for example immigration policies, multiculturalism, affirmative action and political correctness.[13]

In my view, the new radical right has managed to overcome the traditional split between left and right by combining a strong anti-establishment resentment and potent demands for democratic reform with the use of protest and identity as mobilizing agents. Such strategy stands in sharp contrast to the notable inability to conceive of ideological renewal displayed by most traditional parties, unable even to embark upon a critical self-assessment. Faced with the advance of new radical right-wing parties in several Western states, so far, most mainstream parties have tended to ignore their novel features while demonizing them and conflating them with old-type fascism.[14]

Rather than analysing the conditions which have brought about the emergence of the new radical right and seriously examining the reasons why its discourse is being well received by significant sectors of the population, traditional parties seem more eager automatically to delegitimize it and to rule it out as a 'respectable' political option; this is, of course, excluding those occasions on which mainstream parties require their support to form ruling coalitions, as has been the case in Austria, Italy, Switzerland, the Netherlands and New Zealand. The outcome of such a process is a lack of political debate, since both the new radical right and mainstream political parties appeal to the 'fear' of the electorate. The former appeal to 'fear' of a corrupted political elite which is perverting democracy, while the latter invoke 'fear' based on the association of the radical right with old fascist and Nazi regimes.

But is it accurate to conflate new radical right parties with traditional fascism? If we examine the fascist regimes of the 1922–45 period we find a movement, to be precise an anti-movement, in Linz's view, defined as anti-liberalism, anti-parliamentarism, anti-Semitism (except in Italy), anti-communism, partially anti-capitalism and anti-bourgeois, and anti-clerical, or at least non-clerical.[15] All these 'anti-' positions, combined with exacerbating nationalist sentiments, led in many cases to pan-nationalist ideas, which in the past posed a challenge to existing states and accounted for much of the aggressive expansionist foreign policy of some fascist regimes.

In contrast, the new radical right is primarily liberal. It accepts the rules of parliamentary democracy in spite of being strongly anti-establishment, and, in some cases, it endorses anti-Semitism – although it doesn't generally do it in an open manner. Against the corporatist and state-controlled economies defined by a strongly hierarchical political leadership, it favours small government. Anti-communism is no longer its key concern and a major justification for its existence; the collapse of communism and the disintegration of the former USSR after 1989 are responsible for this significant shift. The new radical right accepts market capitalism, and probably one of its main ideological weaknesses concerns the lack of an alternative economic programme to that of mainstream political parties. It has replaced the fascist traditional antipathy towards the bourgeoisie by antipathy – to put it mildly – towards immigrants, asylum-seekers and refugees, in particular if they are non-Western and non-white. The new radical right continues to be mainly non-clerical, although a number of pro-clerical elements can be found within some radical right populist parties, such as the Austrian FPÖ.

In trying to emphasize its closeness to the people and its rejection of the status quo, the new radical right prefers to define itself as a transnational movement, of which we find representatives in Western Europe, the USA and Australia, which reaches far beyond the scope of mainstream political parties.

The dream of a 'white Europe'

In Europe, the new radical right advocates the preservation of Western values, a principle which has turned into the call for 'national preference', that is, citizens should enjoy priority access to social welfare and to the protection of their own culture and language, to the detriment of those of foreigners. Citizenship should determine a sharp boundary between those who belong and those who do not, and the latter should be excluded from the social, economic and political rights associated with it. According to this line of argument, new radical right-wing parties portray themselves as defenders of those citizens who, in their view, have become vulnerable and marginalized within their own societies.

It would be a mistake to consider that the new radical right appeals primarily to those negatively affected by globalization. As Betz stresses, the new parties have done particularly well in some of the most affluent countries and regions in Western Europe, for example in countries such as Austria, Norway, Denmark and Switzerland, and regions such as northeastern Italy and Flanders. In these areas, 'unemployment has generally been significantly below OECD average, and . . . social welfare systems are among the most generous in the world and thus well-positioned to compensate potential losers from globalization.'[16]

Antipathy and, in some instances, open hostility against migration describe radical right-wing parties which, by definition, do not stand against all migration but solely against those immigrants who are deemed to pose a cultural threat to Western values and culture. In particular, the radical right regards the growing number of Muslims settling within Europe and the spread of Islamic fundamentalism as a serious threat to Western culture and values. For instance, both the Italian Lega Nord and the Austrian Freedom Party regard Christianity as a core component of European identity:

> The world order formed by Christianity and the ancient world is the most important intellectual foundation of Europe. The prime intellectual movements from humanism to the Enlightenment are based on them. The cultural character of Christian values and traditions even embraces members of non-Christian religions and peoples without any confession.[17]

The Lega Nord criticizes the fusion between the public and the private sphere, and between religion and politics, which lies at the core of Islam. They see such an amalgamation as a threat to European democracy, political culture and principles, as well as to Catholic values.[18]

The principle of national preference, combined with hostility towards those considered as too different in terms of values and culture, and often skin-colour, should be viewed as part and parcel of a wider project of white resistance, or cultural nativism, destined to protect what is described as an endangered European identity. From this perspective, Nazism is contemplated as an exemplary case of white resistance against non-Western contamination; such a view is in some cases accompanied by statements denying the Holocaust. Also, within radical right-wing circles some claim that the Waffen SS, on account of their avant-garde role against the advance of communism on the Eastern front during the Second World War, should be considered as the proto-European army and a predecessor of NATO.

The precursors of contemporary white resistance and cultural nativism are to be found in some of the reformulations of Nazi and fascist ideas that took place in the 1960s. In 1962 George Lincoln Rockwell (leader of the American Nazi Party, or ANP) and John Colin Campbell Jordan (leader of the British National Socialist Movement, or BNSM) founded the World Union of National Socialists (WUNS), with the aim of uniting the efforts of neo-Nazi activists in Europe and the USA. In their view, fear of communism and Soviet expansion could work in their favour. Rockwell and Jordan defended the idea of Europe as a spiritual and racial entity encompassing those territories – including Europe and beyond – inhabited by white people. It was Rockwell who invented the term 'White Power' as a response to the 'Black Power' nationalist movement in the USA.[19]

According to Casals-Meseguer, in the 1960s three possible options for the future development of ideas stemming from the Nazi and fascist tradition emerged: (1) the construction of a European extreme right movement along the lines of the European Social Movement; (2) the creation of a 'European International', in favour of a united internally borderless Europe, capable of standing up against the USA and the USSR (such an initiative entailed surrendering leadership to transnational organizations such as the European Liberation Front founded by Francis Parker Yockey (1948–9) and the European National Party started by Oswald Mosley in 1962); and (3) the construction of a 'racial international' defining Europe as an Aryan or racially white civilization, as was reflected in the WUNS foundational protocols.[20]

The new radical right, which emerged in the 1980s, exhibits a cultural nativism tinted with populist overtones that connects with the dream of a 'white Europe'. It is crucial to highlight the transnational character of this populist nativism that reaches beyond nationalism by defending the cultural preservation of the European culture. The novelty of the new radical right stems from its adoption of the emerging identity politics discourse to suit its own interest, and it is in this respect that, in spite of its links with the traditional extreme right, it is able to offer a fresh message. The new radical right presents itself as an alternative to traditional political parties and founds its discourse on a critique of democracy, a protest against elites and a concern about the cultural preservation and integrity of national identity understood as part and parcel of European identity. It justifies itself by appealing to the image of a world hostile to Western values and culture.

Against immigrants

The most popular item in the new radical right's political agenda concerns its hostility towards immigrants, asylum-seekers and refugees.[21] To stress this point, Betz mentions that 'more than twice as high a percentage of the French population agreed in 1991 with the Front National's extremist position on immigration than generally voted for the party in regional or national elections', adding that, 'this suggests that xenophobia has become the most significant response in Western Europe toward the second major challenge associated with the transition to post-industrial individualized capitalism, namely the coming of a multiethnic and multicultural world.'[22]

Manfred Küechler establishes a distinction between three possible reactions towards foreigners registered among indigenous populations: racism, xenophobia and self-defence.[23]

The specificity of racism lies in its constant invocation of a difference that attributes superiority to one group to the detriment of another, and favours the growth of hostile feelings towards those who have been defined as 'different'.[24] Xenophobia refers to hatred or fear of foreigners based on the alien character of their culture. According to Pierre-André Taguieff: 'The foreigner is detestable only in that he is postulated as being unassimilable without provoking a destruction of community identity.'[25] The consequences of xenophobia include avoidance of the 'others', exclusion and segregation, as well as various forms of abuse – physical, verbal – and threats/assaults against property. Self-defence, according to Küechler, refers to a 'pattern where there is openness to foreigners, but where the adjustability of the native system has been stretched to the limits, where the native identity and/or legitimate interests of the natives are threatened.'[26]

On racism

It seems to me that a few questions could be posed concerning this typology. For instance, how to assess that a specific 'native system has been stretched to the limits', how to define the 'native identity and/or legitimate interests of the natives' – indeed, not all natives have homogeneous interests – and how to define and assess the nature and consequences of the 'threats' posed by immigrants and refugees. Further to this, it is not clear what type of actions would be 'justified' by self-defence and whether racism and xenophobia could ever be categorized as a 'self-defence' reaction.

In my view, the definition of racism is wider than that initially presented here. Racism involves a negative evaluation of the other that requires an active censorship of any tendency to regard him or her as an equal. This process generates the emergence of boundaries that 'change over time in response to concrete economic, political or ideological conditions'.[27] Among the reasons given by those subscribing to racism are cultural preservation, fear of the unknown and, above all, the maintenance of a political-economic status quo.

The key role of racism since its early manifestations in colonial times has been the denial of social, political and economic participation to certain collectivities and the legitimation of various forms of exploitation. Racism is embedded in power relations. It reflects the capacity of a certain group to formulate an ideology that not only legitimizes a particular power relation between ethnic communities but also represents a useful mechanism for the reproduction of such a relation.

When considering racist attitudes, power fulfils a fundamental role in three different ways. First, power within the racist discourse is epistemologically exercised in the dual practices of naming and evaluating the other.[28] Second, the socio-political consequences of racism depend on the power of the racists. Thus a group may consider their neighbours as endemically inferior, but if they do not possess power to implement their racist views, these would be limited and have no transcendence. What made possible the Holocaust was the combination of a racist discourse with the political, social and economic power to make it effective. Third, when a group imposes a world-view that contains racist elements, the society in question becomes automatically divided between minority and majority groups. Minority groups, Spoonley argues, 'are not necessarily numerically smaller but are those groups who face prejudice and unequal treatment because they are seen as being inferior in some way.'[29] In this context 'minority' reflects relative lack of power. A 'majority group', by contrast, possesses political, economic and ideological power. The 'majority' assumes that its culture is the 'natural' culture of the whole society; its language dominates the private as well as the public sphere. From this perspective, the culture, language and ways of life of different ethnic communities – some of which could have an immigrant origin – are often considered as inferior.

The privileged position of a group generally stems from access to the state apparatus. Race then becomes a political category fixing a well-defined distinction between groups. The power of the state manifests itself in a myriad of ways, encompassing what can be called 'racial definition', to the managing of opportunities for employment, housing and schooling. The state assumes a major role in alleviating or exacerbating racial disadvantage by the policies it adopts.

The impact of immigration in Western Europe

Today, establishing a common legislation affecting migrant workers from Eastern Europe, Africa and Asia into Western Europe is one of the major challenges faced by the European Union. It puts into question moral and economic principles and brings to the fore national differences and interests. A further and extremely important issue related to the accommodation of immigrants into Western societies concerns the conditions for acquiring citizenship. So far, European citizenship is granted solely to those who are already citizens of an EU member state; however, it is possible to envisage in the future the establishment of some kind of European citizenship – detached from membership of a specific nation-state – allowing for the free circulation of some individuals entitled to restricted economic, political and social rights, probably linked to their status as 'free floating labourers' within the EU.

Within the state, usually the 'majority' has the power to decide upon the status of minority groups' members. The 'majority' regards as natural its ability to determine the minority's status and perceives its power as grounded in its unquestionable superiority. Patronage and condescension are likely to emerge in a context in which those considered as inferior play an active part in the established economic structure of production. Yet, a cheap, unproblematic labour force willing to perform any type of job and passively accepting submission is easier to tolerate. The strengthening and growing size of communities of migrant origin settling in Western Europe has the capacity progressively to transform this, by organizing themselves politically, culturally and economically. Notwithstanding, this is a factor which is also regarded with suspicion and resented by the new radical right, sceptical about the idea that immigrants and refugees could make any valuable contribution to their society.

In times of crisis minorities receive harsher treatment. They are blamed for the misfortunes affecting the whole society. They are considered guilty because of their 'inefficiency', 'laziness', 'lack of culture', 'propensity to crime', 'arrogance' or 'economic success'. Any excuse seems appropriate to emphasize the 'difference' and charge it negatively. Racism gains recruits in hard times, when the pre-eminent status of a group is under threat. But an unstable economy is not the only feature which may favour racism. For instance, some ideological factors, such as the perception of a cultural threat capable of endangering national identity, are responsible for raising alarm among the 'dominant' group.

In the last fifteen years or so prejudice, fear and resentment towards immigrants and refugees have been growing within Western societies. The massive influx of refugees from Eastern Europe and Africa received in the 1990s gave rise to talk of an 'invasion of the poor' and expressions such as 'storming Europe'. The following are some of the economic, social, political and cultural arguments employed to justify a negative attitude towards immigrants.

- They alter the labour market by offering cheap and often 'black market' labour.
- They contribute to rising unemployment among the native working-class population.
- They claim welfare benefits, thus stretching an already tight system.
- They generally have high birth rates – higher than those of the native population – and this involves greater demands on welfare and has the potential of altering the political system in the medium term when communities of migrant origin obtain the right to vote. There is also the possibility that higher birth rates among the newcomers – if this was to remain unchanged – could reduce the indigenous population to a minority status.
- They contribute to a rise in violence and crime.
- Their cultures, languages, traditions and ways of life are alien to the indigenous population and they are often regarded as a threat to national identity. Yet not all foreign cultures are perceived as menacing to national identity, and, among those who are, there is a clear gradation. At present, and after the wave of Islamophobia generated by the 9/11 terrorist attacks in New York and Washington, Muslims are singled out as posing the most serious threat to Western civilization, and they are often portrayed as the most alien and difficult to assimilate.

For 'pure' national identities

At a time when a significant number of Western citizens question whether all foreign cultures should be evaluated as a source of cultural enrichment and argue that excessive diversity irremediably leads to the levelling down of native and foreign cultures alike, a bitter debate about whether multiculturalism offers a valid integration model for immigrants has emerged.

Two conceptions of the nation are at stake here: first, a traditionally French idea of the nation as formed by a voluntary union of individuals able to create a general will and present itself as sovereign; and second, a German idea of the nation conceived as a *Volk*, that is, an entity with an organic character that pre-exists and transcends the life of its members.[30] According to the traditionally French conception of the nation, *ius soli* determines citizenship, and national identity is the outcome of the will of the individuals who constitute the sovereign nation at any specific point in time. In contrast, the nation as a *Volk* implies being born and socialized into a specific culture, with its own language, customs and traditions capable of fostering a sense of belonging among those sharing a distinctive national identity. It follows that only those who belong can attain citizenship.

I argue that neither of these ideal types of the nation are found in their pure form within contemporary Western societies and that a mixture of the two seems to prevail. Present concerns on how to maintain social cohesion within societies experiencing an intensification of cultural diversity have opened up a debate on the elements which constitute the core of national identity. Against political theories which base social cohesion solely on adherence to certain civic values and principles (Habermas), the idea that this is not sufficient either to promote a shared national identity or to foster a sense of solidarity among fellow citizens seems to gain relevance. Simultaneously, additional weight is bestowed upon key components of national identity, such as consciousness of a shared culture and history, and the attachment to a territory, myths and symbols capable of generating the emotional bonds which foster social solidarity and cohesion.

In Western Europe, the new radical right has reacted to greater awareness of a rising presence of immigrants and refugees by promoting an organic conception of the nation which regards 'foreign bodies' as a threat to its life and health. Thus, against the idea of society as the outcome of a social contract or the free will of its members, the new radical right considers that it is ontologically impossible to integrate foreigners if they do not assimilate. According to Bruno Mégret, ex-leader of the Front National: 'Democracy cannot take place among a collection of individuals sharing no bonds among themselves, and even less among a juxtaposition of different ethnic groups having incompatible cultural references. To exist and develop [democracy] requires a real people, that is, a community of men and women who recognize each other as close by means of a language, culture, faith, blood and history.'[31] A similar point is made by Georg Haider, leader of the Austrian Freedom Party, who argues that 'Austria certainly does not need a "foreign legion made in Austria" ', and maintains that 'the social organization of Islam stands in opposition to Western values.'[32]

The new radical right exploits a mounting hostility against migrants and refugees and has managed to attract the support of significant sectors of the population who, in other circumstances, would never have considered voting for an extreme right-wing party – people who feel disappointed, neglected and betrayed by conventional political parties.

For instance the Front National argues in favour of stopping all immigration to France, refounding the French nationality, applying the national preference principle and protecting national identity.[33] At the heart of the FN's conception of identity is the idea that France is not merely a territory, so that being French cannot be based exclusively on *ius soli* – *droit du sol*. Such a view would imply a 'materialist assumption ignoring the intellectual, linguistic, cultural and spiritual heritage of the nation while neglecting the true nature of human beings', since, as general Charles De Gaulle argued, 'France is a country of white race, Greco Latin civilization and Catholic religion.'[34]

To strengthen this point the FN mentions that, while in France,

> to be polite, people remove their hats and keep their shoes on; in the East they put a hat on and remove their shoes. Those who don't follow our practices should go, leaving 'mosques in the South and churches in the North'. Foreigners wishing to become French ought to assimilate, start by knowing the language, the history, the practices, to the point of being able to say 'our ancestors the Gauls' without provoking hilarity.[35]

The FN concludes that '*Être français, cela s'hérite ou cela se mérite*' (Being French can either be inherited or obtained by one's own merit),[36] which implies that assimilation is the only way to become a member of the French nation.

The FN condemns the practice of granting citizenship to individuals who do not identify as French and insists on coincidence between citizenship and national identity. Therefore, in its view, allowing for naturalization to precede assimilation is a serious mistake, since, in adopting such a practice, the French nation is failing to defend its distinctive national identity.[37] According to Jean-Marie Le Pen, 'the most serious danger for France is losing its independence for the sake of Europe and losing its identity for the sake of immigration.'[38]

Against multiculturalism

Concerns about the preservation of national identity have led the new radical right to oppose multiculturalism – exemplified by the US 'melting pot' model – as a doctrine, which, in their view, promotes the destruction of individual cultures.

Arguments against multiculturalism adopt different nuances according to different political parties. For instance, in the case of the Austrian Freedom Party (FPÖ), their main argument is that mixing cultures results in levelling down; for this reason they warn against the threat of a foreign invasion from the East and present themselves as defenders of the homeland. In so doing they do not restrict their support to cultural matters; they are also firm defenders of the national preference principle, which often portrays nationals as the victims, as those discriminated against within their own country, and as those in need of the support and protection that the FPÖ is prepared to offer.

The Lega Nord abhors the USA 'melting pot' model. In the words of its leader, Umberto Bossi, 'to transform Italy into a "multi-racial, multi-ethnic and multi-religious country" modelled after the USA mean[s] to keep Italy divided. For "excessive cultural differences, especially if expressed by skin colour, are fatal for social peace. When streets and places are full of coloured people" citizens no longer feel at home and lose their identity.'[39]

A distinctive feature of the Lega Nord is its regionalist nature, which evolved from early demands for devolution, to claims for an independent Padania, changing again to support for a federal Italy after entering into a coalition government during Silvio Berlusconi's second term in office. The Lega, in contrast with other new radical right-wing parties, has been careful to moderate its discourse to avoid accusations of racism and xenophobia.

The Front National points to moral and political problems as the source of what they perceive as France's decline. They are staunch advocates of the principle '*France pour le Français*' ('France for the French') and, in contrast with the FPÖ, which focuses on competitiveness and individual freedom, argue that the preservation of national identity should take precedence over the achievement of economic goals. In line with this idea they are currently moving away from their initial position supporting market liberalism and defending the introduction of economic protectionism.[40]

The new radical right defends Western values and culture and favours European integration. Unable to stop immigration to the EU, it seeks to preserve cultural and ethnic diversity by avoiding cultural intermingling. In its view, the worst possible scenario that could be faced by Westerners and immigrants alike consists of the loss of specific identities by intermixing. The new radical right is in favour of ethnoculturalism and abhors hybridization as a serious threat to national identity. Hence it considers that society should be composed of separate self-contained ethnic and/or cultural units, which should eventually facilitate the immigrants' repatriation.[41]

The new radical right's defence of European identity contrasts with its negative stance towards globalization, identified as the source of many of the illnesses affecting Western societies and certainly as a major contributor to the notable migration movements that the West has been experiencing in recent years.

Beyond a strong concern about the preservation of national identity, great emphasis is also being placed on the need to limit access to welfare benefits. This is the main purpose of the national preference principle endorsed among others by the FN and the FPÖ. The platform Lijst Pim Fortuyn (LPF), created by the Dutch politician Pim Fortuyn – assassinated during the 2002 Dutch electoral campaign – also emphasized this particular point. Fortuyn did not fit into the xenophobic parameters created by the Front National in France; his main concern was not the protection of national identity but the establishment of some kind of 'welfare chauvinism' granting priority to Dutch nationals. In this sense, his discourse was closer to that of the Scandinavian Progress political parties and to the democratic right advocating radical measures against immigration.

Fortuyn spoke openly about his homosexuality and was critical of Islam not because of racist motivations but because he regarded it as intolerant. To strengthen this point, in an interview, Fortuyn declared: 'I not only speak with Muslims, I even go to bed with them.'[42] His style and discourse – very critical of the political class – struck a chord with some sections of a traditionally tolerant Dutch society genuinely preoccupied by increasing immigration and diversity. The Pim Fortuyn List obtained sufficient electoral support to enter into a coalition government (July 2002), but constant internal disputes, lack of political experience and having lost their leader proved too difficult for them, and the coalition government they had helped to create lasted only eighty-six days. In the 2003 election, the LPF lost approximately two-thirds of their parliamentary representatives, moving from twenty-six seats in 2002 to eight in 2003.[43] A much more durable legacy of Pim Fortuyn than the LPF has been his ability to renew the political debate while marginalizing traditional radical right discourses.

The return of white nativism in the USA

One of the possible reactions against large and sustained Hispanic immigration to the USA, and the potential threat to America's language and culture associated with it, could be the revival of white nativism. Undoubtedly, an economic recession could also contribute to trigger a return to white nativism. Samuel Huntington raises this possibility and emphasizes the difference between 'white nativism' and 'extremist fringe groups, such as the militia movements that flourished briefly during the 1990s in Michigan and several Western states or the perennial "hate groups" who are exclusively anti-Jewish or anti-black and reflect prejudice inherited from the Ku Klux Klan.'[44] The main aim of white nativism, in Huntington's view, would not be to exclude non-whites or to focus on racial issues, but to seek to preserve or restore what they see as 'white America'. He is concerned about the pejorative connotations acquired by the term 'nativism' among denationalized elites 'on the assumption that it is wrong vigorously to defend one's "native" culture and identity and to maintain their purity against foreign influences.'[45]

These new nativist movements, if they were to emerge, would be closer to what Carol Swain defines as 'the new white nationalists', that is, groups of primarily white men, 'cultured, intelligent and often possessing impressive degrees from some of America's premier colleges and universities'.[46] They do not advocate white supremacy and they are in favour of racial self-determination and self-preservation. They follow Horace Kallen in linking race, ethnicity and culture in such a way that race is regarded as a source of culture, so that shifting the racial balance would automatically result in the shifting of the cultural balance. They expect that a shift in the cultural balance, when applied to the USA, would result in 'the replacement of the white culture that made America great by black or brown cultures that are different and, in their view, intellectually and morally inferior'.[47]

Huntington does not envisage white nativism resulting in the creation of new radical right parties similar to those that emerged in Europe during the

1990s, for example the Austrian Freedom Party. In his view, the main objective of nativists would be to influence the agenda and the selection of candidates by the two main US political parties.

Ethnopluralism: a response to 'too much diversity'

After the Second World War, a shift from biological to cultural racism took place. In adopting this view, the new radical right sought to distance itself from skinheads and neo-Nazi groups still keen to make open references to biological racism.

The *Nouvelle droite*'s concept of the 'right to cultural difference' constitutes a fundamental ideological and philosophical influence on this new paradigm whose main figures are the French philosopher Alain de Benoist, the French think-tank GRECE (Research Group for the Study of European Civilization) and the *Nouvelle droite*.[48] They oppose racism but share a staunch defence of cultural difference. This, in turn, assumes the need of all cultures – European or not – to maintain their 'purity' by being free from alien influences and avoiding hybridization.

The *Nouvelle droite*'s paradigm assumes that cultural difference involves separation, exclusion and what Benoist refers to as the 'right to difference'. Benoist has subsequently argued that he never intended his theory to be employed against immigrants. In contrast, and while employing a dialectic familiar to critical theory and phenomenology, he has argued that immigrants, with their natural differences, 'provide a dialogue against which one defines one's identity'.[49] In short, the other is seen as a threat to one's own cultural purity and portrayed as a 'quasi-enemy' against whom to construct one's own identity.

The term 'ethnopluralism' has been coined by the new right to advocate respect for cultural and ethnic differences while maintaining that the best strategy to protect them is to avoid their mixing with each other. Its use abandons references to racial or ethnic superiority and presupposes a post-racist discourse based on the preservation of national identity and culture. In so doing the new radical right has appropriated and transformed the definition of 'difference' traditionally employed by the left to promote multiculturalism and respect for diversity. As Taguieff argues, the new right 'claim[s] that true racism is the attempt to impose a unique and general model as the best, which implies the elimination of differences . . . Consequently, true anti-racism is founded on the absolute respect of differences between ethnically and culturally heterogeneous collectives.'[50]

Ethnopluralism, as defined by the new radical right, stands for the protection of national culture and identity while arguing that the national culture and identities of immigrants should also be preserved. To do this successfully, different cultures and identities should not be mixed, because it is in the mixing that culture and identity are weakened, levelled down and eventually destroyed. As Betz writes, 'It is on this basis that Le Pen and others have proclaimed their respect for foreign cultures and identities – as long as their carriers remain in their own countries (Le Pen, leader of the French Front National: 'I love North Africans, but their place is in the Maghreb'. Schönhuber [founder of the German party Der Republikaner], 'I love Turks, but it's in Turkey that I love them most').[51]

In the USA, the conversion to 'non-racialism' of so many conservative, former segregationists, particularly during their attacks on affirmative action, parallels the European new radical right's love of ethnic – *their own* ethnic – diversity. This smacks of apartheid in pluralist clothing.

Ethnopluralism often results in the revival of ethnic nationalism and positions itself against multiculturalism, pointing at the United States of America as an example of a 'levelled society, faceless and anonymous, which inevitably must end in societal chaos and ultimately ethnic and cultural self-destruction'.[52]

The new radical right defends the idea of a 'fortress Europe', which is compatible with the protection of national cultures and identities as well as economic prosperity. It exploits the fears and anxieties of citizens who feel threatened by socio-economic changes and resent a rise in the number of immigrants, asylum-seekers and refugees entering their countries. For many of these citizens, national identity operates as the last resort able to sustain an already damaged sense of self-esteem. For them, identification with the nation offers a source of pride.

Belonging to the nation means participating in all its achievements and replacing the focus on one's own life – which many may regard, although often unconsciously, as a failure or uneventful – by identification with a larger entity – the nation – offering past and present reasons to feel important, valuable, and a member of a distinctive group. In these circumstances, the new radical right skilfully portrays the retreat to a national identity of which citizens can feel proud, as a right, almost as a duty.

All things considered, the new radical right offers strong arguments destined to foster a sense of togetherness among citizens accompanied by a renewed emphasis upon the consolidation of a sense of belonging to the nation and the practical advantages as well as the emotional warmth deriving from it. But its offer comes at a price: the exclusion of those considered 'too different' and the request for them to 'stay away' in order to avoid their own cultural and ethnic contamination. The radical right's defence of 'pure' national identities blatantly hides its hostility towards cultural interchange and dialogue.

National Identity versus Cosmopolitan Identity

Cosmopolitanism was initially formulated by the Stoics – a pre-Socratic philosophical school that criticized the historically arbitrary nature of boundaries of polities and their role in fostering a sense of difference between insiders and outsiders. In their view, the emphasis placed on boundaries contributed to shifting the focus away from the human condition shared by all persons by stressing differences among them rather than commonality. The Stoics sought 'to replace the central role of the *polis* in ancient political thought with that of the *cosmos* in which humankind might live together in harmony'.[1]

During the Enlightenment, the cosmopolitan idea was given a new impetus by Immanuel Kant, who stood in favour of allowing people to 'enjoy a right to the free and unrestricted public use of their reason'[2] by placing themselves beyond the limits – rules, prejudices and beliefs – set up by their polities and by acting as members of a 'cosmopolitan society' defined by its openness. The entitlement to enter the world of open, uncoerced dialogue was adapted and developed in his concept of 'cosmopolitan right'.[3]

In the late 1970s, and partly influenced by the intensification of globalization processes, cosmopolitanism re-emerged once again. Currently, cosmopolitanism has three central separate meanings which are often in tension. First, cultural cosmopolitanism is associated with those individuals who enjoy cultural diversity, are able to travel the world, and tend to enjoy a privileged position which places them well beyond ethnocentric views of culture and identity. Such individuals form a selected transnational elite, and the study of their views on culture and identity belong to the realm of sociological analysis. Second, philosophical cosmopolitanism relates to the adherence to a set of principles and values destined to attain global social justice and, with it, the elimination of dramatic disparities of wealth. This type of cosmopolitanism has a strong ethical nature. It is engaged in the quest for some minimal ethical values to be applicable to the whole of humanity – for instance, the commitment to human rights, as defined by the UN. Third, institutional or political cosmopolitanism refers to the study of how novel forms of governance and political institutions might match up to a more cosmopolitan order.

Yet, in some instances, a tension arises between cultural and philosophical (ethical) cosmopolitanism. For example:

1 The enthusiasm that cultural cosmopolitans show towards cultural creations and diversity often ignores the circumstances of their origins[4] – an issue of paramount significance for ethical cosmopolitans concerned about social justice.
2 They show a different attitude towards difference itself. Hence, while the cultural cosmopolitan praises and enjoys diversity, the ethical cosmopolitan seeks to find some universal standard concerning what ought to be regarded as inalienable rights and principles to be applied to all members of humanity.
3 Each has somehow a different position with regard to inequality. The cultural cosmopolitan enjoys an advantaged position, and his or her open mind is generally associated with the opportunities enjoyed in terms of access to education, travel and the means allowing for a specific life-style. A certain inequality stands at the core of the privileges from which cultural cosmopolitans benefit. Therefore, resentment, lack of trust and criticism of cultural cosmopolitans usually originate among the ranks of less privileged people. According to ethical cosmopolitans, the quest for global social justice requires the mitigation of inequality which, among other things, has allowed an elite to become cultural cosmopolitans. However, a more nuanced approach to this issue leads Sypnowich to argue that 'the idea of global justice involves some idea of cultural evaluation'.[5]

In addition, some further tensions exist between the three notions of cosmopolitanism mentioned above. For instance, a cosmopolitan ethicist could be very sceptical about the possibilities of a cosmopolitan culture, while an institutional cosmopolitan may adhere to a variety of different ethical commitments – not to mention differing views upheld by cosmopolitans with regard to the existing gap between cosmopolitan philosophy and social reality.

The three key principles defended by scholars of philosophical cosmopolitanism – essentially ethical philosophers who focus on the nature and form of ethical justification, such as C. Beitz, Thomas W. Pogge and Brian Barry[6] – are:

1 The principle of individualist moral egalitarianism or egalitarian individualism, that is, all humans are free and equal beings;

2 The principle of reciprocal recognition: 'each person has an equal stake in this universal ethical realm and is, accordingly, required to respect all other people's status as a basic unit of moral interest.'[7]
3 The principle of impartial moral reasoning, which 'requires that each person should enjoy the impartial treatment of their claims – that is, treatment based on principles upon which all could act.'[8]

David Held has formulated the most recent and original work on institutional cosmopolitanism. He argues that cosmopolitan principles – equal worth and dignity; active agency; personal responsibility and accountability; consent; reflexive deliberation and collective decision-making through voting procedures; inclusiveness and subsidiarity; avoidance of serious harm; and the amelioration of urgent need – 'are the principles of democratic public life, but without one crucial assumption – never fully justified in any case in liberal democratic thought, classic or contemporary – that these principles can only be enacted effectively within a single, circumscribed, territorially based political community.'[9] This implies that 'states would no longer be regarded as the sole centres of legitimate political power within their borders, as it is already the case in many places . . . States need to be articulated with, and relocated within, an overarching cosmopolitan framework.'[10]

I understand current accounts of cosmopolitanism to be closely related to the image of the world as a single interconnected place where an unparalleled degree of visibility brought about by the technological revolutions of the late twentieth century has provided unprecedented awareness of political, cultural, linguistic, religious, gender, economic and other forms of difference. Within this novel scenario, increased multilevel interaction strengthens the case for cosmopolitanism as the ethics of the global age.

Cosmopolitan values defend the equality and freedom of all human beings, a principle already accepted and included in some constitutions, international norms and regulations. There is a big gap, however, between the theoretical bow to cosmopolitan principles and social reality, since, at present, not a single institution or organization is recognized by all humans as capable of enforcing compliance with cosmopolitan principles and having sufficient power, legitimacy and means to punish those transgressing them. The global world is not guided by cosmopolitan principles, although there are some signs that a growing transnational movement, if still incipient, is beginning to emerge. Yet some cosmopolitan values are embedded in some international and regional institutions, hence stepping-stones exist.

This chapter is divided into four sections. First, it provides a brief conceptual analysis of the consequences of applying ethical cosmopolitanism to legal, political, economic and cultural issues. Second, it focuses on a sociological issue, that is, the distinction between the concepts of 'global' and 'cosmopolitan' culture. Here, I consider the ethical component absent from most theories of cosmopolitan culture and identity. Third, it compares national and cosmopolitan identity by analysing five dimensions: psychological, cultural, historical, territorial and political. The chapter concludes by assessing whether nationalism and cosmopolitanism are able to coexist and investigates the specific conditions that would render this possible.

Cosmopolitanism: a multilevel theory

Cosmopolitanism operates at different levels and acquires a different meaning according to whether we refer to legal, political, economic or cultural issues.

Legal cosmopolitanism

Legal cosmopolitanism is concerned primarily with global justice and the implementation of human rights. It challenges the almost exclusive capacity of the nation-state to act as the ultimate arbitrator of what should or should not be regarded as an infringement of human rights within its territory.

It is true that respect for human rights can be invoked almost everywhere in the world, but it is equally true that, so far, no institution can force a nation-state actually to respect them. As Habermas puts it, 'Human rights are Janus-faced, looking simultaneously toward morality and the law . . . Like moral norms, they refer to every creature "that bears a human face", but as legal norms they protect individual persons only insofar as the latter belong to a particular legal community – normally the citizens of a nation-state.'[11]

In recent years, some significant progress has been made in connection with the use of references and 'on paper' commitment to global justice and human rights on behalf of nation-states and some international and transnational organizations and institutions. In spite of this, the main remaining problem relates both to their implementation and to the sanctioning of those who trespass them.

Political cosmopolitanism

Political cosmopolitanism transcends national sovereignty[12] by moving beyond both internationalism and those forms of supranationalism based exclusively on national sovereignty. For instance, a European Union based upon supranational institutions ruled according to national categories and particular interests – as exemplified by the so far pre-eminently intergovernmentalist nature of the EU – could lead to some kind of European supranationalism rather than tending towards cosmopolitanism.[13]

Globalization has contributed to the generation of novel political spaces where interaction among a wide range of national, international, transnational and supranational actors, as well as other organizations and institutions, takes place. I regard the emergence of these new 'global political spaces' as a double edged phenomenon which can either contribute to the progressive defense of cosmopolitan principles or, quite the opposite, utilize its unprecedented influence to promote values hostile to global justice and the defence of human rights. As is the case with other new opportunities opened up by globalization, it is impossible to predict the ways in which technological innovation will be employed and the principles it will be set up to defend.

It is true that globalization has created unique opportunities for the rise of new kinds of connectivity leading to a reconfiguration of the social beyond the traditional limits imposed by the nation-state. Nevertheless it is not only cosmopolitanism that could take advantage of such new forms of connectivity. I argue that authoritarian, neo-fascist doctrines, as well as novel fundamentalisms, could employ them to build up a world opposed to the ideals of cosmopolitanism.

It is not at all clear whether we are moving towards a freer and more equal world or, quite the reverse, whether we are to be faced with new forms of tyranny. For instance, the perception of terrorism as an ever present threat – real, potential or imagined – could be employed to curtail civil liberties, expand surveillance mechanisms and limit the free movement of people. Populist authoritarian political parties capitalizing on anti-immigrant sentiments across the Western world could occupy new global political spaces and promote various forms of exclusion. Furthermore, hostility to secularism and Western values could lead to the expansion of political regimes based on various forms of religious fundamentalism.

Kwame Anthony Appiah points to a new brand of 'counter-cosmopolitans' formed by neo-fundamentalists – violent or not – defending the idea of 'universalism without toleration'.[14] They include some Muslims as well as Christians. Oliver Roy has analysed 'radical neo-fundamentalists' – that is, Muslims who want to turn jihad, interpreted as literal warfare against the West, into the sixth pillar of Islam. Roy argues that, for them, 'Globalization is a good opportunity to dissociate Islam from any given culture and to provide a model that could work beyond any culture.'[15]

In my view, the institutional and procedural outlook of an eventual cosmopolitan political order remains largely undefined, since it is unclear what type of institutions, political culture and models of democracy ought to operate within it. A series of 'contradictions, ambivalences and paradoxes', as pointed out by Beck and Grande,[16] such as the idea that strengthening democracy alone will not create cosmopolitanism, highlight the dilemmas faced by political cosmopolitanism.

Economic cosmopolitanism

Economic cosmopolitanism consists of applying cosmopolitan principles to trade and labour relations throughout the world. Complying with cosmopolitanism would automatically entail the end of political and economic doctrines based on the exploitation of 'others', regardless of how these are to be defined. It is to be expected that a full commitment to cosmopolitanism would signal the end of doctrines based on making profit out of the exploitation of people. Consequently, I envisage a forceful resistance to its implementation.

Cultural cosmopolitanism

I argue that a clear-cut distinction needs to be drawn between global and cosmopolitan culture. By 'global culture' I refer to a worldwide culture formed by a mixture of elements originating from a wide range of traditions. By 'cosmopolitan culture' I refer to a type of culture which, in addition to being global in scope, ought to be committed to cosmopolitan values. It is precisely the compliance with these values that should ultimately determine whether or not a particular item of a specific culture, which might have become a global cultural artefact, could also be considered as a component of a cosmopolitan culture. It is in this respect that I understand a 'cosmopolitan culture' to be a moral culture – that is, a type of culture moving well beyond the traditional remit of the nation, but also beyond emerging supranational cultures such as the now incipient European culture promoted by the EU. In my view, some democratic progressive social movements, such as feminism, anti-apartheid and environmentalist movements, can be considered as examples of an avant garde of cultural cosmopolitanism.

On global culture

Currently, a single global culture does not exist, despite the fact that a limited but growing number of cultural elements are becoming almost global in scope. To date, the world is formed by a rich variety of cultures, most of them based, created and promoted by particular nations. So far, the most efficient creator and disseminator of a homogenizing culture and language among a territorially circumscribed and generally diverse population has been the nation-state.

In my view, a global culture would be constituted by a limited number of cultural elements, including certain images, mores, ideas and procedures drawn from various traditions, to be superimposed upon already existing national, ethnic and local cultures. This process would entail the emergence of national and local versions of global cultural artefacts rising elsewhere with the aim of adapting them to local styles, customs and taste. After having an initial homogenizing effect, I expect that the rise of a global culture, if this were to emerge, would result in the proliferation of novel forms of cultural diversification. A global culture would depend on worldwide telecommunications networks for its dissemination, by far its greatest challenge being to ensure that its components retain the power to move and inspire populations, something that national and local cultures have repeatedly proved achievable.[17]

On cosmopolitan culture

A cosmopolitan culture aspires to become a moral culture shared by humanity and able to permeate national and other cultures. But could this ever be accomplished? And, if so, then how could such a culture be created? A cosmopolitan culture, if it were ever to emerge, would be formed by a mixture of elements originating from various national, ethnic and other cultures, to be selected according to whether or not each specific element complies with cosmopolitan values.[18] In this respect, a cosmopolitan culture could be defined as a hybrid and moral culture destined to overcome ethnocentrism and ready to defend the principles of ethical cosmopolitanism when applied to cultural elements and practices. Such a culture would be fluid, dynamic and opened to change. It would add a thin layer of identity – containing a strong moral outlook – on people's national, local and other identities.

Some of the main issues associated with the eventual rise of a cosmopolitan culture refer to questions about who should act as its creator, who should fund its dissemination and who decide on its content. A further dilemma concerns how to avoid its becoming a replica of some more or less elaborate Western political principles and traditions spiced up with some folkloric elements originating elsewhere. If this were the case, then such a type of cosmopolitan culture could easily be discarded as 'alien' by non-Western peoples in fear of experiencing a new wave of colonization.

Yet, as once happened with Marxism – an all-embracing ideology willing to change the world by freeing it from exploitation, alienation and inequality – it is unclear what the outcome would be if cosmopolitans were faced with the dilemma of either remaining loyal to their views or complying with their governments' request to join their national armies in the fight against their fellow human beings, some of whom might well share their cosmopolitan outlook. Let's for a moment remember the devastating impact upon ideas of world socialism effected by the decision adopted by large numbers of European socialist workers massively to support their national armies in the First World War and again in the Second World War, thus ignoring the advice of the Second International of Socialist Workers. On those occasions, national loyalty took precedence over social-class solidarity, and I expect that, if the occasion came up, national attachments would take precedence over cosmopolitan commitments too.

In my view, a cosmopolitan culture should aim at combining a global outlook free from ethnocentric leanings with the commitment to cosmopolitan values, that is, cultural and ethical cosmopolitanism should be able to interact. The philosophical principles, which should underpin a truly cosmopolitan culture, are as follows.

1 The *principle of egalitarian individualism* assumes that all humans are free and equal beings. However, I do not understand it to mean, when applied to culture, that all cultures are equal – at least, not if we were to adopt a cosmopolitan outlook according to which a distinction should be established between those cultural elements that comply with the philosophical principles of cosmopolitanism and those that do not. For instance, a cosmopolitan culture should exclude those values, principles and social practices present in some national and other types of culture which deny the equal worth and dignity of all human beings. It should reject all aspects of particular cultures tolerating, defending and promoting discrimination and inequality on grounds of gender, age, health, race, religious faith, social status and other mechanisms utilized for setting people apart as inferior and for preventing their freedom. This would be highly controversial due to the different meaning attributed to social practices and value systems across the globe.

2 The *principle of reciprocal recognition* assumes that individuals can only be free and equal if they recognize each other as such. It is not for an external

Leviathan, constitution or law to impose cosmopolitanism, since, to exist, it necessitates the active engagement of all individuals without exception. Yet we could appeal to consent, collective decision-making and agency as principles requiring freedom and equality among all humans. Dialogic democracy should act as the mechanism by means of which agreements and decisions could be reached. The recognition of equal value attributed to citizens' votes in a parliamentary democracy further illustrates this point. The acknowledgement of cultural diversity and the value attributed to it should result in the avoidance of ethnocentrism and the rise of a more cosmopolitan outlook defined in cultural terms.

3 The *principle of impartial moral reasoning* assumes that all humans should be able to transcend their national and local cultures in order to attain a playing field free from prejudices and stereotypes within which they could engage in the free and unrestricted use of reason. It is incorrect to state that a cosmopolitan culture celebrates difference, diversity and hybridity without further qualifying such an assumption. In my view, diversity, difference and hybridity can be deemed as components of an eventual cosmopolitan culture if and only if they respect the principles of philosophical cosmopolitanism. There are numerous examples of a wide variety of cultural elements which contribute to an unqualified celebration of diversity, difference and hybridity within an already incipient 'global' culture. However, many of them would never make it into a truly 'cosmopolitan' culture if this were ever to emerge and be true to its name.

Cosmopolitanism: a Western theory

It should not escape our analysis that theories of cosmopolitanism originated in the West and that it is within the West that they find most of their supporters. We should be aware that, hitherto in the developing world, many regard cosmopolitanism as a new strategy of the West in its long-term quest to dominate the rest of the globe.

But suspicion of cosmopolitanism understood in sociological (cultural), philosophical and institutional terms is not confined to the developing world. In fact, many Western working-class and lower-middle-class people associate cosmopolitanism with a relatively glamorous life-style available only to the few. They regard it as a luxury item at the disposal of an elite who can afford it, while the vast majority continues either ignorant or indifferent. In Western societies access to a humanist education including knowledge of various cultural traditions remains, to a considerable extent, determined by social class. Access to high culture is restricted primarily to the elites, while the rest of the population tends to rely on the national mass media and enjoys fewer opportunities to access alternative cultural outlooks and value systems. This has a strong impact on the construction of national and other forms of identity among elites and the majority of the population.

Political participation and political opinion are heavily influenced by the media and various other sources providing partial and sometimes even false information and promises to the masses, who, in spite of having the right to vote, are ill-prepared and ill-informed about the meaning of their various political options. For many of them cosmopolitanism represents yet a further tool of the few to acquire and consolidate their own power and influence.

'National' versus 'cosmopolitan' identity

On cosmopolitan identity

Various forms of cosmopolitan identity, restricted to a selected elite, have existed since ancient times. In its modern form, cosmopolitan identity is intrinsically bound up with the intensification and expansion of globalization processes allowing us, for the first time in history, to have a reasonably accurate idea of the composition, numbers and features of humanity. Previous images of the world were incomplete to the point of neglecting millions of peoples. Limited awareness of other cultures and civilizations resulted in partial accounts of human diversity entirely mediated by the particular experiences and circumscribed knowledge of various peoples who sought to describe the world from their own perspective and according to their own cultural parameters.

By definition, a cosmopolitan identity is fluid, dynamic, open and a prerogative of a selected elite. Today's cosmopolitans belong to the middle and upper classes, tend to speak English[19] as a mother tongue or as a *lingua franca*, enjoy sufficient resources to take advantage of the goods and life-styles associated with post-industrial societies, and feel comfortable using the continually emerging new ranges of sophisticated information technology and communications goods bombarding the market. Cosmopolitans represent a new class free from national attachments and eager to transcend the limits of their national and local communities. They enjoy travelling a world that, for them, has truly become a single place.

In my view, it is necessary to move beyond a type of cosmopolitan identity blind to the ethical principles of philosophical cosmopolitanism. Praising and savouring cultural diversity for its own sake regardless of the social inequalities and injustices that might, in some cases, be associated with it should be replaced by a greater concern for global social justice. Further to adopting a critical and constructive attitude towards existing national cultures – one's own as well as those of others – a truly cosmopolitan identity should engage in an active struggle against those ideologies, value systems and social practices impeding the fulfilment of human freedom and equality. The desire to transcend ethnocentrism, while achieving a radical transformation of the social, can never be achieved if cosmopolitan identity is made to fit the outlook of a single culture.

Steps towards the construction of an incipient cosmopolitan identity should involve dialogue, exchange, understanding and reciprocal respect for each other's cultural practices while taking into account the specific temporal and geographical social milieu within which they have been constructed. At present, I consider cosmopolitan identity the privilege of an elite, and I do not envisage its expansion among the masses in the foreseeable future.

In what follows I examine the relevance of the psychological, cultural, historical, territorial and political dimensions I attribute to national identity[20] when applied to cosmopolitan identity.

Psychological dimension

National identity is extremely valuable to individuals because it provides them with a sense of dignity regardless of their class, gender, achievements, status and age. By belonging to the nation, individuals identify with and, up to a point, regard as their own the accomplishments of their fellow nationals. It is by identifying with the nation that individuals' finite lives are transcended and that the nation comes to be revered as a higher entity. One of the most outstanding features of national identity is its ability to cut across class divisions while strengthening a sentiment of belonging to an artificial type of extended family, the nation.

As Margalit and Raz argue, a 'people's self-respect is bound up with the esteem in which their national group is held. If a culture is not generally respected, then the dignity and self-respect of its members will also be threatened.'[21] It is my concern that when this occurs, in some cases, the national elite constructs a victimizing discourse founded on the promotion of a siege mentality based on the real or potential threat posed by those who do not 'comprehend and value' the nation's qualities. This involves closing down the community to external influences – in as much as this remains a feasible alternative – portraying certain nations or particular groups as enemies, and promoting a sense of hostility and lack of trust towards foreigners as bearers of a real or potential threat to the besieged nation. The power and resources enjoyed by the nation, as well as its predominant political ideology, strongly contribute to determining the extent of the closure and the mechanisms applied to set it up and maintain it.

In other cases, nationals lose their self-esteem; they adopt a passive attitude and become either isolated or engaged in a rampage of socio-political and cultural decay while often enduring external domination. Sometimes external power acts as a *stimulus* and contributes towards awakening a resistance movement.

National identity fosters closeness, empathy and solidarity among fellow nationals. By emphasizing what is unique about a specific nation, it singles it out from the rest and generates a sentimental attachment to it. But, does awareness of being a 'citizen of the world' foster sentiments of solidarity and closeness among human beings? I do not think so, at least not in the first instance, although up to a point – usually a theoretical point and among certain sectors of the population – it might. In practice, it is incredibly hard to sustain an emotional attachment to such a vast number of unknown people. Indeed, we could consider whether humanity forms a community and feels as a community or, on the contrary, whether it stands as a large aggregate of individuals forming a myriad of distinct and separate peoples. If the latter is true, then what are the mechanisms which could promote the rise of some incipient solidarity and a shared sense of identity among peoples who, throughout history, have spent most of their time fighting each other?

To identify with somebody we need to speak his or her language and understand his or her culture, and, above all, we need the sensitivity to know what it would feel like to be in his or her place. We also need the capacity to suffer and rejoice with the other – dare we say, the art to love each other. In my view, most people do not tend to identify with those deemed too different, remote or alien. Nonetheless, an entirely different matter concerns whether people should, in spite of all differences, be able to share an attitude in favour of the recognition and promotion of respect, dignity, equality and freedom for all.

Relations among people, in particular among strangers, do not tend to be based on cosmopolitan principles; the contrary seems to be the norm. To illustrate this, let's just consider the incredible amount of violence present in human relations – personal and collective – a degree of violence that, if we were truly to identify with the other, would not exist.

A raw test assessing the degree of mutual identification among people could consist of analysing whether individuals are able to inflict pain and use violence against those with whom they identify. It is my view that only by emphasizing the otherness of victims are individuals capable of inflicting pain and suffering upon them.

There are numerous examples – war, conflict, crime, repression, rape and torture – in which individuals – pursuing their own private interest or just for the sake of it – strip fellow human beings of their human condition. In order to justify their violence, they degrade their victims by turning them into strangers, enemies, animals or even monsters.

Individuals have a limited capacity to feel for others, or at least to feel with intensity. This is not to deny that people can empathize and, in a superficial manner, identify with strangers whenever their humanity – limited to those traits to which they can relate – is brought to the fore. For example we can, up to a point, feel for – that is, identify within some unspecified manner – the hunger, suffering, illnesses and deprivation endured by others when they are made visible to us. But the enormous amount of avoidable suffering which continues to exist, not only miles away from us but also within our own societies, shows that identification with strangers is slight and often remains associated with the belief that people should take responsibility for their own lives and that we cannot aspire to resolve social problems, simply because these are huge and there are far too many of them.

Acquiring a cosmopolitan identity is a matter of personal choice. In this respect it differs from national identity, which most Westerners have experienced since the moment when they were born and to which they have been socialized within their own specific cultures endowed with their own specific languages.

The eventual materialization of a genuine cosmopolitan identity, in my view, would involve a militant attitude in favour of human freedom and equality. I am aware of the controversial character of these assertions because, first of all, cosmopolitan principles ought to be defined cross-culturally and they cannot be implemented until a global shared meaning is agreed. I envisage a process similar to that resulting in the Declaration of Human Rights to be applied to the search for genuinely cosmopolitan principles.

But does cosmopolitan identity require the weakening and even the renunciation of national identity? In my view, cosmopolitan identity urges a critical attitude towards non-cosmopolitan principles present within national cultures as well as the commitment to change them. This implies neither the renunciation of national identity nor the outright condemnation of a particular culture, but denotes the preparedness to change it from within. I do not regard cosmopolitanism as a synonym of disengagement with the national; on the contrary, I regard it as founded upon a set of ethical principles able to inform political action with the aim of permeating national and other forms of culture with a cosmopolitan outlook.

For example, let's imagine a citizen of a country where after a *coup d'état* a dictatorship has taken over. Would this justify some citizens in being disloyal to the dictator's rule? From a cosmopolitan perspective, we obtain a positive response, since disloyalty to a specific political regime on the grounds of its anti-democratic non-cosmopolitan credentials should not be confused with disloyalty to the nation. A response from a nationalist perspective has to be nuanced. Yet, whenever a nation is defined as an open, democratic society, all attempts to reverse this are to be condemned. It is from this perspective that disloyalty to a non-democratic regime might become an ethical imperative.

Cultural dimension

The quest for a cosmopolitan identity should best be described as the endeavour towards the addition of a moral layer, defined by respect for cosmopolitan principles, to national, ethnic and other cultures.

While key components of national identity such as culture, language, national symbols, heroes, rituals, sacred places, memories, traditions and ways of life are internalized by individuals and emotionally charged, so far, a comparable process concerning cosmopolitan identity has yet to take place. An eventual cosmopolitan identity could only come into being within societies endowed with sophisticated telecommunications and information technology networks enabling simultaneous interaction between the peoples of the world. In a similar manner, the construction of national cultures and identities has evolved within industrial societies competent to effect the cultural and linguistic homogenization of their citizens.

A sense of common nationhood acts in tension with deep societal cleavages, preventing fellow citizens from identifying each other as members of the same nation. National cohesion can only be attained if differences among citizens are upheld within certain limits, and it seems to me that a similar point including the whole of humanity should be made regarding the eventual rise of a cosmopolitan culture and identity.

The worldwide expansion of cosmopolitan principles, including access to sufficient resources for all to live with dignity, is indispensable for the eventual rise of an incipient cosmopolitan identity. The unlikely fulfilment of this condition stands as a serious obstacle to the advent of cosmopolitanism in the near future. In so far as humanity remains fractured by deep social, political and economic cleavages, such as those currently in place, it will be impossible to envisage the coming to light of a cosmopolitan identity beyond the remit of a privileged elite. Let's bear in mind that, throughout history, the progress and advantage acquired by some nations as well as by some social classes has almost invariably been built on the disadvantage and the exploitation endured by others, and this continues to be the case.

Historical dimension

Antiquity acts as a source of legitimacy for the nation and the national identity associated with it. Elites are eager to remind their fellow nationals that the nation pre-dated their very existence and will transcend their own lifespan. Instead of looking at the past, a cosmopolitan identity will focus on the future, since turning back in time would reveal a fragmented picture dominated by memories of war, conflict, alliances and rivalries among various peoples.

The history of humanity is based upon the immemorial division of its peoples. To the present, conquest, war and conflict have contributed to the emergence of distinct national and ethnic identities. Opposition to the other has proven key to fostering particular identities – individual as well as collective. Identifying with our ancestors by celebrating their successes and remembering their tragedies is central to the construction of national identity. However, from the perspective of a cosmopolitan identity, such activities can only contribute further to the consolidation and deepening of existing divisions among various peoples.

If cosmopolitan principles were to be taken seriously, then, how could Spaniards celebrate the conquest of the Americas after the devastation it caused to the indigenous populations of the New World? To what extent could the British Empire be celebrated after the suffering it inflicted on millions of people in India alone? How could slavery be integrated into a colonial history to be proud of? Or, indeed, how could the British, French, Dutch and other European peoples engaged in the colonization of North America ignore that the actions and policies of their ancestors brought indigenous peoples – First Nations – to near extinction? Similar remarks could be made about the Maori and the Aboriginal peoples in New Zealand and Australia, as well as regarding the effects of European colonization upon the peoples of Africa and the Middle East. The list of events reinforcing a view of the world based on the primacy of some peoples over others is long and tainted with blood.

The collective memory shared by the national community emphasizes continuity over time and differentiation from others while strengthening its unity. The selective use of the past – including some joyous as well as some painful events – makes up the backdrop against which intellectuals engage in the construction of a shared national history – one usually based on a myth of common origin connected with a sentiment of forming an extended family. Besides, the experience of sharing the present and a sense of mission, including a common project for the future, crucially reinforces the sentimental bond uniting fellow nationals. Of course, the intensity and specific content of this sentiment varies among individuals, but, in spite of this, a sufficiently strong sense of communality tends to remain in place.

The consciousness of forming a nation, once acquired, remains alive for generations, although in some instances it may remain hidden for a long period of time and then, suddenly, re-emerge as a response to particular events or to the call of some national mobilizers.

Territorial dimension

Within a cosmopolitan identity, the sentimental attachment to the nation's territory should be replaced by an attachment to the whole planet. Probably the cosmopolitan principle, which has gained greatest prominence worldwide in the last few years, is the principle of sustainability. The reasons for its current relevance derive from serious concerns about global warming and other irreversible alterations of the ecological equilibrium prompted by human action. For most peoples and their governments, the preservation of the environment becomes a priority only and in so far as its continuous degradation poses a direct threat to themselves and to their successors.

The relationship with territory established by a cosmopolitan identity would be founded on the 'lifting out' of cultural experiences from their traditional anchoring.[22] It is envisaged that a cosmopolitan identity will entail disembedding cultural practices from the territories – spaces – within which they have emerged and portraying them as shared by all without privileging specific groups and peoples.

Political dimension

The nation is a political community willing to decide upon its future, be it as an independent nation-state, an autonomous entity, a member of a federation, a province or a region. The terminology is subject to various nuances according to each particular case. Those sharing a distinct national identity regard themselves as forming a *demos* with the capacity to reach and express a common will and to act upon it. As previously indicated, nations may or may not have a state of their own.

In contrast, the human community has never regarded itself as a single *demos* or acted as one. The eventual rise of a cosmopolitan identity would change this. By emphasizing the significance of sharing the human condition and the dignity, respect, freedom and equality attributed to it, humanity as a whole would be able to express itself as a single *demos*. But, hitherto, the mechanisms for cosmopolitan political representation as well as the institutions and political culture associated with them remain largely undefined. I expect that the emergence of an incipient cosmopolitan identity would, in time, foster the constitution of cosmopolitan institutions with legislative, executive and judicial powers – a move burdened with issues concerning how to make compatible and adapt the value systems of particular national cultures to the requirements of cosmopolitan principles.

Currently, not only national and local interests but also international and transnational ones take precedence over the common interests of humanity as a whole, and only rarely has a shared global interest, such as the need to preserve the environment, been identified. A cosmopolitan identity would call for a shared language to further communication and understanding among world citizens. Even if English is spoken by large sections of the world's population, it is still far from being a *lingua franca* at the global level. In my view, it is impossible to generate a shared sense of identity among people who do not understand one another.

Sharing a vernacular language is paramount to national identity. Conversely, whenever a nation enjoys a distinct language this becomes a strong, if not the strongest, marker of the community, one that allows individuals to recognize each other as fellow nationals.

The minorization of vernacular languages spoken by only a small percentage of the population could be a product of different reasons, among them the current or past proscription of the language, leading to a reduction in the number of its speakers; the influx of a large number of immigrants unwilling or unable to learn the vernacular language of the host society; and the influence of a non-vernacular which progressively takes over as the primary language. The replacement of a vernacular by another language almost invariably weakens the sense of distinctiveness attributed to the nation in the eyes of its own members and others.

Wherever a vernacular language has ceased to exist or has been brought to practical extinction while being replaced by another nation's language – usually a nation occupying a position of power over it – the specific accent adopted by individuals speaking the 'foreign' language turns into an identity marker for insiders and outsiders. For instance, Scots speaking English can easily be identified by their distinctive accent. Even more crucially, the use of a common language among those sharing a national identity confirms that 'the political community really does belong to the people and not to the elite.'[23]

Sharing a national identity facilitates a mutual understanding between fellow nationals and contributes to the unfolding and consolidation of democratic citizenship. It is difficult to envisage how such a function might be performed at a cosmopolitan level. As argued by Kymlicka, 'democracy requires the adjudication of conflicting interests, and so works best when there is some sort of common identity that transcends these conflicting interests.'[24]

Cosmopolitanism versus nationalism

Cosmopolitanism and nationalism are often portrayed as being in opposition to each other. Being a nationalist is frequently regarded as an obstacle to adopting a cosmopolitan outlook, as being in direct opposition to it. Why is this so? Are there any particular circumstances in which both cosmopolitanism and nationalism can coexist and be compatible? Or, on the contrary, are we faced with two irreconcilable ideologies?

On nationalism

Nationalism has traditionally been an uncomfortable topic for social scientists. In the nineteenth and early twentieth centuries, we encounter numerous examples of major scholars who paid scant attention to what clearly was one of the major political forces of their time. As I have shown elsewhere, Max Weber, a German nationalist himself, never provided a systematic theory of nationalism. Weber revealed his German nationalism through his opposition to Polish immigration in eastern Germany, his support of German nationalists during the First World War, and his reaction against the Treaty of Versailles. He encouraged and correctly foresaw a movement of German irredentism after the First World War.[25]

Émile Durkheim and Karl Marx predicted that nationalism would soon disappear, and they understood it as an ideology that needed to be transcended. Durkheim's and Marx's approaches are slightly different. Durkheim's position could be described as 'pan-nationalist'. By this I mean that his stance puts 'human' aims above 'national' ones. According to Durkheim, the *'patrie'* has a key role in the process of moralization, since it is the 'highest organized society that exists'.[26]

In contrast, Marx's attitude can be described as 'internationalist'. His main objective was 'universal emancipation', and he envisaged some kind of world solidarity. But he recognized that this could only be possible if nations were free from their conquerors, because only then could the workers think in international terms about a working-class solidarity.[27]

History has proved Marx and Durkheim to be wrong. Instead, nationalism has played a key role in the modern age, and it currently manifests itself as a potent force. Nationalism, however, has often been portrayed in intellectual circles as a sign of backwardness and as a doctrine opposed to the cosmopolitan ideal once formulated by Kant.[28] Such uneasiness towards nationalism stems from its potent emotional dimension, which clearly differs from the ideal of rationality defended by the *philosophes* and which up to now has remained unchallenged. On these grounds, the indiscriminate rejection of all forms of nationalism, including the democratic nationalism of some nations without states, should be carefully assessed, since it often hides a simplistic approach to one of the most influential ideologies of our time.

The study of nationalism requires a thorough analysis of the specific situations in which it arises. The political ideologies to which nationalism is attached are crucial to understanding the significance and character of nationalism in each particular case. Above all, we should realize that the complexity, flexibility and great appeal of nationalism are connected to its multifaceted character. Therefore, nationalism is sometimes associated with those who advocate xenophobia and ethnic cleansing, while in other cases it is applied to describe those who defend their right to exist and peacefully cultivate a particular culture which makes them 'different' from other groups.

The eighteenth-century concept of popular sovereignty was designed for the 'whole people'. When the revolutionaries stated that the principle of sovereignty resides essentially in the nation, it may be taken as their having asserted that the nation was more than the king and the aristocracy. National self-determination turned out to be one of the most frequent interpretations of popular sovereignty.

The new ideas of the *philosophes*, emphasizing the cult of liberty, equality and, in particular, the idea of state power rooted in popular consent, were initially applied to the construction and consolidation of the nation-state.

At present, democratic nationalist movements in nations without states invoke the principle of consent and the idea of popular sovereignty to legitimate their claims to self-determination, a concept embracing a wide range of options encompassing political decentralization, devolution, federation and independence. The recognition of the right to self-determination has the capacity to challenge the nation-state as a political institution, which, in most cases, has been created through the attempt to seek the cultural and political homogenization of its citizens, paying scant attention to its own internal national diversity.

Democratic nationalism and cosmopolitanism

A type of nationalism based on belief in the superiority of a particular ethnic group – ethnocentrism – aiming to dominate and exploit other peoples economically, culturally, military or politically, is not compatible with cosmopolitanism. This type of nationalism, which I refer to as 'non-democratic nationalism', wants to expand its nation's borders and is concerned primarily with acquiring sufficient power to achieve its aims. Non-democratic nationalism tends to embrace political ideologies infused with authoritarian, dictatorial or fascist ideas. It fosters unequal relations and tends to promote illiberal and undemocratic forms of government. But not all nationalisms define their objectives and the means to achieve them by subscribing to the use of force and a disregard for the well-being of strangers.

When studying the possible compatibility between nationalism and cosmopolitanism, it is important to acknowledge the sometimes almost visceral rejection of anything related to nationalism on behalf of some defenders of cosmopolitanism, for whom nationalism is merely associated with backwardness, ethnocentrism, emotions and violence. Instead of engaging in a serious analysis of the meanings of nationalism, they tend to stick to inaccurate and simplified definitions of it and ignore that cosmopolitanism and democratic nationalism share some powerful common enemies; these are xenophobia, intolerance and injustice.

Being a cosmopolitan involves a commitment to global equality, but is it possible to sustain such a commitment and defend the preferential treatment of fellow nationals? This is the crux of the matter when analysing whether cosmopolitanism and nationalism can be compatible. The response is a nuanced one. Basically we need a definition of global equality and also an account of the meaning and limitations of the so-called priority thesis for fellow nationals.

To define global equality is a difficult task, because the meaning of words such as 'sufficient' and 'basic needs' is subject to variations according to different cultures and locations; still, this should not prevent us from offering a more general definition. I understand that the basic tenets of global equality are the avoidance of death by poverty and the fulfilment of human rights as defined by the UN.

A clash between cosmopolitanism and nationalism comes to light whenever the nation, through its policies, contributes to global poverty and the transgression of human rights. Pogge writes: 'Our failure to make a serious effort toward poverty reduction may constitute not merely a lack of beneficence, but our active impoverishing, starving, and killing millions of innocent people by economic means.'[29] In my view, whether or not nationalism is compatible with cosmopolitanism depends on the political ideology with which nationalism is associated. That is, a democratic form of nationalism – associated with social democracy, socialism or liberalism, to mention but a few political ideologies that usually inform nationalist political action – subscribing to the principles of social justice, deliberative democracy and individual freedom plainly shares its values with cosmopolitanism. In contrast, non-democratic forms of nationalism associated with fascist and authoritarian ideologies stand in opposition to cosmopolitanism and democratic nationalism alike.

Among the arguments commonly neglected by cosmopolitans when assessing the moral value of nationalism and its nuanced compatibility with cosmopolitanism are:

- the idea that many nationalists perceive national membership as a good in itself and not as a mere instrument;
- the assumption that the solidarity bonds shared by members of the nation make national belonging valuable and meaningful to individuals;
- the conviction that the attachment to a national culture provides individuals with a 'context of choice'[30] and a basis for self-identity;
- the belief that sentiments of national belonging generate a 'community of obligation in the sense that their members recognize duties to meet the basic needs and protect the basic interests of other members',[31] thus providing a foundation for the development of social justice;
- the idea that national attachments have moral value since, by instilling social justice, trust and respect among fellow citizens, they are setting up the foundations for a democratic society.

Yet the compatibility between nationalism and cosmopolitanism still hinges on whether the cosmopolitan commitment to global equality can be reconciled with the nationalist principle of granting priority to fellow nationals. At this point, we could push this a bit further and ask whether the commitment to global equality is compatible with giving priority to family members and friends. Cosmopolitans adopt two broad positions concerning this issue: basically they all accept the principle of egalitarian individualism; nevertheless, they attribute different weight to the various modes of interpretation of other principles.

David Miller establishes a distinction between 'strong' and 'weak' versions of cosmopolitanism.[32] According to the former, 'all moral principles must be justified by showing that they give equal weight to the claims of everyone, which means that they must either be directly universal in their scope, or if they apply only to a select group of people they must be secondary principles whose ultimate foundation is universal.'[33]

In contrast, 'weak' cosmopolitanism 'holds only that morality is cosmopolitan in part; there are some valid principles with a more restricted scope', so that 'we may owe certain kinds of treatment to all other human beings regardless of any relationship in which we stand to them, while there are other kinds of treatment that we owe only to those to whom we are related in certain ways, with neither sort of obligation being derivative of the other.'[34] Among the main advocates of 'strong' cosmopolitanism are Martha C. Nussbaum and Bryan Barry; defenders of 'weak' cosmopolitanism include Michael Walzer and Kor Cho Tan.

I agree with Tan in that a theory of global justice should accommodate and properly account for the special ties and obligations established among fellow nationals[35] and, I would also add, among members of the same family and people sharing friendship bonds. In this respect, some liberal nationalists argue that the subordination of national commitments to cosmopolitan justice fails properly to accommodate people's national allegiances and undervalues the moral significance of national identity. Moreover, 'nationalists who reject the subordination of nationality to cosmopolitan justice do not necessarily reject the idea of global justice *per se*. What they reject is the cosmopolitan egalitarian ideal that the terms of distributive justice ought to be defined independently of people's national commitments . . . National allegiances must be allowed to shape the terms of global justice, and not the other way round as cosmopolitans hold.'[36]

By being able to develop a sense of national solidarity and duty towards their fellow nationals, individuals move beyond the immediate family circle of solidarity and trust. In a similar manner, a nationalism embracing cosmopolitan values will efficiently contribute to the generation of attachments stretching from the national to the global level. Attachment to fellow nationals does not imply denigration and disrespect for others. On the contrary, the main argument for defending the so-called compatriot priority claim assumes that we have a duty towards compatriots because they are members in a democratic political body that we, as active citizens, have a duty to sustain and improve.[37]

*   *   *

In my view, the 'priority thesis' is founded on the specific type of relationship established among individuals forming a community – in this case, the nation. It is my concern that the sentiments of solidarity that individuals tend to develop towards members of their own community have the capacity to generate a sense of special duty and care towards them. Being prepared to support your fellow nationals, as well as the expectation that one would be assisted by them when in need, constitutes a major tenet of social cohesion, that is, a situation in which a minimum set of values and principles able to maintain a sense of unity and common purpose are shared among the members of a particular society who are also prepared to make sacrifices for the well-being of the community.

But, why is national solidarity so important? Basically, because we do not live in a cosmopolitan world within which individuals feel free, equal and secure and are treated with dignity wherever they go, regardless of their origin, gender, age, class and culture. Nations are engaged in a constant competition with each other, their relations being determined by their own power and status within the international community. Most of the time, nations feel threatened in political, economic or cultural terms, and their members rely on, identify with and contribute to their own nations as the communities within which they matter and enjoy certain rights.

The nation versus the global society

Tönnies's distinction between *Gesellschaft* and *Gemeinschaft* becomes relevant when trying to account for the relationship between the nation and the global society. The former is a community – with a shared history, culture, territory and the wish to decide upon its political destiny – capable of creating a bond of sentiment and a sense of belonging among its members.

The term 'global society' refers to humanity as a whole. It embraces the wide range of cultures and peoples sharing the planet which, so far, have proven unable both to imagine themselves as forming a single community and to act as a single *demos*.

Tönnies's distinction between community (*Gemeinschaft*) and society (*Gesellschaft*) is based on the different degree of coherence and solidarity which regulates life in both situations. He writes:

> The theory of the *Gesellschaft* deals with the artificial construction of an aggregate of human beings, which superficially resembles the *Gemeinschaft*

in so far as the individuals peacefully live, and dwell together. However, in the *Gemeinschaft* they remain essentially united in spite of all separating factors, whereas in the *Gesellschaft*, they are essentially separated in spite of all uniting factors.[38]

In *Gesellschaft*, individuals are isolated and 'there exists a condition of tension against all others'. People only have and enjoy what belongs to them to the exclusion of all others; 'something that has a common value does not exist.'[39] A contractual relation lies at the basis of *Gesellschaft*.

In my view, some useful parallels could be drawn between the attributes of *Gesellschaft* and those defining global society. For instance, although some basic human rights are theoretically granted to all – as established by the UN and sanctioned by most nation-states – no contractual relation exists among the peoples of the world, and there are no global legislative and judicial institutions recognized and respected worldwide. Global society is formed by an aggregate of human beings whose interaction is often mediated by the nation-state and, increasingly, by other international and supranational organizations and institutions. Social coherence is non-existent, and some type of 'global' solidarity tends to materialize only in extremely specific circumstances.

Gesellschaft describes a society in which individuals compete most of the time, except when they form a coalition to confront a common enemy. All relations are permeated by material interests and 'based upon comparison of possible and offered services'.[40] Tönnies would go even further and argue that, 'before and outside convention and also before and outside of each special contract, the relation of all to all may therefore be conceived as potential hostility or latent war.'[41]

Finding a common enemy to global society, one capable of triggering a global response, is not easy. For instance, global warming and environmental degradation could be regarded as potential common enemies, but even so, not all nation-states are prepared to endorse global measures to fight them, primarily because the commitment to such measures would almost invariably come at an economic cost to the nation and its citizens. Moreover, the 'potential hostility' that Tönnies attributes to *Gesellschaft*, with few exceptions, accurately describes global relations.

Let's now turn to Tönnies's conception of *Gemeinshaft* and explore its relevance when seeking to understand the nation. 'Blood, place (land), and mind, or kinship, neighbourhood, and friendship' are, according to Tönnies, the three pillars of *Gemeinschaft*, which are encompassed in the family. He stresses the primordial role of the land as the place where the community's life evolves. The land is the area occupied by the community throughout different generations and links individuals to their ancestors, prompting the sacralization of certain shrines. What Tönnies writes about the land when applied to *Gemeinschaft* can perfectly be applied to the territory of the nation as portrayed in nationalist discourses.

Habits, mores and folkways are also attributed particular significance in a *Gemeinschaft*. Similarly, customs and beliefs are an important component of the nation. The image of the family, employed by Tönnies to exemplify *Gemeinschaft*, has often been used to portray the nation. But, this does not mean that nations are ideal communities free from internal conflict and diversity; rather their members may hold conflicting images of the nation and envisage dissimilar national projects.

Democratic nationalist movements accept and encourage dialogue between people who may differ in their conception of the nation but who share a sense of belonging. They conceive national membership as open, and are prepared to engage in a dialogic process leading towards national development. It would be naïve, though, to ignore the fact that non-democratic forms of nationalism do not subscribe to these principles and that some nations seek to enhance their unity and identity by implementing undemocratic homogenizing policies.

On liberal nationalism and cosmopolitanism

It is the contention of some liberals that a particular type of nationalism – liberal nationalism – is compatible with cosmopolitanism, since 'it is within the context of a national culture that the core liberal values of individual autonomy and self-identity, social justice and democracy are best realized.'[42]

Liberal nationalism focuses on the connection between liberal democracy and the nation. Three basic principles define liberal democracy – social justice, deliberative democracy and individual freedom – and it is the liberal nationalists' view that they are all better achieved within the nation.

Social justice

It is the belief of many liberals that moral cosmopolitanism – that is, the commitment to global social justice – is better accomplished by being fostered within the nation-state rather than by the creation of some kind of – still non-existent – global state. The construction of a welfare state can be regarded as a step towards social justice within a particular society, and, as its name indicates, the state is its creator and designer. A 'nebulous cosmopolitan order' does not provide welfare-state programmes, public education, religious liberty and tolerance or prohibit racial and sexual discrimination.[43] Furthermore, a theory of social justice ignoring the particular ties and obligations shared by fellow nationals cannot be considered suitable for humanity, since it blatantly ignores the role of the nation as the political space within which social justice emerges as a consequence of the bonds of solidarity uniting nationals.[44]

Liberal nationalism depends on the sovereign state to implement its principles and relies on national identity as the glue holding together an otherwise diverse population. It is through the commitment to liberal democratic values that the state becomes an organ of global social justice. But it is also through the commitment to liberal democratic values that the state creates the conditions that make it possible for its citizens to become sensitive to the spread of democratic values beyond their national borders and prepares them to embrace cosmopolitanism as an attitude in favour of freedom and equality for all.

Although some relevant attempts have been made recently aiming at the adoption of principles destined to promote global social justice, the scope of their impact is minimal when compared with those principles according supremacy to the nation-state. Currently sovereign states have the greatest power to grant and sustain rights, and it is hard to see how this could be fundamentally changed in the foreseeable future. In addition, it would be naïve to presume that all nation-states' actions are necessarily conducive to social justice. For instance, it is true that, in some cases, nation-states seeking their own benefit or trying to protect themselves have sabotaged global initiatives destined to tackle specific transnational issues related to social justice, such as global warming, genocide, and the status and treatment of immigrants and refugees, as well as of national minorities, to mention but a few.

Deliberative democracy

Deliberative democracy entails 'a system of collective deliberation and legitimation that allows all citizens to use their reason in political deliberation'.[45] It requires a high level of trust and a mutual understanding among citizens, which, so far, only the nation has been able to generate. In a corresponding manner, global democracy 'is best achieved through the promotion of democratic citizenship at national level. If anything, the goals of moral cosmopolitanism are furthered rather than thwarted by liberal nationalism.'[46]

Democracy, tolerance and respect within a given society can never be fully attained through the strict compliance with the law – although the law and, in particular, the threat of punishment tend to persuade those inclined to act otherwise to comply with it. These are attitudes and values that need to be learned, internalized and regarded as so precious that individuals should be prepared to make sacrifices to preserve them.

In my view, a democratic political culture is difficult to achieve. It cannot be improvised and relies heavily on democratic values being introduced through education, political practice and public debate. A commitment to democracy presupposes readiness to engage in a dynamic process that recognizes dialogue as a means to reach solutions and overcome differences. Democracy, if applied only to the political arena, does not guarantee the construction of a democratic society. I regard democracy as a vital attitude defining private and public relations and occurring in the political, social and economic milieu.

Individual freedom

The relationship between individual autonomy and national culture is a complex one. Liberals argue that national identity 'makes individual freedom meaningful'.[47] By offering individuals a specific value system, a way of life and traditions, national culture bestows meaning upon specific social practices and situates the individual at a vantage point from which to relate to, understand and value those of others. This is why national culture makes individual freedom meaningful.

National identity offers a moral anchor to individuals by means of the specific corpus of knowledge and values it embodies. This represents the context within which individuals make choices and foster solidarity bonds with fellow nationals. Trust and mutual respect are likely to emerge among people socialized within a shared culture including a value system. In this regard, learning to be an active member of a national community ruled by liberal principles prepares the individual for active membership of the world community by 'providing the requisite grounding and motivation for social justice commitments among citizens'.[48]

In Nielsen's view, 'a truly liberal nationalist should also be a cosmopolitan nationalist and cohere with the quintessential cosmopolitan principle of normative individualism and ethical universalism.'[49] Thus the cosmopolitan commitment to global egalitarianism can be reconciled with the national principle, in so far as this is informed by liberal nationalism, as an ideology prepared to protect the integrity of the nation while adopting an internationalist and egalitarian outlook.

In my view, one of the major weaknesses of liberal nationalism is its emphasis on individual rights and its disregard for collective rights, a concept of supreme significance for democratic nationalists. I consider that individual rights cannot be fully enjoyed if they are not conceived in a context of respect for collective rights. Thus, for an individual to be able to develop all his or her potentialities, he or she should be considered not in isolation but as a member of one or more groups. Two sets of different rights which complement each other need to be taken into account: those concerning the individual as a free agent, and those related to the social dimension of individuals who live within specific communities. In late modernity, these communities tend to be nations.

After years of developing and promoting individual rights, we are now confronted with the socio-political need to counteract an exceedingly individualistic society threatened by a fragmentation resulting from a growing lack of civic coherence.

On cosmopolitan nationalism

We live in a world of nations within which national identity compels individuals to social and political action and where national loyalty takes precedence over cosmopolitan allegiances. We do not live within a cosmopolitan order, and I do not envisage such an order emerging in the foreseeable future. At present, the cosmopolitan ideal remains a utopia far removed from the constant competition, conflict and war defining international relations. It is within this context that individuals turn towards their own nations as a source of identity but also as an environment within which they enjoy some rights.

Democratic nationalism and cosmopolitanism agree in their commitment to human rights, tolerance, cultural interchange and international peace and cooperation, and I believe that they both share sufficient aims to coexist. Cosmopolitanism, that is, world citizenship free from national prejudices, could only emerge under the following conditions:

1 the establishment of democratic constitutions in all nation–states as a guarantee of respect for freedom, equality before the law, and national, ethnic, cultural and gender diversity;
2 the predominance of democracy as the principle governing international relations, which should involve a relationship of equality between nations;
3 the enactment of a 'cosmopolitan law', which would provide for what Immanuel Kant called 'universal hospitality', that is, the right of any foreigner − not a citizen of the specific state − to be treated without hostility in the country of arrival, supposing that he or she behaves peacefully.[50]

A cosmopolitan order could only come into being if the above conditions were to be fulfilled. In such an ideal situation the discrimination, repression and attempted annihilation endured by some nations and ethnic groups will cease to exist. It is not morally sound to demand from a nation engaged in a struggle for its own cultural and political survival that it declare itself 'cosmopolitan' (*kosmos polites*), simply because to be able to do so this nation should be free, and freedom is not an option for a nation faced by constant threats to its own social, cultural, economic, political or territorial existence while being denied the right to form a part of this 'cosmos'.

This is a point totally ignored by Martha C. Nussbaum, who offers a largely US-centred analysis. She considers patriotic pride as 'both morally dangerous and, ultimately, subversive of some of the worthy goals [it] sets out to serve'.[51] She insists on the need to encourage a sense of world citizenship among US students – a laudable thing to do – but never talks about how students from 'other' countries – developed or not – may feel about her insistence on world citizenship. She ignores what Tagore clearly spelled out at a time fraught with internationalist discourses:

> Races, communities, nations were constantly urged to abolish their frontiers, destroy their distinctive attributes, cease from mutual strife, and combine into one great universal society. This was well enough as an ultimate ideal: it would fit a world where peoples were of approximately equal strength and status; but so long as vast inequalities existed, these sermons addressed to the weak – who are still seeking recognition, or even elementary justice, or the means of survival – had they been listened to, would merely . . . have achieved for them the unity which the kid achieved with the tiger when it was swallowed by it. . . . Those who are scattered, weak, humiliated, oppressed must first be collected, strengthened, liberated, given opportunity to grow and develop at least to some degree by their own natural resources, on their own soil, in their own languages, with unborrowed memories, and not wholly in perpetual debt, cultural or economic, to some outside benefactor.[52]

Democratic nationalism is legitimate. It defends the right of nations to exist and develop while recognizing and respecting internal diversity. It rejects the territorial expansion of nations and shows a commitment to increasing the morality of the nations' citizens by promoting democracy, social justice, freedom, equality, and mutual respect concerning cultural and other differences. Only by being committed to these principles can democratic nationalism become cosmopolitan.

In my view, all nations – with and without states – should be encouraged to set up the conditions favouring the emergence of cosmopolitanism as an attitude compelling individuals to add a further dimension to their care and concern for fellow nationals by raising awareness about the respect, dignity, freedom and equality that should be granted to all human beings.

I am convinced that the political agenda for the future of nations should include the commitment to cosmopolitan ideals and values capable of informing political action and adding a new moral dimension to national identity. The advent of cosmopolitanism requires the pledge to eradicate social, political and economic ideologies based upon the exploitation of individuals and nations. In so far as this remains out of reach, cosmopolitanism will continue to be a utopian ideology. Its strength as a political and moral ideology will depend on its own ability to act as a transformative force leading a multidimensional process destined to change the relations of power in society. I envisage that it will encounter fierce opposition.

Conclusion

At the beginning of the new millennium, the identity of nations remains strong and acts as a powerful political mobilizer. National identity now, however, is different from that at other periods of time, simply because, in the global age, national identity is simultaneously more solidly constructed by efficient strategies of nation-building and much more open to alien influences impossible to control and exclude from the national space.

National identity has acquired a new dimension that makes it more open and able to include foreign elements without fundamentally changing its core. To put it another way, national identity tolerates a higher degree of hybridity and fuzziness at the margins than in previous times.

The state nurtures national identity by promoting a shared culture, language, symbols and rituals among a diverse population and is actively engaged in a number of strategies destined to foster bonds of solidarity and feelings of social cohesion among its citizens; the means to achieve them are far greater than ever before. National identity cannot survive indefinitely without the active support of some elites that need not necessarily be associated with the state; we should bear in mind that not all nations have states of their own.

Currently, the identity of nations is being challenged from below – that is, by the claims of national minorities – from above – that is, by the construction of supranational institutions and organizations such as the European Union – and from within – by internal challenges posed by ethnic minorities of migrant origin.

The acceptance of liberal democratic principles by most Western countries has implied, among other things, a much more receptive attitude on behalf of the nation-state towards the accommodation of its national minorities. As the cases considered here – Britain, Canada and Spain – demonstrate, devolution has strengthened regional identities but, so far, has not brought about the independence of new nations.[1] On the contrary, devolution seems to have contributed to taming secessionist claims while fostering the peaceful coexistence of multiple identities within a single state. Even more crucially, devolution has promoted the emergence of new regional identities where they did not previously exist.

An incipient European identity seeks to add a further layer to already strong national and regional identities. Yet, Europe has never before constituted a community of fate as have most of its constituent regions and nations – at least those sharing a strong sense of identity. Europe does not share a common language, culture and history. Its territorial boundaries are fuzzy and have fluctuated throughout time. Furthermore, only recently, some European elites decided to engage in the construction of a common project personified in the European Union.

Even so, the recent failure to endorse a European constitution, concerns about the EU's democratic deficit, disagreement about how the EU should evolve, a gap between European elites and the majority of the population, disagreement on the content of a common foreign and security policy, plus the inability to agree on the future institutional structure and mission of the EU emphasize the great difficulties that elites encounter when faced with the task of generating a shared European identity.

Still, the biggest challenge yet to be faced by Western nations concerns how to maintain social cohesion in the light of the realization that, within their borders, some ethnic minorities of immigrant origin have managed to create urban enclaves ruled by their own laws, culture and religion – that is, they have formed ghettos completely alien to mainstream society, its national identity, culture and values.[2]

In many Western nations, some of these ghettos are based on an outright rejection of the principles and political culture of the host society. That this situation has come to the fore and acquired an unpredicted new dimension proves that a radicalized form of Islam, which has been associated with some terrorist actions, is gaining adherents. Some form of fundamentalist Islam is thought to be behind the legitimation of the terrorist attacks of 11 September 2001 in New York and Washington, the March 2004 bombings in Madrid and the July 2005 bombings in London, but also of the murder of the Dutch film director Theo van Gogh in 2004 for allegedly insulting Islam. The most recent and violent example (early 2006) was the angry worldwide reaction to the publication in Denmark of some cartoons portraying the Prophet Mohammed in a manner deeply offensive to Muslims.

Across the Western world, political and intellectual elites wonder what has gone wrong with multiculturalism. In Britain, this turned out to be a particularly poignant question after it was revealed that the perpetrators of the London bombings were British citizens, who obviously did not feel for their fellow citizens or share any loyalty towards the nation within which they were brought up and educated. They were people whose national identity had either remained elsewhere or been replaced by some kind of religious identity which permitted the association of their actions with martyrdom. Melanie Phillips writes: 'Incredibly, London had become the hub of the European terror networks. Its large and fluid Muslim and Arab population fostered the growth of myriad radical Islamist publications spitting hatred of the West, and its banks were used for fundraising accounts funnelling money into extremist and terrorist organizations.'[3]

Suddenly, claims to preserve national identity have come to the fore, accompanied by a renewed and unprecedented insistence on the need for immigrants to integrate. In Britain, it has prompted the introduction of British history and culture tests for immigrants prior to their acquiring full citizenship, the latter involving a ceremony in which an oath of allegiance to the monarch has to be taken – a process and ceremony echoing those already in place in the United States of America and Canada, among other countries.

Beyond this, the most fundamental issue, not only for Britain but also for the USA and other Western countries, is how to maintain social cohesion by generating a minimal sense of shared identity among a diverse citizenry including some sectors of the population who clearly despise Western culture, laws, principles and way of life.

Of course, not all Muslims follow radical Islam and are critical of Western mores, and even fewer are prepared to commit acts of violence. But a small number of them do, and they defend their right to 'opt out' of a common project. In short, they wish to dissociate themselves from the national identity of the host society. At the same time, many Muslims across Europe and North America are justified in feeling that Western societies look at them with suspicion and that, in some instances, they are treated as potential terrorists. For example, many feel disadvantaged within Britain, are outraged by some British actions abroad, and are dismayed at their own prospects for social and economic mobility; a similar point could be made about some ethnic minorities in France, Denmark or the Netherlands. One reaction feeds the other.

Western nations feel under threat from within. They are uncertain about how tolerant they should be and about what they should tolerate. Tragically, the West is unsure about the content of its own values and principles and, in some cases, it seems prepared to nurture the seeds of its own decline as a civilization. It defends multiculturalism and, in its name, it blindly fosters and funds cultural diversity, taking no notice of whether or not some of the values and principles being promoted comply with human rights and the

Western values of freedom, gender equality, equality before the law, tolerance, and the separation of state and church.

Western countries such as Britain are eager to learn about religious beliefs,
ceremonies and rituals which originated beyond their shores, and yet are
ready to abandon and overlook the values at the root of the Judeo-Christian
tradition. They are geared up to be lax about disrespect towards their own
traditional religions while showing great concern not to offend the sensibili-
ties of other groups of believers such as Muslims. Is it only because offence
to the latter may result in violence while the former is bound to issue only
a verbal protest? More than this, among some sectors of Western society,
criticism of traditional religion is often perceived as a sign of being 'progressive' – that is, free from religious prejudice, free from what Marx denounced
as the 'people's opium'.

We would be mistaken to think that Judeo-Christian values are being
replaced by some other religion; this is seldom the case. Generally, the West
swaps its traditional religious values for the values of secularization, and this
is legitimate; however, often religious values are simply not replaced at all,
because accepting a philosophical distinction between what is 'good' and
what is 'bad' seems to be increasingly difficult and, as a consequence, people
are frequently left with their own individual judgement. Individualism is
taken to its ultimate consequences and, as a result, feelings of social cohesion
and solidarity are increasingly losing strength. It is only when society is suddenly shaken by the consequences of this process – for instance, after the
London bombings in July 2005 or the violent incidents in the Paris *banlieues*
in December 2005 and again in autumn 2006 – that some people begin to
react.

In my view, respect for cultural diversity and the belief that all cultures
possess some valuable components does not involve a blind endorsement
of those traditions and values that stand against the principles governing
liberal democratic societies. I argue that liberal democracies should not
tolerate – promote or fund – alternative cultures which do not respect the
principles of democracy, equal rights, freedom and tolerance. The limit of
toleration should be placed right at the point where an aspect of a specific
culture undermines the very principles of the democratic society that allows
it to exist and develop within its borders.

I do not believe that immigrants should be expected immediately to adopt
the culture and ways of life of their new society; this is a process generally
realized in subsequent generations and which, in my view, should not result
in complete assimilation. It is important for people's sense of self-esteem to
maintain and feel a particular attachment to their origins as a crucial part of

their own individual identity. I defend the right of immigrants to preserve their own culture, but I also wish to stress their duty to accept the values entrenched in the political culture and institutions of the host society, to learn its language, values and traditions.

To be sure, immigrants should be welcomed into the host society, be granted social and economic rights and, in due course, acquire political rights. They should not be exploited and marginalized. I am aware that this can only result through well-developed procedures able to control the numbers of immigrants, simply because resources are not infinite. In principle, a chaotic immigration system is bad for the immigrant and for the indigenous population alike, except for those who seek to benefit from it.

It is a fact that the identity of nations will progressively be transformed by immigration, as it always has been. It is undeniable that subsequent waves of immigration and settlement will enlarge already existing ethnic communities. Further immigration also holds the potential to create new ethnic communities and, in time, immigrants will become full members of a society they are helping to construct. There is a distinction, however, between contributing to a slow transformation of the culture and ways of life of a particular society by means of increasing interaction and cooperation among all its members and aspiring or actively struggling fundamentally to alter the principles governing it.

The recognition of the right to self-determination of nations involves the right to cultivate and promote one's own culture, language and traditions while respecting internal diversity. But respect for internal diversity neither implies renouncing one's own identity nor assumes that others ought fully to comply. However, it does assume that, in order that everyone should live together and form a society with a sufficient degree of cohesion, respect for the basic tenets of that society ought to be upheld.

Many Western nations are unsure about how much strength, if any, they can invest in reinforcing and promoting their national identity. In Britain, feelings of guilt associated with its colonial past – including an almost complete disregard for colonial cultures and political systems – a significant weakening of its worldwide status after the demise of its imperial era, and claims for devolution arising from its own national minorities have revealed great difficulty in defining British identity. Furthermore, blind tolerance of diversity has resulted in the free evolvement of radical Islamic fundamentalism and terrorism on British soil.

Two powerful reactions running in opposite directions are currently challenging national identity: the proliferation and strengthening of radical right-wing populist parties advocating the preservation of what I have referred to as 'pure identities'; and the expansion of cosmopolitanism as a doctrine aiming to transcend national allegiances by replacing them with feelings of worldwide citizenship. Both ideologies target national identity yet, while the former is concerned with the preservation of its integrity, the latter stands in favour of its progressive dissolution. The two ideologies tend to appeal to different sections of the population; as I have shown, there is evidence that the radical new right finds most of its supporters among the working class and the petite bourgeoisie. Cosmopolitanism, in turn, appeals to middle-class educated people of left-wing leanings. Of course, this is an overtly simplified picture, because probably one of the most outstanding features of both ideologies is their ability to resonate well beyond their supporters and, in the case of the new radical right, their proven capacity to influence public policy.

The new radical right is mostly populist. It criticizes corruption and the establishment and plays by the rules of democratic governance. It constructs its discourse around the need to preserve national identity, which in its view is fatally threatened by growing non-Western immigration. It is of non-Western values, cultures and traditions, and in particular those associated with Islam, that the new radical right is most critical. It defends giving priority to citizens rather than overstretching welfare systems to accommodate large numbers of immigrants, regarded as a source of crime, lower wages, unemployment and the gradual erosion of national identity.

Nations have reacted to the social, cultural and economic challenges posed by greater immigration by tightening their laws,[4] by revising multiculturalism and, since 9/11, by holding greater suspicion of Islamic fundamentalism and those associated with it. In my view, immigration and the discourse of the radical right are forcing nations to redefine their own identities much more tightly than previously.

The new radical right seems to benefit from a split between, on the one hand, the majority of the working and lower middle classes and, on the other, elites concerning the impact of immigration upon their own societies. Thus, some businesses benefit from cheap immigrant labour – legal or not – and some middle-class families take advantage of affordable domestic and care support provided by immigration. Nevertheless, the middle classes do not live in the same neighbourhoods as immigrants, or visit the same shops, restaurants and entertainment venues. It is the working class that often competes for jobs with low-skilled immigrant labour – by far the largest contingent, since only a small minority are highly skilled immigrants who tend to integrate easily within the middle-class ranks of the indigenous population. It is also the working class that mostly perceives immigration as an extra burden on an already overstretched welfare system.

Furthermore, the fact should not be ignored that recent waves of immigration have often encountered stark opposition from migrants who have already settled within particular societies and have colonized certain jobs within specific areas. Competition and conflict between migrants of different origin has already taken place in areas around Birmingham, in the East End of London, in Rotterdam and in New York, as well as in the Paris *banlieues*, to mention just a few examples.

Cosmopolitanism is primarily a secular ideology based on the premise that all persons are in a fundamental sense equal and free and deserve equal political treatment regardless of their origin. It focuses on the world as a point of reference and considers national attachments as an obstacle to the recognition of freedom and equality for all. Cosmopolitanism, at least the acceptance of its principles, has already been incorporated into numerous constitutions, although not a single institution has been able actually to sanction those transgressing them.

Often, cosmopolitans neglect the role of the nation-state as a rights-giver within its own territory and undervalue the function of national identity – that is, of sharing bonds of solidarity and a sense of common purpose – in facilitating the everyday practice of democracy. In my view, adopting a cosmopolitan attitude does not imply renouncing national identity; rather, it is a matter of adding a cosmopolitan layer to it. Yet, by actively endorsing the principles of freedom and equality for all, national identity would be made compatible with cosmopolitanism. At this point, it would be possible to speak about a cosmopolitan nationalism.

Cosmopolitanism holds the potential further to reinforce national identity and culture by actively promoting and respecting different ways of 'being in the world', all of them united by shared respect for the principles of democratic public life. I regard cosmopolitanism as an attitude that should pervade national identity and which presupposes a constant effort on behalf of all people to free their cultures from those aspects which do not comply with the values of freedom and equality for all.

To conclude, national identity remains strong, and it is likely to be further strengthened in the foreseeable future as nations are faced with renewed pressure to accommodate and coexist with alternative forms of identity, while being compelled actively to encourage the preservation and promotion of their own distinct cultures. In the medium term, I envisage a backlash against multiculturalism across Europe and the USA, resulting in tightened immigration controls, a qualified endorsement of multiculturalism, a renewed emphasis on integration and, in some cases, the return of assimilation. I also expect that calls for charismatic leadership are likely to return to the political arena.

National identity becomes stronger as it becomes more porous, but pressure for 'pure identities' could never mean the return to a time when cultural isolation was possible. The identity of nations simultaneously reacts and contributes to the consolidation of regional and supranational identities. It is hard to predict whether the West will respond in time to fundamental challenges being posed to the very principles sustaining it.

Notes

Introduction

1 *Constitución Española*, 1978, Artículo 2.
2 Phillips (2006).
3 Phillips (2005).
4 Weber ([1968] 1978, p. 389).

Chapter 1 What is National Identity?

1 Baumeister (1986, p. 29).
2 Quoted in Guibernau (1996, p. 72).
3 Baumeister (1986, p. 59).
4 Melucci (1982, p. 62).
5 Ibid., p. 88.
6 Guibernau (1996, p. 47).
7 For instance, Smith (2002, p. 15).
8 See Connor (1994a).
9 Ibid., p. 202.
10 Deutsch ([1953] 1966, p. 97).
11 Smith (1998, p. 167).
12 Gellner (1983).
13 Anderson (1983).
14 Hobsbawm and Ranger (1983).
15 See Smith (1986).
16 See Shils (1957).
17 Geertz (1973, p. 260).
18 Cohen (1969).
19 Eriksen (2001, p. 45).
20 Ibid.
21 Ibid., p. 46.
22 Weber (1979).
23 Connor (1994, p. 157).
24 Ibid.
25 Gellner (1983, p. 38).
26 Ibid.
27 Gellner (1987, p. 16).
28 Gellner (1983, p. 55).
29 Nairn (1977, p. 340).
30 Anderson (1983).
31 Guibernau (1996, p. 47).

32   Kohn ([1955] 1965, p. 26).
33   See Guibernau (2001, pp. 242–68).
34   See point 4 on pp. 95–6.
35   Soysal (1994).
36   Held (2002, p. 315).
37   Ibid.
38   See Gellner (1983).

Chapter 2   National Identity, Devolution and Secession

1   Keating (2001), p. 78.
2   Ibid., pp. 78–9.
3   Ibid., p. 80.
4   Fitzmaurice (1985), pp. 201–39.
5   See Brown (1990).
6   Cook, Saywell and Ricker (1963), p. 83.
7   McRoberts (1997), p. 40.
8   Ibid., p. 42.
9   McRoberts (2001), p. 58. See also McRoberts (2004).
10   McRoberts (2001), p. 63.
11   See Oliver (1991); Laforest (1995); and Bashevkin (1991).
12   Gagnon (1998), pp. 163–71.
13   McRoberts (2001), p. 107.
14   Conway (1992), p. 70.
15   Ibid., p. 73.
16   See Harrison and Marmen (1994).
17   Kymlicka (1998).
18   Ottawa, House of Commons, Debates, 8 October 1971, 8581.
19   Throughout this chapter, the term 'Quebecker' refers to all Quebec citizens, while the term 'Québécois' refers only to 'nationalist Quebeckers'. This follows a current use in Quebec studies.
20   B&B Commission (1967), Book I, p. xxxiii.
21   Bissoondath (1994).
22   McRoberts (2001), p. 132; see also Resnick (1994).
23   McRoberts (2001), p. 135.
24   See Cummins and Danesi (1990) and Manning (1992).
25   Breton (1986).
26   Gagnon (2004b).
27   *Le Devoir*, 3 December 1981; McWhinney (1982), p. 137.
28   Russell (1993).
29   Quoted by Gagnon (2003), p. 302.
30   Ibid.
31   Tully (1995), p. 6.
32   McRoberts (2001), p. 164.
33   Ibid., p. 170; see also Russell (1993) and Laforest (1995).
34   Schneiderman (1998), p. 159.
35   Seymour (2005), p. 4; McRoberts (2001), p. 172.
36   McRoberts (2001), p. 174.
37   The Lévesque government formulated its proposal in the document *Quebec-Canada: A New Deal* (Quebec Government, 1979).
38   Quebec Chief Electoral Office (1995).
39   For a set of proposals on reconciliation between Quebec and Canada, see Gibbins and Laforest (1998).

40 Cairns (1996) and Whitaker (1995).

41 Dion (1996).

42 Rocher and Verrelli (2003), p. 208.

43 Ibid., p. 209.

44 Noël (2000).

45 Lajoie (2004).

46 Seymour (2005), p. 7.

47 G. Smith (1995), p. 4.

48 Burgess and Gagnon (1993), p. 5.

49 Elazar (1987), p. 12.

50 CRIC, *Opinion Canada*, vol. 5, no. 17, 8 May 2003.

51 Ibid.

52 CRIC, *Portraits of Canada*, 2004.

53 See http://quebeclibre.net/sondage1.html (accessed 22 September 2005). Support for sovereignty-partnership has obtained similar results (54 per cent) in a recent opinion poll carried out by Leger Marketing (May 2005).

54 CRIC, *Portraits of Canada*, 2004.

55 Riquer and Culla (1989) and Balcells (1996).

56 See Preston (1986); Preston (2003); and Solé Tura (1985).

57 Fossas (1999).

58 Guibernau (2004b), pp. 70–84.

59 Requejo (2000). See also Requejo (2001) and Keating (2000).

60 Keating (1999).

61 This project was launched on 27 September 2002 by José María Ibarretxe, *lehendakari*, or president, of the Basque autonomous government, and obtained the support of the Basque parliament.

62 Note that the Spanish Constitution recognizes 'a single Spanish nation patria of all Spaniards' (Article 2) and refers to Catalonia, the Basque Country and Galicia as 'nacionalidades históricas' (historical nationalities). There is a fundamental difference between the Great Britain which acknowledges Scotland, England and Wales as 'nations' and Spain which only recognizes the existence of 'a single Spanish nation'.

63 CIS (2003).

64 Resina (2002).

65 In 2003, the ERC managed to double its 1999 results. It obtained a record twenty-three seats, corresponding to 16.47 per cent of the vote, and became consolidated as the third political force in Catalonia – one with the capacity to play a key role in the constitution of a future government, since neither the CiU (Convergència i Unió; the federation of Convergència Democràtica de Catalunya and Unió Democràtica) nor the PSC (Partit dels Socialistes de Catalunya) had achieved a majority.

In the Catalan election on 1 November 2006, the ERC obtained twenty-one seats (two fewer than in the previous election; 14.06 per cent of the vote), and remains a key player in the constitution of the government of Catalonia. As in 2003, it decided to form a coalition including the PSC (PSC–PSOE) (the federation of Partit dels Socialistes de Catalunya and Partido Socialista Obrero Español), which had obtained thirty-seven seats (26.81 per cent of the vote), and the ICV–EUiA (Iniciativa per Catalunya Verds–Esquerra Unida i Alternativa), which had obtained twelve seats (9.56 per cent of the vote). The CiU won the election by obtaining forty-eight seats (31.52 per cent of the vote), but it was short of achieving the necessary majority to form a government.

66 Osmond (2000), p. 40; Tomaney (2000).

67 For a comprehensive analysis and statistical data concerning support for devolution in Scotland, see McCrone and Paterson (2002).

68 National Centre for Social Research (2003), p. 42.

69   Slightly different percentages for the year 2002 are provided by Lindsay Paterson in 'Attitudes to Scottish Independence and to the SNP'; www.institute-of-governance. org/onlinepub/sa/paterson_attitudes_tables.html (accessed 15 March 2005).

70   National Centre for Social Research (2003), pp. 39–41.

71   Ibid., p. 59.

72   CIS (2003).

73   CRIC, *Opinion Canada*, vol. 5, no. 17, 8 May 2003.

74   Ibid.

75   CIS (2003).

76   Alternative data concerning Catalonia provided by the Institut de Ciències Polítiques i Socials (ICPS) varies slightly from that produced by the CIS. According to the 2003 ICPS opinion poll, 9 per cent of Catalan citizens feel 'only Spanish'; 4 per cent feel 'more Spanish than Catalan'; 41 per cent feel 'as Spanish as Catalan'; 27 per cent feel 'more Catalan than Spanish'; and 16 per cent feel 'only Catalan'. *Sondeig d'Opinió 2003* (Barcelona: ICPS 2004), p. 84.

77   National Centre for Social Research (2003).

78   Similar data for Scotland can be found in McCrone (2002).

79   Keating (1999). See also Seymour (2004).

80   Keating (2001), p. 64.

81   Ibid., p. 134.

82   Weber ([1968] 1978), p. 389.

83   Guibernau (2000), pp. 1003–4.

Chapter 3   The Impact of Migration on National Identity

1   Historians have shown that the volume of internal and international migration per head of population was greater in the nineteenth century (up to 1914) than in the twentieth. See Lucassen (2002), Moch (2003) and Hoerder (2003).

2   Furnivall (1948) and Smith (1965); see Eriksen (1993).

3   Castles and Miller ([1993] 1998), p. 30.

4   Weber ([1968] 1978), p. 389.

5   Ibid.

6   Ibid.

7   Guibernau (1996), p. 47.

8   Weber (1948), p. 78.

9   Walzer (1992).

10   See also Tamir (1993); Spinner-Halev (1994); and Kymlicka (1989).

11   Kymlicka (2001), pp. 23–4.

12   Marshall (1973).

13   Castles and Miller ([1993] 1998), p. 43.

14   Ibid.

15   Ibid., p. 230.

16   See Bauböck (1994).

17   Park and Burgess ([1921] 1969), p. 735.

18   Park (1930), p. 281.

19   Gordon (1964), pp. 80–1.

20   Alba and Nee (1997), p. 829.

21   See Finkielkraut (1987); Taguieff (1994); and Todd (1994).

22   Brubaker (2001), p. 538.

23   Huntington (2004), p. 61.

24   See Rex and Singh (2004); Rex (2005); and Wieviorka (1996a).

25   Castles and Miller ([1993] 1998), p. 245.

26 Ibid.
27 As Castles and Miller point out, multiculturalism has different meanings. For instance, 'in the USA it mainly refers to demands for rethinking history and culture to include the role of minorities, and may thus even include women's studies. In Western Europe, multiculturalism is often used pejoratively to refer to a policy of ethnic separatism (in the sense of a "nation of tribes"). In Canada, Australia and Sweden, multiculturalism usually denotes a certain type of government policy, combining cultural rights and social equality for minorities. It might be more appropriate to use a more neutral term, such as "pluralism", or "inclusionary citizenship", but multiculturalism has become too well established in public debates to be easily displaced' (ibid., p. 302).
28 Ibid., p. 248.
29 Ibid.
30 Rex (1997), p. 208.
31 Stone (1975).
32 Taylor (1994), p. 25.
33 Ibid., p. 26.
34 Ibid., p. 33.
35 Ibid., p. 38.
36 Parekh (1999), p. 3.
37 Ibid., p. 4.
38 Schlesinger (1992).
39 Bissoondath (1994).
40 Ibid., p. 111.
41 Glazer (1997), p. 92.
42 Ibid., p. 14.
43 Parekh (1997).
44 Forst (1997).
45 Parekh (1985), p. 59.
46 Kymlicka (2001), p. 155.
47 Ibid., p. 158.
48 Ibid., p. 161.
49 See Haller et al. (1996).
50 The 1919 constitution was re-established in its 1929 version.
51 Bruckmüller (2003), p. 290.
52 Spohn (2005), p. 60.
53 Ibid.
54 Bruckmüller (2003), p. 307.
55 Ibid., p. 308.
56 Spohn (2005), pp. 60–1.
57 See Erdmann (1985).
58 Bruckmüller (2003), p. 311.
59 Ibid., p. 371.
60 Ibid., p. 389.
61 Spohn (2005), p. 63.
62 Bauböck (1999), p. 104.
63 Bruckmüller (1998), p. 70.
64 See Programme of the Austrian Freedom Party, adopted 30 October 1997, ch. 3, 'Austria First!'. Article 1 states: 'Austria is more than a simple administrative unit. Its people are linked by a will for independence and belong together in regional diversity. This will is expressed by the democratic federal and constitutional Republic of Austria. (1) Austria's patriotism is expressed in the will for the independence and unity of Austrians, in the will to preserve democracy, human rights, the rule of law and federal-

ism, and in the will to cultivate Austria's cultural heritage and protect its environment, countryside and nature. (2) Austria's identity is formed by a variety and multitude of regional identities. After a painful past the Austrian people have demonstrated a will to be together within the bounds of regional peculiarities.'

65   Bruckmüller (1998), p. 70.
66   Bruckmüller (2003), p. 41.
67   National Contact Point Austria (2004), p. 5.
68   Ibid., p. 10.
69   Ibid.
70   Ibid., p. 11.
71   According to the 1951 United Nations Convention Relating to the Status of Refugees and its 1967 Protocol, refugees are defined as 'persons with a well-founded fear of persecution in their own country for reasons of race, religion, nationality, membership of a particular social group or political opinion'.
72   Bauböck (1999), p. 108.
73   Ibid.
74   National Contact Point Austria (2004), p. 12.
75   Ibid., p. 12.
76   Ibid., p. 13.
77   Bauböck (1999), p. 132.
78   National Contact Point Austria (2004), p. 13.
79   See www.statistik.at (accessed 7 June 2005).
80   Alba and Nee (1997).
81   National Contact Point Austria (2004), p. 20.
82   Ibid., p. 21.
83   Ibid., p. 22.
84   Ibid.
85   Ibid., p. 23.
86   Alba and Nee (1997).
87   Council of Europe (2001), p. 12.
88   Ibid.
89   Ibid., p. 11.
90   As I have already pointed out elsewhere (Guibernau, 1999), I understand ethnic groups as well as nations as internally heterogeneous, and I have considered in detail the strategies employed by the state in the construction of national identity (chapter 1). Yet while from an analytical perspective I accept the value of considering groupness 'as a contextually fluctuating conceptual variable', as argued by Brubaker (Brubaker, 2002, p. 167), I have serious concerns about the political consequences of his approach. For instance, if groups are not recognized as constant – accepting that being constant does not imply remaining the same – how can they pose political demands? How can they become the subject of specific rights? How can they be considered as political actors? Is it just a matter of arguing that 'race, nation, ethnie' (in Brubaker's terms) do not exist as groups because rights are not granted to 'events', as Brubaker seems to point out?
91   Council of Europe (2001), pp. 12–13.
92   National Contact Point Austria (2004), p. 38.
93   Wiener Integrationsfonds (1999), p. 43.
94   Council of Europe (2001), p. 13.
95   Ibid.
96   National Contact Point Austria (2004), pp. 38–9.
97   Fleck (1995).
98   Council of Europe (2001), p. 53.
99   Bauböck (2002), p. 246.

100   Bauböck (1999), p. 132.
101   For an interesting comparative analysis between the values and ways of life of German-speaking and Italian-speaking communities in Alto Adige, see Haller et al. (1986). See also Haller (1991).
102   Programme of the Austrian Freedom Party, adopted 30 October 1997, ch. 7, Art. 4.
103   Spohn (2005), p. 65.
104   Haller et al. (1996).
105   Cited in National Contact Point Austria (2004), p. 30.
106   Cited ibid.
107   See Kraler and Sohler (2005).
108   Cited in National Contact Point Austria (2004), p. 33.
109   Between October and December 2004 and May 2006 I carried out a series of in-depth semi-structured interviews with Austrian politicians and academics. The selection included members and sympathizers of mainstream political parties, independent academics and some academics with open political allegiances. I conducted face-to-face interviews in Vienna with forty people, the average interview time being 1 hour 30 minutes.
110   European Monitoring Centre on Racism and Xenophobia (2005), p. 33.
111   Ibid., p. 32.
112   Ibid., p. 34.
113   The FPÖ obtained 10 per cent of the vote of blue-collar workers in 1986, 21 per cent in 1990, 29 per cent in 1994, and 34 per cent in 1995. See Wodak (2002), pp. 28–9.
114   Ter Wal (2002), p. 161.
115   Ibid.
116   Gärtner (2002), p. 23.
117   Quoted in Ter Wal (2002), p. 165.
118   Quoted ibid., p. 161.
119   *Die Presse*, 21 August 1995, p. 6 (with reference to a television interview of 20 August 1995). Quoted in Bruckmüller (2003), p. 38.

Chapter 4   On European Identity

 1   Burgess (1997), p. 67.
 2   Guibernau (1996), p. 75.
 3   Thompson (1990), p. 132.
 4   Smith (1991).
 5   Huntington (1996).
 6   Quoted in Burgess (1997), p. 67.
 7   Ibid., p. 69.
 8   Enlightenment humanism emerged in France and involved establishing a distinction between those parts of the world engaged in the pursuit of the ideas of rationality and progress, which lie at the heart of the Enlightenment, and those enmeshed in pre-rational practices and beliefs. In spite of the superiority which the *philosophes* attributed to their revolutionary way of thinking, the Enlightenment that they represented did not result in a diminished interest in other areas of the world.
 9   Den Boer (1995), p. 70.
10   Crouch (1999), p. 20.
11   Burgess (1997), p. 91.
12   Giddens (1985), p. 140.
13   Crouch (1999), p. 397.
14   Ibid., pp. 366–89. See also Guibernau (2006).

15 Crouch (1999), p. 399.
16 See Giddens (2006).
17 Mazower (1998), p. 404.
18 Urwin (1993), p. 18.
19 European Commission (1998), pp. 1–4.
20 *Sociological Review*, 3/4 (1994).
21 Mayall ([1990] 1992), ch. 4.
22 Point no. 5 reads: 'A free, open-minded, and absolutely impartial adjustment of all colonial claims, based upon a strict observance of the principle that in determining all such questions of sovereignty the interest of the populations concerned must have equal weight with the equitable claims of the government whose title is to be determined.'
23 See Davies (1996); Goddard, Llobera and Shore (1996).
24 *Maastricht Treaty for the EU* (1992) p. 1; www.eurotreaties.com/maastrichtext.html.
25 See Hayward (1996) and Pérez-Díaz (1998).
26 Guibernau (1999), p. 25.
27 Guibernau (2004a), p. 140.
28 *Eurobarometer 62/*, fieldwork Oct–Nov 2004, p. 8; http://europa.eu/ (accessed 3 December 2005).
29 *Eurobarometer 64/*, fieldwork Oct–Nov 2005, p. 9; http://europa.eu/ (accessed 8 Nov 2006).
30 Ibid., p. 10.
31 Ibid.
32 Ibid., p. 14.
33 Ibid.
34 Ibid., p. 16.
35 Haller (1999), p. 272. See also Puntscher-Riekmann (1998).
36 Mazower (1998), p. xii.
37 Ibid., p. 3.
38 Ibid., p. 405.

Chapter 5   Rethinking American Identity

1 The term 'Hispanic' refers to Spanish-speaking immigrants originating from Latin American countries. At present, the largest contingent of Hispanics comes from Mexico (although all Mexicans are Hispanics, not all Hispanics are Mexicans).
2 Myrdal (1944).
3 Huntington (2004), p. 129.
4 Ibid., p. 86.
5 Ibid., p. 85.
6 Ibid., p. 103.
7 Fukuyama (2007), p. 31.
8 Thernstrom (1995). See also Glazer and Moynihan (1970); Lipset (1963); and Lipset (1996).
9 King (2005), pp. 6–7; Putnam (2000).
10 King (2005), p. 29. See also Meyer (1980).
11 Huntington (2004), pp. 196–7.
12 See Glazer (2002).
13 See Takaki (2002) and Steinberg (1995).
14 Bloom (1987), p. 37.
15 Hirsch (1987).
16 Huntington (2004), pp. 212–13.

17 US Immigration and Naturalization Service (2002), p. 19; US Census Bureau (2001), p. 45.
18 Schlesinger (2002), p. 257.
19 Schlesinger (1992), pp. 135–6.
20 Schlesinger (2002), p. 259.
21 Brimelow (1995).
22 Ibid., p. 264.
23 Fukuyama (1995).
24 See Borjas (1990) and Borjas and Freeman (1992).
25 Brimelow (1995), p. 144.
26 Ibid.
27 Ibid., ch. 9 (pp. 178–90).
28 Taub (1995).
29 Beck (1996) and Briggs (2003).
30 Ungar (1998), p. 366.
31 Salins (1997), p. 40.
32 Isbister (1996).
33 Huntington (2004).
34 Wolfe (2005).
35 Michaels (2006a).
36 Wolfe (2005), ch. 1.
37 Ibid., pp. 169ff.
38 Michaels (2006b), p. 4.
39 Ibid.
40 Ibid.
41 The studies of Harvard economists Alberto Alesina and Edward Glaeser argue that 'American racial heterogeneity explains about half the gap between American and European welfare spending, and Thomas and Mary Edsall's 1991 classic "Chain Reaction" described how a backlash against the civil rights movement resulted in a waning public willingness to support the welfare state through taxes.' See Caldwell (2006), p. 1.
42 *The Economist*, 24 August 2002, pp. 21–2; quoted by Huntington (2004), p. 224.
43 McCormick and Franklin (2000), p. 316.
44 Huntington (2004), p. 225.
45 Contemporary Mexicans lay claim to territories lost to the USA in both the War of Independence (1835–6) and the Mexican–American War of 1846–8. Such territories include most of Arizona, California, Nevada, New Mexico, Texas and Utah.
46 Samuelson (2002), p. 217.
47 Ibid., p. 218.
48 Huntington (2004), p. 231.
49 Alba and Nee (1997), p. 847.
50 Márquez (2003), p. 14.
51 Kryder (1997), p. 7.
52 Woods (2003b).
53 King (2005), p. 85.
54 Henderson (2000), p. 339.
55 See Foner (1990) and Rable (1984).
56 McCormick and Franklin (2000), p. 318.
57 Cruse (1967).
58 Quoted in Henderson (2000), p. 339.
59 Steinberg (2005), p. 2.
60 Ibid., pp. 2–3.

61   Ibid., p. 10.
62   Herrnstein and Murray (1995).
63   Steinberg (2005), p. 13.
64   Ibid., p. 14.
65   This particular point would be addressed in the 9 January 1973 response from the White House to the Indians' Twenty Points March (3–9 November 1972): 'Over one hundred years ago the Congress decided that it was no longer appropriate for the United States to make treaties with Indian tribes. By 1924, all Indians were citizens of the United States and of the states in which they resided. The citizenship relationship with one's government and the treaty relationship are mutually exclusive; a government makes treaties with foreign nations, not with its own citizens. If renunciation of citizenship is implied here, or secession, these are wholly backward steps, inappropriate for a nation which is a Union.' Quoted in Deloria (1985), p. viii.
66   Ibid., pp. 23–4.
67   See American Indian Capital Conference on Poverty: A Statement made for the Young People by Melvin Thom, May 1964; quoted in Josephy (1971).
68   Josephy (1971), p. 226.
69   Nixon said: 'This resolution would explicitly affirm the integrity and right to continued existence of all Indian tribes and Alaska native governments, recognizing that cultural pluralism is a source of national strength. It would assure these groups that the United States Government would continue to carry out its treaty and trusteeship obligations to them as long as the groups themselves believe that such a policy was necessary or desirable . . . For years we have talked about encouraging Indians to exercise greater self-determination, but our progress has never been commensurate with our promises. Part of the reason for this situation has been the threat of termination. But another reason is the fact that when a decision is made as to whether a Federal program will be turned over to Indian administration, it is the Federal authorities and not the Indian people who finally make that decision.' Quoted ibid., pp. 228–9.
70   Robbins (1992), p. 110.
71   Parman (1994).
72   Novak (1971).
73   Tischauser (2002), p. 198.
74   See Bell (1975).
75   Alba (1990), p. 315.
76   Ibid., p. 318.
77   Ibid., p. 319.
78   Lee and Edmonston (2005), p. 1.
79   Ibid., p. 2.
80   Ibid., p. 3.
81   Duster ([1991] 2003), p. 188.
82   King (2005), p. 170.
83   Guibernau (2001), p. 263.

Chapter 6   Reactions to the End of 'Pure' National Identities

1   Zaslove (2004), p. 102.
2   See Ignazi (2003).
3   Betz (1994), p. 169.
4   For a comprehensive analysis of the various motivations explaining voting behaviour, see van der Brug, Fennema and Tillie (2000); van der Brug and Fennema (2003).
5   Eatwell (2003), p. 53.
6   Norris (2005), p. 147.

7   Ibid., p. 257.
8   Ibid., p. 18.
9   Ibid., p. 185.
10   Ibid., p. 186.
11   Ignazi (2003), p. 215.
12   Betz (2003), p. 78.
13   Ibid., p. 79.
14   Gregor (2006), p. 75.
15   See Linz ([1976] 1991), p. 15.
16   Betz (2003), p. 86.
17   Programme of the Austrian Freedom Party, adopted 30 October 1997, ch. 5, art. 1.
18   Zaslove (2004), p. 106.
19   Casals-Meseguer (2003), p. 170.
20   Ibid., p. 173.
21   See Boswell (2002); Spencer (2006).
22   Betz (1994), p. 172.
23   Küechler (1994), pp. 51ff.
24   Guibernau (1996), pp. 86–7.
25   Taguieff (1994), p. 120.
26   Küechler (1994), p. 1.
27   Anthias and Yuval-Davies (1993), p. 4.
28   Goldberg (1993), p. 150.
29   Spoonley (1993), p. 4.
30   Mény and Surel (2000), pp. 206–7.
31   Mégret (1997), ch. 3; quoted by Mény and Surel (2000), p. 207.
32   Quoted by Mény and Surel (2000), p. 211.
33   Le   Front   National,   http://www.frontnational.com/doc_prop_identite.php#
     immigration (accessed 17 February 2006).
34   Le Front National (2000) *Les Argumentaires: L'Identité*: www.frontnational.com/
     argumentaires/identite.php, p. 1 (translated from French by the author).
35   Ibid., p. 2.
36   Ibid., p. 3.
37   Ibid.
38   Le Pen (2005), p. 4.
39   Quoted in Betz (1994), p. 122.
40   Ibid., p. 128.
41   Casals-Meseguer (2003), p. 293.
42   Ibid., p. 103.
43   Norris (2005), p. 235.
44   Huntington (2004).
45   Ibid., p. 310.
46   Swain (2000), p. 4.
47   Huntington (2004), p. 312.
48   Taguieff (1994).
49   Gregor (2006), p. 73; Benoist (1986).
50   Taguieff (1994), p. 111.
51   Betz (1994), p. 183.
52   Ibid., p. 184.

Chapter 7   National Identity versus Cosmopolitan Identity

1   Held (2005), p. 10.
2   Schmidt (1998), p. 424.

3   O'Neill (1990), p. 194.
4   Sypnowich (2005), p. 57.
5   Ibid., p. 58.
6   See Beitz (1979); Beitz (1998); Pogge (1994a); Pogge (1994b); Barry (1999).
7   Pogge (1994b), p. 90.
8   Held (2002), p. 311.
9   Held (2005), p. 21.
10   Ibid., p. 27.
11   Habermas (2001), p. 118.
12   Grande (2006), p. 94.
13   Ibid., p. 96.
14   Appiah (2006), p. 140.
15   Roy (2004), p. 25.
16   Delanty (2005), p. 416.
17   Smith ([2000] 2003), pp. 278–81.
18   Human rights had to be agreed and sanctioned by representatives of nation-states. It
      was for them to concur on their formulation and meaning. In a similar manner, the
      components of a 'cosmopolitan culture' will have to be considered by a wide range
      of people representing the different cultures and civilizations worldwide. Cultural
      principles and various elements ought to comply with cosmopolitan principles – that
      is, they should imply the recognition that each person is regarded as equally worthy
      of respect and consideration.
19   Norris ([2000] 2003), p. 294.
20   Guibernau (2004), pp. 135ff.
21   Margalit and Raz (1990), pp. 447–9.
22   Tomlinson ([2000] 2003), p. 273.
23   Kymlicka (2001), p. 218.
24   Ibid., p. 239.
25   Guibernau (1996), p. 40.
26   Giddens ([1972] 1987), p. 202.
27   See Guibernau (1996), p. 41.
28   See Kant ([1795] 1996b).
29   Pogge ([2000] 2003), p. 550.
30   Tan (2004), p. 91.
31   Miller (1995), p. 83.
32   David Held refers to 'thick' and 'thin' cosmopolitanism. See Held (2005), p. 17.
33   Miller (1998), pp. 166–7.
34   Ibid.
35   Tan (2005), p. 164.
36   Ibid., p. 167.
37   Kleingeld (2000), p. 327.
38   Tönnies (1955), p. 74.
39   Ibid., pp. 74–5.
40   Ibid., p. 90.
41   Ibid., p. 88.
42   See Kymlicka (2001); Gutman (1994); Tamir (1993); Miller (1995); and Nielsen (1999).
43   Himmelfarb (1996), p. 77.
44   Tan (2005), p. 164.
45   Kymlicka (2001), p. 226.
46   Tan (2004), p. 96.
47   Kymlicka (2001), p. 227.
48   Tan (2004), p. 91.

49 Nielsen (1999), pp. 448–50.
50 See Kant (1996a), p. 329.
51 Nussbaum (1996), p. 4.
52 Berlin (1996), p. 264.

Conclusion

1 A different matter concerns the break-up of the Soviet Union and the subsequent independent status acquired by some of its former republics – a process exemplified in the continuing tensions and political demands posed by various national and ethnic minorities within the former USSR.
2 Phillips (2005).
3 Phillips (2006), p. 12.
4 See Weil (2006).

References and Bibliography

Alba, Richard D. (1990) *Ethnic Identity: The Transformation of White America*. New Haven and London: Yale University Press.

Alba, Richard, and Nee, Victor (1997) 'Rethinking Assimilation Theory for a New Era of Immigration', *International Migration Review*, 31/4, pp. 826–74.

Alex-Assensoh, Yvette, and Hanks, Lawrence J. (eds) (2000) *Black and Multiracial Politics in America*. New York and London: New York University Press.

Anderson, Benedict (1983) *Imagined Communities: Reflections on the Origins and Spread of Nationalism*. London: Verso.

Anthias, Floya, and Yuval-Davies, Nira (1993) *Racialized Boundaries: Race, Nation, Gender, Colour and Class and the Anti-Racist Struggle*. London: Routledge.

Appiah, Kwame Anthony (2006) *Cosmopolitanism: Ethics in a World of Strangers*. London and New York: Allen Lane.

Ashmore, Richard D., Jussim, Lee, and Wilder, David (2001) *Social Identity, Intergroup Conflict, and Conflict Reduction*. Oxford: Oxford University Press.

Balcells, A. (1996) *Catalan Nationalism*. London: Macmillan.

B&B Commission (1967) *Report of the Royal Commission on Bilingualism and Biculturalism*. Ottawa: Queen's Printer.

Barry, B. (1999) 'Statism and Nationalism: a Cosmopolitan Critique', in Shapiro, Ian, and Brilmayer, Lea (eds), *Global Justice*. New York: New York University Press, pp. 12–66.

Bashevkin, S. (1991) *True Patriot Love: The Politics of Canadian Nationalism*. Toronto: Oxford University Press.

Bauböck, Rainer (1994) *Transnational Citizenship: Membership and Rights in International Migration*. Cheltenham: Edward Elgar.

Bauböck, Rainer (1999) 'Immigration Control without Integration Policy: An Austrian Dilemma', in Brochmann, Grete, and Hammar, Tomas (eds), *Mechanisms of Immigration Control: A Comparative Analysis of European Regulation Policies*. Oxford: Berg, pp. 94–134.

Bauböck, Rainer (2002) 'Constructing the Boundaries of the Volk: Nation-Building and National Populism in Austrian Politics', in Wodak, Ruth, and Pelinka, Anton (eds), *The Haider Phenomenon in Austria*. New Brunswick, NJ, and London: Transaction, pp. 231–53.

Baumeister, R. (1986) *Identity: Cultural Change and the Struggle for Self*. Oxford: Oxford University Press.

Beck, Roy (1996) *The Case against Immigration: The Moral, Economic, Social, and Environmental Reasons for Reducing US Immigration back to Traditional Levels.* New York: W. W. Norton.

Beitz, C. (1979) *Political Theory and International Relations.* Princeton, NJ: Princeton University Press.

Beitz, C. (1998) 'Philosophy of International Relations', in *Routledge Encyclopedia of Philosophy.* London: Routledge.

Bell, Daniel (1975) 'Ethnicity and Social Change', in Glazer, N., and Moynihan, D. P. (eds), *Ethnicity: Theory and Experience.* Cambridge, MA: Harvard University Press.

Benoist, Alain de (1986) *Europe, tiers monde, même combat.* Paris: Robert Laffont.

Berlin, Isaiah (1996) *The Sense of Reality: Studies in Ideas and their History*, ed. Henry Hardy. London: Pimlico.

Berman, Yizhak (ed.) (1995) *Integration and Pluralism in Societies of Immigration.* Vienna: European Centre for Social Welfare Policy and Research [Eurosocial report 54/1995].

Betz, Hans-Georg (1994) *Radical Right-Wing Populism in Western Europe.* London: Macmillan.

Betz, Hans-Georg (2003) 'The Growing Threat of the Radical Right', in Merkl, Peter H., and Weinberg, Leonard (eds), *Right-Wing Extremism in the Twenty-First Century.* London: Frank Cass, pp. 74–93.

Bissoondath, N. (1994) *Selling Illusions: The Cult of Multiculturalism in Canada.* Toronto: Penguin.

Bloom, Allan (1987) *The Closing of the American Mind.* New York: Simon & Schuster.

Borjas, George J. (1990) *Friends or Strangers: The Impact of Immigrants on the U.S. Economy.* New York: Basic Books.

Borjas, George, and Freeman, Richard B. (eds) (1992) *Immigration and the Work Force: Economic Consequences for the United States and Source Areas.* Chicago: University of Chicago Press.

Boswell, Christian (2002) *European Migration Policies in Flux: Changing Patterns of Inclusion and Exclusion.* Oxford: Oxford University Press.

Breton, R. (1986) 'Multiculturalism and Canadian Nation-Building', in Cairns, Alan, and Williams, Cynthia (eds), *The Politics of Gender, Ethnicity and Language in Canada.* Toronto: University of Toronto Press, pp. 27–66.

Briggs, Vernon, Jr. (2003) *Mass Immigration and the National Interest: Policy Directions for the New Century.* 3rd edn, New York: M. E. Sharpe.

Brimelow, Peter (1995) *Alien Nation: Sense about America's Immigration Disaster.* New York: Random House.

Brochmann, Grete, and Hammar, Tomas (eds) (1999) *Mechanisms of Immigration Control: A Comparative Analysis of European Regulation Policies.* Oxford: Berg.

Brock, Gillian, and Brighouse, Harry (eds) (2005) *The Political Philosophy of Cosmopolitanism.* Cambridge: Cambridge University Press.

Brown, C. (ed.) (1994) *Political Restructuring in Europe: Ethical Perspectives*. London: Routledge.

Brown, J. L. (1990) 'The Meech Lake Accord in Historical Perspective', in Burgess, M. (ed.), *Canadian Federalism: Past, Present and Future*. Leicester: Leicester University Press, pp. 72–93.

Brubaker, Rogers (2001) 'The Return of Assimilation? Changing Perspectives on Immigration and its Sequels in France, Germany and the United States', *Ethnic and Racial Studies*, 24/4, pp. 531–48.

Brubaker, Rogers (2002) 'Ethnicity without Groups', *Archives of European Sociology* 43/2, pp. 163–89.

Bruckmüller, Ernst (1998) 'The Development of Austrian National Identity', in Luther, Kurt Richard, and Pulzer, Peter (eds), *Austria 1945–1995: Fifty Years of the Second Republic*. Aldershot: Ashgate, pp. 67–8.

Bruckmüller, Ernst (2003) *The Austrian Nation: Cultural Consciousness and Socio-Political Processes*. Riverside: CA: Ariadne Press.

Burgess, Anthony (1997) *Divided Europe*. London: Pluto Press.

Burgess, M., and Gagnon, A. G. (1993) *Comparative Federalism and Federation*. London: Harvester Wheatsheaf.

Cairns, A. C. (1996) 'Looking Back from the Future', in Trent, J. E. et al. (eds), *Québec–Canada: What is the Path Ahead? Nouveaux sentiers vers l'avenir*. Ottawa: University of Ottawa Press, pp. 77–80.

Caldwell, Christopher (2006) 'Affirmative Distraction', *New York Times*, 24 December; http://www.nytimes.com (accessed 28 February 2007).

Carens, J. H. (ed.) (1995) *Is Quebec Nationalism Just? Perspectives from Anglophone Canada*. Montreal and Kingston: McGill–Queen's University Press.

Casals-Meseguer, Xavier (2003) *Ultrapatriotas*. Barcelona: Crítica.

Castles, Stephen, and Miller, Mark J. ([1993] 1998) *The Age of Migration*. 2nd edn, London: Macmillan.

CIS (Centro de Investigaciones Sociológicas) (2003) 'Datos de Opinión: Instituciones y autonomías', *Boletín 31*. Madrid: CIS; http://www.cis.es (accessed 16 February 2004).

Cohen, Abner (1969) *Custom and Politics in Urban Africa: A Study of Hausa Migrants in a Yoruba Town*. London: Routledge & Kegan Paul.

Cohen, Joshua (ed.) (1996) *For Love of Country: Debating the Limits of Patriotism: Martha C. Nussbaum with Respondents*. Boston: Beacon Press.

Connor, Walker (1994a) *Ethno-Nationalism: The Quest for Understanding*. Princeton, NJ: Princeton University Press.

Connor, Walker (1994b) 'When is a Nation?', in Hutchinson, John, and Smith, Anthony D. (eds), *Nationalism*, vol. 1. Oxford: Oxford University Press, pp. 154–9.

Conway, J. F. (1992) *Debts to Pay: English Canada and Quebec from the Conquest to the Referendum*. Toronto: James Lorimer.

Cook, R., Saywell, J. T., and Ricker, J. C. (eds) (1963) *Canada: A Modern Study*. Toronto: Clarke Irwin.

Council of Europe, Council for Cultural Co-operation, Culture Committee (2001) *Cultural Policy and Cultural Diversity, National Report, Austria.* Strasbourg, 20–2 February; http://www.coe.int.

Couture, Jacqueline, and Nielsen, Kai (2005) 'Cosmopolitanism and the Compatriot Priority Principle', in Brock, G., and Brighouse, H. (eds), *The Political Philosophy of Cosmopolitanism.* Cambridge: Cambridge University Press, pp. 180–95.

Crouch, Colin (1999) *Social Change in Western Europe.* Oxford: Oxford University Press.

Cruse, Harold (1967) *The Crisis of the Negro Intellectual.* New York: Morrow.

Cummins, J., and Danesi, M. (1990) *Heritage Languages: The Development and Denial of Canada's Linguistic Resources.* Toronto: Our Schools/Our Selves Foundation.

Davies, N. (1996) *Europe: A History.* London: Pimlico.

Delanty, Gerard (2005) 'The Idea of a Cosmopolitan Europe: On the Cultural Significance of Europeanization', *International Review of Sociology,* 15/3, pp. 405–21.

Deloria, Vine, Jr. (1985) *Behind the Trail of Broken Treaties.* Austin: University of Texas Press.

Den Boer, Pim (1995) 'Europe to 1914: The Making of an Idea', in Wilson, K., and van der Dussen, J. (eds), *The History of the Idea of Europe.* London: Routledge.

Deutsch, Karl ([1953] 1966) *Nationalism and Social Communication.* New York: MIT Press and Wiley.

Dion, J. (1996) 'Un Bureau d'information vantera les vertus de Canada', *Le Devoir,* 10 July.

Duster, Troy ([1991] 2003) 'Understanding Self-Segregation on the Campus', *Chronicle of Higher Education,* September; quoted in Yanow, Dvora, *Constructing 'Race' and 'Ethnicity' in America: Category-Making in Public Policy and Administration.* Armonk, NY: M. E. Sharpe.

Eatwell, Roger (2003) 'Ten Theories of the Extreme Right', in Merkl, Peter H., and Weinberg, Leonard (eds), *Right-Wing Extremism in the Twenty-First Century.* London: Frank Cass, pp. 47–73.

Elazar, D. (1987) *Exploring Federalism.* Tuscaloosa, AL: University of Alabama Press.

Erdmann, Karl Kietrich (1985) 'Drei Staaten – zwei Nationen – ein Volk? Überlegungen zur deutsche Geschichte seit der Teilung', *Geschichte in Wissenschaft und Unterricht,* 36, pp. 671–83.

Eriksen, Thomas Hylland (1993) *Ethnicity and Nationalism.* London: Pluto Press.

Eriksen, Thomas Hylland (2001) 'Ethnic Identity, National Identity and Intergroup Conflict', in Ashmore, Richard D., Jussim, Lee, and Wilder, David (eds), *Social Identity, Intergroup Conflict, and Conflict Reduction.* Oxford: Oxford University Press, pp. 42–68.

Eurobarometer 62/ fieldwork Oct–Nov. 2004. Publication December 2004. http://europa.eu.int/com/public-opinion/index-en.htm.

European Commission, Forward Studies Unit (1998) *Survey on National Identity and Deep-Seated Attitudes towards European Integration in the Ten Applicant Countries of Central and Eastern Europe,* working paper.

European Monitoring Centre on Racism and Xenophobia (2005) *Majorities' Attitudes Towards Minorities: Key Findings from the Eurobarometer and the European Social Survey Summary.*

Finkielkraut, Alain (1987) *La Défaite de la pensée.* Paris: Gallimard.

Fitzmaurice, J. (1985) *Quebec and Canada: Past, Present and Future.* London: C. Hurst.

Fleck, Elfie (1995) 'Intercultural Education in Austria', in Berman, Yizhak (ed.), *Integration and Pluralism in Societies of Immigration.* Vienna: European Centre for Social Welfare Policy and Research [Eurosocial report 54/1995].

Foner, E. (1990) *A Short History of Reconstruction, 1863–1877.* New York: Harper & Row.

Forst, Rainer (1997) 'Foundations of a Theory of Multicultural Justice', *Constellations*, 4/1, pp. 63–71.

Fossas, Enric (1999) 'Asimetría y plurinacionalidad en el estado autonómico', in Fossas, Enric, and Requejo, Ferran, *Asimetría federal y estado plurinacional.* Madrid: Trotta, pp. 275–301.

Fossas, Enric, and Requejo, Ferran (1999) *Asimetría federal y estado plurinacional.* Madrid: Trotta.

Fukuyama, Francis (1995) 'Alien Nation Review', *National Review*, 47/8, p. 77.

Fukuyama, Francis (2007) 'Identity and Migration', *Prospect*, February, pp. 26–31.

Furnivall, J. S. (1948) *Colonial Policy and Practice.* Cambridge: Cambridge University Press.

Gagnon, Alain (1998) *Quebec y el Federalismo Canadiense.* Madrid: Consejo Superior de Investigaciones Científicas.

Gagnon, Alain (2003) 'Undermining Federalism and Feeding Minority Nationalism', in Gagnon, A., Guibernau, M., and Rocher, F. (eds), *The Conditions of Diversity in Multinational Democracies.* Montreal: IRPP, pp. 295–312.

Gagnon, Alain (ed.) (2004a) *Quebec: State and Society.* 3rd edn, Toronto: Broadview Press.

Gagnon, Alain (2004b) 'Quebec-Canada's Constitutional Dossier', in Gagnon, A. (ed.), *Quebec: State and Society.* 3rd edn, Toronto: Broadview Press, pp. 127–49.

Gagnon, Alain, and Iacovino, Raffaele (2007) *Federalism, Citizenship and Quebec: Debating Multinationalism.* Toronto: University of Toronto Press.

Gagnon, Alain, Guibernau, Montserrat, and Rocher, François (2003) *The Conditions of Diversity in Multinational Democracies.* Montreal: IRPP.

Gärtner, Reinhold (2002) 'The FPÖ, Foreigners, and Racism in the Haider Era', in Wodak, Ruth, and Pelinka, Anton (eds), *The Haider Phenomenon in Austria.* New Brunswick, NJ, and London: Transaction, pp. 17–31.

Geertz, Clifford (1973) *The Interpretation of Cultures.* London: Fontana.

Gellner, Ernest (1983) *Nations and Nationalism.* Oxford: Blackwell.

Gellner, Ernest (1987) *Culture, Identity and Politics.* Cambridge: Cambridge University Press.

Gibbins, Roger, and Laforest, Guy (eds) (1998) *Beyond the Impasse: Toward Reconciliation*. Montreal: IRPP.

Giddens, Anthony (1985) *The Nation-State and Violence*. Cambridge: Polity.

Giddens, Anthony ([1972] 1987) *Durkheim on Politics and the State*. London: Fontana.

Giddens, Anthony (2006) *Europe in the Global Age*. Cambridge: Polity.

Giner, Salvador (2001) *Teoría sociológica clásica*. Barcelona: Ariel.

Giner, Salvador (2003) *Carisma y razón*. Madrid: Alianza.

Glazer, Nathan (1996) 'Limits of Loyalty', in Cohen, Joshua (ed.), *For Love of Country: Debating the Limits of Patriotism: Martha C. Nussbaum with Respondents*. Boston: Beacon Press, pp. 61–5.

Glazer, Nathan (1997) *We Are All Multiculturalist Now*. Cambridge, MA: Harvard University Press.

Glazer, Nathan (2002) 'The Emergence of an American Ethnic Pattern', in Takaki, Ronald (ed.), *Debating Diversity: Clashing Perspectives on Race and Ethnicity in America*. Oxford and New York: Oxford University Press, pp. 7–22.

Glazer, Nathan, and Moynihan, Daniel Patrick (1970) *Beyond the Melting Pot*. 2nd edn, Cambridge, MA: MIT Press.

Goddard, V., Llobera, J., and Shore, C. (eds) (1996) *The Anthropology of Europe*. Oxford: Berg.

Goldberg, D. T. (1993) *Racist Culture: Philosophy and the Politics of Meaning*. Oxford: Blackwell.

Gordon, Milton (1964) *Assimilation in American Life*. Oxford: Oxford University Press.

Grande, E. (2006) 'Cosmopolitan Political Science', *British Journal of Sociology*, 57/1, pp. 87–111.

Gregor, A. James (2006) *The Search for Neofascism: The Use and Abuse of Social Science*. Cambridge: Cambridge University Press.

Guibernau, M. (1996) *Nationalisms: The Nation-State and Nationalism in the Twentieth Century*. Cambridge: Polity.

Guibernau, M. (1999) *Nations without States*. Cambridge: Polity.

Guibernau, M. (2000) 'Nationalism and Intellectuals in Nations without States: The Catalan Case', *Political Studies*, 48/5, pp. 989–1005.

Guibernau, M. (2001) 'Globalization and the Nation-State', in Guibernau, M., and Hutchinson, J., *Understanding Nationalism*. Cambridge: Polity, pp. 242–68.

Guibernau, M. (2004a) 'Anthony D. Smith on Nations and National Identity: A Critical Assessment', *Nations and Nationalism*, 10/1–2, pp. 125–41.

Guibernau, M. (2004b) *Catalan Nationalism: Francoism, Transition and Democracy*. London: Routledge.

Guibernau, M. (2006) *Governing Europe: The Developing Agenda*. Milton Keynes: Open University Press.

Guibernau, M., and Hutchinson, J. (2001) *Understanding Nationalism*. Cambridge: Polity.

Guibernau, M., and Rex, J. (eds) (1997) *The Ethnicity Reader: Nationalism, Multiculturalism and Migration.* Cambridge: Polity.

Gutmann, Amy (ed.) (1994) *Multiculturalism: Examining the 'Politics of Recognition'.* Princeton, NJ: Princeton University Press.

Habermas, J. (2001) *The Postnational Constellation: Political Essays.* Cambridge: Polity.

Haller, Max (1991) 'L'identità regionale in Europa', paper of the working group 'Promozione delle Culture Regionali' at the Convention of the Assembly of the Regions of Europe, Trento 9–10 October 1990, Trento, 1991.

Haller, Max (1999) 'Voiceless Submission or Deliberate Choice? European Integration and the Relation between National and European Identity', in Kriesi, H. et al. (eds), *Nation and National Identity: The European Experience in Perspective.* Chur: Rüegger, pp. 263–96.

Haller, Max et al. (1986) *Social Survey 1986: Opinioni, valori et modi di vita in Alto Adige: Resultati di una indagine rappresentativa.* Bolzano: Instituto Provinciale di Statistica della Provincia Autonoma di Bolzano–Alto Adige.

Haller, Max et al. (1996) *Identität und Nationalstolz der Österreicher: Gesellschaftliche Ursachen und Funktionen, Herausbildung und Transformationen seit 1945, internationaler Vergleich.* Vienna: Böhlau.

Harrison, B. R., and Marmen, L. (1994) *Languages in Canada.* Ottawa: Statistics Canada.

Hayward, J. (1996) *Elitism, Population and European Elites.* Oxford: Oxford University Press.

Hazell, R. (ed.) (2000) *The State and the Nations.* Exeter: Imprint Academic.

Held, David (2002) 'Cosmopolitanism: Ideas, Realities and Deficits', in Held, David, and McGrew, Anthony (eds), *Governing Globalization: Power, Authority and Global Governance.* Cambridge: Polity, pp. 305–24.

Held, David (2005) 'Principles of Cosmopolitan Order', in Brock, Gillian, and Brighouse, Harry (eds), *The Political Philosophy of Cosmopolitanism.* Cambridge: Cambridge University Press, pp. 10–27.

Held, David, and McGrew, Anthony (eds) (2002) *Governing Globalization: Power, Authority and Global Governance.* Cambridge: Polity.

Held, David, and McGrew, Anthony ([2000] 2003) *The Global Transformations Reader.* 2nd edn, Cambridge: Polity.

Henderson, Errol A. (2000) 'War, Political Cycles, and the Pendulum Thesis', in Alex-Assensoh, Yvette M., and Hanks, Lawrence J. (eds), *Black and Multiracial Politics in America.* New York and London: New York University Press, pp. 337–74.

Herrnstein, Richard J., and Murray, Charles (1995) *The Bell Curve: Intelligence and Class Structure in American Life.* New York: Free Press.

Himmelfarb, G. (1996) 'The Illusions of Cosmopolitanism', in Cohen, Joshua (ed.), *For Love of Country: Debating the Limits of Patriotism: Martha C. Nussbaum with Respondents.* Boston: Beacon Press, pp. 72–7.

Hirsch, E. D. (1987) *Cultural Literacy: What Every American Needs to Know.* Boston: Houghton Mifflin.

Hobsbawm, Eric, and Ranger, Terence (eds) (1983) *The Invention of Tradition*. Cambridge: Cambridge University Press.

Hoerder, Dirk (ed.) (2003) *The Historical Practice of Diversity*. Oxford and New York: Berghahn.

Hudon, R., and Pelletier, R. (eds) (1991) *L'Engagement intellectuel: Mélanges en l'honneur de Léon Dion*. Sainte-Foy: Presses de l'Université Laval.

Huntington, Samuel P. (1996) *The Clash of Civilizations and the Remaking of World Order*. New York: Simon & Schuster.

Huntington, Samuel P. (2004) *Who Are We? The Challenges to America's National Identity*. New York: Simon & Schuster.

Hutchinson, John (2005) *Nations as Zones of Conflict*. London: Sage.

Ichijo, Atsuko, and Spohn, Willfried (eds) (2005) *Entangled Identities: Nations and Europe*. Aldershot: Ashgate.

Ignazi, Piero (2003) *Extreme Right Parties in Western Europe*. Oxford: Oxford University Press.

Isbister, John (1996) *The Immigration Debate: Remaking America*. West Hartford, CT: Kumarian Press.

Jaimes, Annette (ed.) (1992) *The State of Native America: Genocide, Colonization, and Resistance*. Boston: South End Press.

Josephy, A., Jr. (1971) *Red Power: The American Indians' Fight for Freedom*. New York: American Heritage Press.

Kant, Immanuel (1996a) *Practical Philosophy*. Cambridge: Cambridge University Press.

Kant, Immanuel (1996b) 'Toward Perpetual Peace' [1795], in *Practical Philosophy*. Cambridge: Cambridge University Press, pp. 311–52.

Keating, Michael (1999) 'Asymmetrical Government: Multinational States in an Integrating Europe', *Publius: The Journal of Federalism*, 29/1, pp. 71–86.

Keating, Michael (2000) 'The Minority Nations of Spain and European Integration: A New Framework for Autonomy', *Journal of Spanish Cultural Studies*, 1/1, pp. 29–42.

Keating, Michael (2001) *Nations against the State: The New Politics of Nationalism in Quebec, Catalonia and Scotland*. 2nd edn, London: Palgrave.

Kershen, Anne (2005) *Strangers, Aliens and Asians: Huguenots, Jews and Bangladeshis in Spitalfields 1660–2000*. London: Taylor & Francis.

King, Desmond (2005) *The Liberty of Strangers: Making the American Nation*. Oxford: Oxford University Press.

Kleingeld, P. (2000) 'Kantian Patriotism', *Philosophy and Public Affairs*, 29/4, pp. 313–41.

Kohn, H. ([1955] 1965) *Nationalism: Its Meaning and History*. Rev. edn, Princeton, NJ: Van Nostrand.

Kraler, Albert, and Sohler, Karin (2005) *Active Civic Participation of Immigrants in Austria* (Country Report prepared for the European research project Politis), Oldenburg: Carl Von Ossietzky Universität; http://www.uni-oldenburg.de/politis-europe.

Kriesi, H. et al. (eds) (1999) *Nation and National Identity: The European Experience in Perspective*. Chur: Rüegger.

Kryder, Daniel (1997) 'War and the Politics of Black Militancy in the Twentieth Century', paper presented to the annual conference of the American Political Science Association, Washington, DC, August.

Küechler, Manfred (1994) 'The Germans and the "Others": Racism, Xenophobia, or Legitimate Conservatism?' *German Politics*, 3, pp. 47–74.

Kymlicka, Will (1989) *Liberalism, Community and Culture*. Oxford: Oxford University Press.

Kymlicka, Will (1998) 'Multinational Federalism in Canada: Rethinking the Partnership', *Policy Options* [Montreal], March, pp. 5–9.

Kymlicka, Will (2001) *Politics in the Vernacular: Nationalism, Multiculturalism and Citizenship*. Oxford: Oxford University Press.

Lacqueur, Walter (ed.) ([1976] 1991) *Fascism: A Reader's Guide*. Cambridge: Scolar Press.

Laforest, Guy (1995) *Trudeau and the End of a Canadian Dream*. Montreal and Kingston: McGill–Queen's University Press.

Lajoie, A. (2004) 'The Clarity Act in its Context', in Gagnon, A. (ed.), *Quebec: State and Society*. 3rd edn, Toronto: Broadview, pp. 151–64.

Lee, Sharon, M., and Edmonston, Barry (2005) *New Marriages, New Families: US Racial and Hispanic Intermarriage*, *Population Bulletin*, 60/2, pp. 1–22; http://www.prb.org (accessed 26 February 2007).

Le Pen, Jean-Marie (2005) '1er mai 2005: Le discours du NON au référendum sur la Constitution européenne', www.frontnational.com/doc_interventions_detail.php?id_inter=36 (accessed 17 February 2006).

Linz, Juan ([1976] 1991) 'Some Notes toward a Comparative Study of Fascism in Sociological Historical Perspective', in Lacqueur, Walter (ed.), *Fascism: A Reader's Guide*. Cambridge: Scolar Press.

Lipset, Seymour Martin (1963) *The First New Nation*. New York: Basic Books.

Lipset, Seymour Martin (1996) *American Exceptionalism: A Double-Edged Nation*. New York: W. W. Norton.

Lucassen, Leo (2002) 'Bringing Structure Back in: Economic and Political Determinants of Immigration in Cities, 1920–1940', *Social Science History*, 26/3, pp. 503–29.

Luther, Kurt Richard, and Pulzer, Peter (eds) (1998) *Austria 1945–1995: Fifty Years of the Second Republic*. Aldershot: Ashgate.

McCormick, Joseph, and Franklin, Sekou (2000) 'Expressions of Racial Consciousness', in Alex-Assensoh, Yvette, and Hanks, Lawrence J. (eds), *Black and Multiracial Politics in America*. New York and London: New York University Press, pp. 315–36.

McCrone, David (2002) 'National Identity in Scotland', briefing paper, Institute of Governance, University of Edinburgh, 10 January; www.institute-of-governance.org/onlinepub/mccrone/bp_scottish_identity.html (accessed 15 March 2005).

McCrone, David, and Paterson, Lindsay (2002) 'The Conundrum of Scottish Independence', *Scottish Affairs*, no. 40, pp. 54–75.

McRoberts, Kenneth (1997) *Misconceiving Canada: The Struggle for National Unity.* Toronto: Oxford University Press.

McRoberts, Kenneth (2001) *Catalonia: Nation Building without a State.* Oxford: Oxford University Press.

McRoberts, Kenneth (2004) 'The Future of the Nation-State and Quebec–Canada Relations', in Seymour, M. (ed.), *The Fate of the Nation State.* Montreal and Kingston: McGill–Queen's University Press, pp. 390–402.

McWhinney, E. (1982) *Canada and the Constitution, 1960–1978.* Toronto: University of Toronto Press.

Manning, Peter (1992) *The New Canada.* Toronto: Macmillan.

Margalit, Avishai, and Raz, Joseph (1990) 'National Self-Determination', *Journal of Philosophy*, 87/9, pp. 439–61.

Márquez, Benjamin (2003) *Constructing Identities in Mexican-American Political Organizations: Choosing Issues, Taking Sides.* Austin: University of Texas Press.

Marshall, T. H. (1973) *Class, Citizenship and Social Development.* Westport, CT: Greenwood Press.

Mayall, James ([1990] 1992) *Nationalism and International Society.* Cambridge: Cambridge University Press.

Mazower, Mark (1998) *Dark Continent: Europe's Twentieth Century.* London: Allen Lane.

Mégret, Bruno (1997) *L'Alternative nationale.* Paris: Éditions nationales.

Melucci, Antonio (1982) *L'invenzione del presente: Movimenti, identità, bisogni individuali.* Bologna: Il Mulino.

Mény, Yves, and Surel, Yves (2000) *Par le peuple, pour le people.* Paris: Fayard.

Merkl, Peter H., and Weinberg, Leonard (eds) (2003) *Right-Wing Extremism in the Twenty-First Century.* London: Frank Cass.

Meyer, Stephen (1980) 'Adapting the Immigrant to the Line: Americanization in the Ford Factory, 1914–1921', *Journal of Social History*, 14, pp. 76–102.

Michaels, Walter Benn (2006a) *The Trouble with Diversity: How We Learned to Love Identity and Ignore Equality.* New York: Metropolitan Books.

Michaels, Walter Benn (2006b) 'The Trouble with Diversity', *American Prospect*, 9 December, pp. 1–7; http://www.prospect.org/web/ (accessed 28 February 2007).

Miller, David (1995) *On Nationality.* Oxford: Oxford University Press.

Miller, David (1998) 'The Limits of Cosmopolitan Justice', in Mapel, D., and Nardin, T. (eds), *International Society: Diverse Ethical Perspectives.* Princeton, NJ: Princeton University Press.

Moch, Leslie Page (2003) *Moving Europeans: Migration in Western Europe since 1650.* Bloomington: Indiana University Press.

Myrdal, Gunnar (1944) *An American Dilemma.* 2 vols, New York: Harper & Row.

Nairn, Tom (1977) *The Break-Up of Britain: Crisis and Neo-Nationalism.* London: New Left Books.

Nash, Mary (2005) *Inmigrantes en nuestro espejo: Inmigración y discurso periodístico en la prensa Espanola*. Barcelona: Icaria.

National Centre for Social Research (2003) *Devolution and Constitutional Change, 2001* (SN 4766); www.data-archive.ac.uk (accessed 16 February 2004).

National Contact Point Austria (2004) *The Impact of Immigration on Austria's Society: A Survey of Recent Austrian Migration Research*. Vienna: National Contact Point Austria with the European Migration Network; www.emn.at.

Nielsen, Kai (1999) 'Cosmopolitan Nationalism', *Monist*, 82/1, pp. 446–90.

Noël, Alain (2000) 'Without Quebec: Collaborative Federalism with a Footnote', *Policy Matters*, 1/2, pp. 1–26.

Norris, Pippa ([2000] 2003) 'Global Governance and Cosmopolitan Citizens', in Held, D., and McGrew, A. (eds), *The Global Transformations Reader*. 2nd edn, Cambridge: Polity.

Norris, Pippa (2005) *Radical Right: Voters and Parties in the Electoral Market*. Cambridge: Cambridge University Press.

Novak, Michael (1971) *The Rise of the Unmeltable Ethnics*. New York: Macmillan.

Nussbaum, Martha C. (1966) 'Patriotism and Cosmopolitanism', in Cohen, Joshua (ed.), *For Love of Country: Debating the Limits of Patriotism: Martha C. Nussbaum with Respondents*. Boston: Beacon Press, pp. 2–20.

Oliver, M. (1991) 'Laurendeau et Trudeau: leurs opinions sur le Canada', in Hudon, R. and Pelletier, R. (eds), *L'Engagement intellectuel: Mélanges en l'honneur de Léon Dion*. Sainte-Foy: Presses de l'Université Laval, pp. 339–68.

O'Neill, O. (1990) 'Enlightenment as Autonomy: Kant's Vindication of Reason', in Jordanova, L., and Hulme, P. (eds), *The Enlightenment and its Shadows*. London: Routledge.

Osmond, John (2000) 'A Constitutional Convention by Other Means: The First Year of the National Assembly for Wales', in Hazell, Robert (ed.), *The State and the Nations*. Exeter: Imprint Academic, pp. 37–77.

Parekh, Bhikhu (1997) 'Dilemmas of a Theory of Multicultural Citizenship', *Constellations*, 4/1, pp. 54–62.

Parekh, Bhikhu (1999) 'What is Multiculturalism?', *Seminar*, December, pp. 1–8; http://www.india-seminar.com.

Parekh, Bhikhu (2000) *The Future of Multi-Ethnic Britain: The Parekh Report*. London: Profile Books.

Park, Robert Ezra (1930) 'Assimilation, Social', in Seligman, E., and Johnson, A. (eds), *Encyclopedia of the Social Sciences*. New York: Macmillan.

Park, Robert Ezra, and Burgess, E. ([1921] 1969) *Introduction to the Science of Sociology*. Chicago: University of Chicago Press.

Parman, D. L. (1994) *Indians and the American West in the Twentieth Century*. Bloomington: Indiana University Press.

Pérez-Díaz, V. (1998) 'The Public Sphere and a European Civil Society', in Alexander, J. (ed.), *Real Civil Societies*. London: Sage.

Phillips, Melanie (2006) *Londonistan: How Britain is Creating a Terror State Within*. London: Gibson Square.

Phillips, Trevor (2005) 'After 7/7: Sleepwalking to Segregation', speech to Manchester Council for Community Relations, 22 September; http://www.cre.gov.uk (accessed 18 November 2006).

Pogge, Thomas W. (1994a) 'An Egalitarian Law of Peoples', *Philosophy and Public Affairs*, 23, pp. 195–224.

Pogge, Thomas W. (1994b) 'Cosmopolitanism and Sovereignty', in Brown, C. (ed.), *Political Restructuring in Europe: Ethical Perspectives*. London: Routledge, pp. 89–102.

Pogge, Thomas W. ([2000] 2003) 'Priorities of Global Justice', in Held, D., and McGrew, A. (eds), *The Global Transformations Reader*. 2nd edn, Cambridge: Polity, pp. 548–58.

Preston, P. (1986) *The Triumph of Democracy in Spain*. London: Routledge.

Preston, P. (2003) *Juan Carlos: Rey de un pueblo*. Barcelona: Plaza y Janés.

Puntscher-Riekmann, Sonja (1998) *Die kommissarische Neuordnung Europas*. Berlin: Springer Verlag.

Putnam, Robert (2000) *Bowling Alone*. New York: Simon & Schuster.

Quebec Chief Electoral Office (1995) *Rapport préliminaire des résultats du dépouillement des votes le soir du scrutin: Référendum du 30 octobre 1995*, Quebec City: Bibliothèque nationale du Québec.

Quebec Government (1979) *Quebec–Canada: A New Deal: The Government's Proposal for a New Partnership between Equals: Sovereignty Association*. Quebec City: Éditeur official.

Rable, G. C. (1984) *But There Was No Peace: The Role of Violence in the Politics of Reconstruction*. Athens: University of Georgia Press.

Requejo, Ferran (2000) 'Democràcia, partits i escenaris de futur', *Idees*, no. 6, April–June, pp. 108–14.

Requejo, Ferran (ed.) (2001) *Democracy and National Pluralism*. London: Routledge.

Resina, Joan Ramon (2002) 'Post-National Spain? Post-Spanish Spain?', *Nations and Nationalism*, 8/3, pp. 377–96.

Resnick, P. (1994) *Thinking English Canada*. Toronto: Stoddart.

Rex, John (1997) 'The Concept of Multicultural Society', in Guibernau, M., and Rex, J. (eds), *The Ethnicity Reader: Nationalism, Multiculturalism and Migration*. Cambridge: Polity, pp. 205–20.

Rex, John (2005) *Theoretical Essays on Race and Ethnic Relations*. Paris: L'Harmattan.

Rex, John, and Singh, G. (2004) *Governance within Multicultural Societies*. Aldershot: Ashgate.

Riquer, Borja de, and Culla, Joan B. (1989) *El Franquisme i la transició democràtica (1939–1988)*, vol. 7 of Vilar, Pierre (ed.), *Història de Catalunya*. Barcelona: Edicions 62.

Robbins, R. L. (1992) 'Self-Determination and Subordination', in Jaimes, Annette (ed.), *The State of Native America: Genocide, Colonization, and Resistance*. Boston: South End Press.

Rocher, F., and Verrelli, N. (2003) 'Constitutional Democracy in Canada: From the Canadian Supreme Court Reference on Quebec Secession to the Clarity Act', in

Gagnon, A., Guibernau, M., and Rocher, F. (eds), *The Conditions of Diversity in Multinational Democracies*. Montreal: IRPP, pp. 207–40.

Roy, Oliver (2004) *Globalized Islam: The Search for a New Ummah*. New York: Columbia University Press.

Russell, P. H. (1993) *Constitutional Odyssey: Can Canadians become a Sovereign People?* Toronto: University of Toronto Press, pp. 1–33.

Salins, Peter (1997) *Assimilation American Style*. New York: Basic Books.

Samuelson, Robert J. (2002) 'The Limits of Immigration', in Takaki, Ronald (ed.), *Debating Diversity: Clashing Perspectives on Race and Ethnicity in America*. Oxford and New York: Oxford University Press, pp. 217–18.

Schlesinger, Arthur M. (1992) *The Disuniting of America*. New York: W. W. Norton.

Schlesinger, Arthur M. (2002) 'The Return of the Melting Pot', in Takaki, Ronald (ed.), *Debating Diversity: Clashing Perspectives on Race and Ethnicity in America*. Oxford and New York: Oxford University Press, pp. 257–9.

Schmidt, J. (1998) 'Civility, Enlightenment and Society: Conceptual Confusions and Kantian Remedies', *American Political Science Review*, no. 92, pp. 419–27.

Schnapper, Dominique (2000) *Qu'est-ce que la citoyenneté?* Paris: Folio.

Schnapper, Dominique (2006) *Providential Democracy: An Essay on Contemporary Equality*, trans. John Taylor. New Brunswick, NJ, and London: Transaction.

Schneiderman, D. (1998) 'Human Rights, Fundamental Differences? Multiple Charters in a Partnership Frame', in Gibbins, R. and Laforest, G. (eds), *Beyond the Impasse: Toward Reconciliation*. Montreal: IRPP, pp. 147–76.

Seymour, M. (ed.) (2004) *The Fate of the Nation State*. Montreal and Kingston: McGill–Queen's University Press.

Seymour, M. (2005) 'Quebec Nationalism and Canadian Federalism', in http://pages.infinit.net/mseymour/apage/cambridge.

Shapiro, Ian, and Brilmayer, Lea (eds) (1999) *Global Justice*. New York: New York University Press.

Shils, Edward (1957) 'Primordial, Personal, Sacred and Civil Ties', *British Journal of Sociology*, 7, pp. 13–45.

Smith, Anthony D. (1986) *The Ethnic Origins of Nations*. Oxford: Blackwell.

Smith, Anthony, D. (1991) *National Identity*. London: Penguin.

Smith, Anthony D. (1995) *Nations and Nationalism in a Global Era*. Cambridge: Polity.

Smith, Anthony D. (1998) *Nationalism and Modernism*. London: Routledge.

Smith, Anthony D. (2002) 'When is a Nation?' *Geopolitics*, 7/2, pp. 5–32.

Smith, Anthony D. ([2000] 2003) 'Towards a Global Culture?', in Held, D., and McGrew, A. (eds), *The Global Transformations Reader*. 2nd edn, Cambridge: Polity, pp. 278–96.

Smith, Graham (1995) *Federalism: The Multiethnic Challenge*. London: Longman.

Smith, M. G. (1965) *The Plural Society in the British West Indies*. Berkeley and Los Angeles: University of California Press.

Solé Tura, J. (1985) *Nacionalidades y nacionalismos en Espana: Autonomías, federalismo, autodeterminación.* Madrid: Alianza.

Soysal, Yasemin N. (1994) *Limits of Citizenship: Migrants and Postnational Membership in Europe.* Chicago and London: University of Chicago Press.

Spencer, Sarah (ed.) (2006) *The Politics of Migration: Global Capital, Migrant Labour and the Nation-State.* Aldershot: Ashgate.

Spinner-Halev, Jeff (1994) *The Boundaries of Citizenship: Race, Ethnicity, and Nationality in the Liberal State.* Baltimore and London: Johns Hopkins University Press.

Spohn, Willfried (2005) 'Austria: From Habsburg Empire to a Small Nation in Europe', in Ichijo, Atsuko, and Spohn, Willfried (eds), *Entangled Identities: Nations and Europe.* Aldershot: Ashgate, pp. 55–71.

Spoonley, P. (1993) *Racism and Ethnicity.* Auckland: Oxford University Press.

Steinberg, Stephen (1995) *Turning Back: The Retreat from Racial Justice in American Thought and Policy.* Boston: Beacon Press.

Steinberg, Stephen (2005) 'Immigration, African Americans, and Race Discourse', *New Politics,* 10/3, pp. 1–19; http://www.wpunj.edu/newpol/issue39/Steinberg39.htm (accessed 15 February 2007).

Stone, John (1975) 'The "Migrant Factor" in a Plural Society: A South African Case Study', *International Migration Review,* 9/1, pp. 15–28.

Swain, Carol M. (2000) *The New White Nationalism in America: Its Challenge to Integration.* New York: Cambridge University Press.

Sypnowich, C. (2005) 'Cosmopolitans, Cosmopolitanism, and Human Flourishing' in Brock, Gillian, and Brighouse, Harry (eds), *The Political Philosophy of Cosmopolitanism.* Cambridge: Cambridge University Press, pp. 55–74.

Taguieff, Pierre-André (1994) *Sur la Nouvelle droite: jalons d'une analyse critique.* Paris: Descartes.

Takaki, Ronald (ed.) (2002) *Debating Diversity: Clashing Perspectives on Race and Ethnicity in America.* Oxford and New York: Oxford University Press.

Tamir, Yael (1993) *Liberal Nationalism.* Princeton, NJ: Princeton University Press.

Tan, K. C. (2004) *Justice without Borders: Cosmopolitanism, Nationalism and Patriotism.* Cambridge: Cambridge University Press.

Tan, K. C. (2005) 'The Demands of Justice and National Allegiances', in Brock, G., and Brighouse, H. (eds), *The Political Philosophy of Cosmopolitanism.* Cambridge: Cambridge University Press, pp. 164–79.

Taub, Mark (1995) 'Alien Nation Review: The Far Right Leans into the Bell Curve', *The Guardian,* 5 May.

Taylor, Charles (1994) 'The Politics of Recognition', in Gutmann, Amy (ed.), *Multiculturalism.* Princeton, NJ: Princeton University Press, pp. 25–74.

Ter Wal, Jessica (2002) 'Anti-Foreigner Campaigns in the Austrian Freedom Party and the Italian Northern League: The Discursive Construction of Identity', in Wodak, Ruth, and Pelinka, Anton (eds), *The Haider Phenomenon in Austria.* New Brunswick, NJ, and London, Transaction, pp. 157–75.

Thernstrom, Stephan (1995) 'Has the Melting Pot Begun to Boil?', *Washington Post*, 2 April.

Thompson, John B. (1990) *Ideology and Modern Culture*. Cambridge: Polity.

Tischauser, Leslie V. (2002) *The Changing Nature of Racial and Ethnic Conflict in United States History*. New York: University Press of America.

Todd, Emmanuel (1994) *Le Destin des immigrés: assimilation et ségrégation dans les démocraties occidentals*. Paris: Seuil.

Tomaney, J. (2000) 'The Regional Governance of England', in Hazell, R. (ed.), *The State and the Nations*. Exeter: Imprint Academic, pp. 117–22.

Tomlinson, J. ([2000] 2003) 'Global and Cultural Identity', in Held, D., and McGrew, A. (eds), *The Global Transformations Reader*. 2nd edn, Cambridge: Polity.

Tönnies, Ferdinand (1955) *Community and Association (Gemeinschaft und Gesellschaft)*, trans. Charles P. Loomis. London: Routledge & Kegan Paul.

Trent, J. E. et al. (eds) (1996) *Québec–Canada: What is the Path Ahead? Nouveaux sentiers vers l'avenir*. Ottawa: University of Ottawa Press.

Tully, James (1995) 'Let's Talk: The Quebec Referendum and the Future of Canada', Austin–Hempel Lecture, Dalhousie University, 23–4 March.

Ungar, Sanford, J. (1998) *Fresh Blood: The New American Immigrants*. New York: Simon & Schuster.

US Census Bureau (2001) *Statistical Abstract of the United States 2001*. Washington, DC: Government Printing Office.

US Immigration and Naturalization Service (2002) *1999 Statistical Yearbook of the Immigration and Naturalization Service*. Washington, DC: Government Printing Office.

Urwin, Derek W. (1993) *The Community of Europe*. London: Longman.

van der Brug, Wouter, and Fennema, Meindert (2003) 'Protest or Mainstream? How the European Anti-immigrant Parties Developed into Two Separate Groups by 1999', *European Journal of Political Research*, 42, pp. 55–76.

van der Brug, Wouter, Fennema, Meindert, and Tillie, Jean (2000) 'Anti-immigrant Parties in Europe: Ideological or Protest Vote?' *European Journal of Political Research*, 37/1, pp. 77–102.

Vilar, Pierre (ed.) (1989) *Història de Catalunya*. Barcelona: Edicions 62.

Walzer, Michael (1992) 'Comment', in Gutmann, Amy (ed.), *Multiculturalism and the 'Politics of Recognition'*. Princeton, NJ: Princeton University Press, pp. 99–103.

Weber, Eugène (1979) *Peasants into Frenchmen: The Modernization of Rural France, 1870–1914*. London: Chatto & Windus.

Weber, Max (1948) *From Max Weber: Essays in Sociology*, ed. and trans. H. H. Gerth and C. Wright Mills. London: Routledge & Kegan Paul.

Weber, Max ([1968] 1978) *Economy and Society*, vol. 1. Berkeley: University of California Press.

Weil, Patrick (2006) 'A Flexible Framework for a Plural Europe', *Papers on the European Social Model Project*. London: London School of Economics.

Whitaker, R. (1995) 'Quebec's Self-Determination and Aboriginal Self-Government', in Carens, J. H. (ed.), *Is Quebec Nationalism Just? Perspectives from Anglophone Canada*. Montreal and Kingston: McGill–Queen's University Press, pp. 193–220.

Wiener Integrationsfonds (ed.) (1999) *MigrantInnen in Wien 1999: Daten & Fakten & Recht*. Report 98, Part II, Vienna.

Wieviorka, Michel (1996a) 'Culture, société et démocratie', in Wieviorka, Michel (ed.), *Une société fragmentée? Le multiculturalisme en débat*. Paris: La Découverte, pp. 11–60.

Wieviorka, Michel (ed.) (1996b) *Une société fragmentée? Le multiculturalisme en débat*. Paris: La Découverte.

Wilson, K., and van der Dussen, J. (eds) (1995) *The History of the Idea of Europe*. London: Routledge.

Wodak, Ruth (2002) 'Discourse and Politics: The Rhetoric of Exclusion', in Wodak, Ruth, and Pelinka, Anton (eds), *The Haider Phenomenon in Austria*. New Brunswick, NJ, and London: Transaction, pp. 33–60.

Wodak, Ruth, and Pelinka, Anton (eds) (2002) *The Haider Phenomenon in Austria*. New Brunswick, NJ, and London: Transaction.

Wolfe, Alan (2005) *Return to Greatness: How America Lost its Sense of Purpose and What it Needs to Do to Recover It*. Princeton, NJ: Princeton University Press.

Woods, Randall B. (ed.) (2003a) *Vietnam and the American Political Tradition*. Cambridge: Cambridge University Press.

Woods, Randall B. (2003b) 'World War II, Congress and the Roots of Postwar American Foreign Policy', in Woods, Randall B. (ed.), *Vietnam and the American Political Tradition*. Cambridge: Cambridge University Press, pp. 42–57.

Yanow, Dvora (2003) *Constructing 'Race' and 'Ethnicity' in America: Category-Making in Public Policy and Administration*. Armonk, NY: M. E. Sharpe.

Zaslove, Andrej (2004) 'Closing the Door? The Ideology and Impact of Radical Right Populism on Immigration Policy in Austria and Italy', *Journal of Political Ideologies*, 9/1, pp. 99–118.

Index